Academic Ethos Management

Academic Ethos Management

Building the Foundation for Integrity in Management Education

Agata Stachowicz-Stanusch

business**expert**
Press

Academic Ethos Management: Building the Foundation for Integrity in Management Education
Copyright © Business Expert Press, 2012.

Reviewer:
Charles Wankel, PhD
Professor of Management
St. John's University, New York

First published in 2012 by
Business Expert Press, LLC
222 East 46th Street, New York, NY 10017
www.businessexpertpress.com

ISBN-13: 978-1-60649-456-1 (paperback)

ISBN-13: 978-1-60649-457-8 (e-book)

DOI 10.4128/9781606494578

Business Expert Press Principles of Responsible Management Education collection

Collection ISSN: Forthcoming (print)
Collection ISSN: Forthcoming (electronic)

Cover design by Jonathan Pennell
Interior design by Exeter Premedia Services Private Ltd., Chennai, India

First edition: 2012

10 9 8 7 6 5 4 3 2 1

Printed in the United States of America.

For my daughter, Natalie

Abstract

This topical and much needed book constitutes an important part of the debate on the integrity in an academic context as a sine qua non of responsible management education. This discussion in management education occurred partly in reaction to highly publicized corporate scandals and instances of management misconduct that have eroded public faith. Concomitantly, management scholars and educators have begun to question the assumptions underlying the traditional management education, which in their view not only contributed to a recent moral crisis but has also failed to prepare students and executives for coping with the responsible leadership challenges and ethical dilemmas that face managers in contemporary corporations.

The past decade, which might be called an epoch of moral catastrophes, sets for universities the stage for effectively performing their missions through conscious and consequent incorporating the core values of academic ethos into academic activities.

This book discusses with stimulating examples how universities should bring alive their core values constituting academic ethos. Using case studies and examples from universities from all over the world, this book offers what few other titles are able to offer: conceptual framework of academic integrity based on Positive Academic Ethos, a new, holistic approach involving developing academic integrity based on human fulfillment and development of man's virtuous nature as well as practical advice and guidance, explaining in detail how administrators and educators should discover, articulate, and institutionalize core values of academic ethos into daily academic activities and create a foundation for academy integrity. The universities, educators, and instructors committed to socially responsible management education will find many valuable tools and pragmatic strategies to effectively spread practices of integrity based on academic ethos core values across organizational institutions. It also provides valuable teaching case studies and should be used by course leaders at undergraduate, master's, and MBA level in all business schools.

Keywords

academic ethos, core values of academic ethos, academic integrity, responsible management education, academic ethos management, positive academic ethos

Contents

Acknowledgments...xi

Introduction xiii

Chapter 1   The Erosion of Academic Ethos *Quo Vadis* Higher
            Education?..1

Chapter 2   Discovering and Developing the Core Values
            of Academic Ethos..19

Chapter 3   Enacting the Core Values of Academic Ethos...................39

Chapter 4   Communicating Core Values of Academic Ethos.............61

Chapter 5   Maintaining Core Values of Academic Ethos 79

Chapter 6   Core Values Management at the University—Insights
            from USA..95

Chapter 7   Core Values Management at the University—Insights
            from International Case Studies....................................137

Chapter 8   Core Values Management at the World's Oldest
            Universities...165

Chapter 9   Recommendations from Cases—Toward the Concept
            of Academic Integrity Development by Academic
            Ethos Management..201

Chapter 10 Positive Academic Ethos—the Frame for Integrity
            in Managerial Education...205

Conclusion 223

Notes..229

References 247

Index 263

Endorsements..267

Acknowledgments

This book is a result of the efforts of many people whom I would like to thank. I express my sincere appreciation to the following people for their invaluable inputs and assistance in conducting research for this book:

J. Michael Bernstein, Wright State University, USA

Ásta Bjarnadóttir, Reykjavik University, Iceland

Katarzyna Frankowicz, Jagiellonian University in Krakow, Poland

Svafa Grönfeldt, Reykjavik University, Iceland

Steinn Jóhannsson, Reykjavik University, Iceland

Þóranna Jónsdóttir, Reykjavik University, Iceland

Matthias Kleinhempel, IAE Business School—Universidad Austral, Argentina

Alfred Lewis, Hamline University, USA

Marcelo Paladino, IAE Business School—Universidad Austral, Argentina

Joseph A. Petrick, Wright State University, USA

Þröstur Olaf Sigurjónsson, Reykjavik University, Iceland

Robert Sweeney, Wright State University, USA

Marco Tavanti, DePaul University, USA

and the members of the Strategic Planning Committee from Hamline University, USA

I would particularly like to acknowledge the reviewer of this book, Professor Charles Wankel. His thoughtful suggestions truly enriched the content.

To each of above I would like to say once again:

THANK YOU.

Agata Stachowicz-Stanusch

Introduction

Why Is a Book about Academic Ethos Management Needed Now?

Why is it important to conduct scholarly studies of bolstering integrity in the world of academia through the process of academic ethos management? And why is now the appropriate time to do so? Following are some compelling reasons.

First, over the past few years we have been witnesses to an ever-growing interest among scholars, educators, and managers with regard to integrity in business and management education. This movement is partly a reaction to highly publicized corporate scandals and instances of management misconduct that have eroded public faith. From the beginning of the millennium, the business press has presented a growing list of corrupt practices among various organizations (Enron, WorldCom, Global Crossing, Tyco, Quest, and Adelphia, to name a few). Corruption seems to be omnipresent in enterprises, nonprofit organizations, and even in religious organizations. Moreover, corrupt behavior seems to be strongly connected not only to individuals within organizations, but also to whole organizations that more often become corrupt entities. That is why corruption concerns not only particular enterprises, but also entire business sectors or even nations. It seems to be justified to ask a question as to whether higher education and especially business schools have forgotten their prime objective: not only promoting the discovery and exchange of knowledge and ideas, but also educating wise people who will be equipped with knowledge and integrity. Questions also rise as to whether the academic environment truly shapes the moral attitudes of young people and creates the appropriate examples for them. Do the core values of academic ethos really mold the behavior of an academic community?

The time has come to redefine academic ethos in the context of recent economic crises stemming from the unethical behavior of corporations;

such behavior has fostered a growing distrust in interpersonal relations, an atrophy of organizational bonds, and a decreasing level of intraorganizational social capital. The new focus on academic ethos, redefining core values of a higher school, should be one of the answers of academic world for the corruption phenomenon and its proliferation within its own environment.

Second, the quest for integrity in business and education is not only a reaction to highly publicized corruption scandals, but also a result of the expectations that stakeholders of contemporary corporations and their leaders will take more active roles in the fight against the most important problems in the world, such as environmental degradation, abuse of human rights, and corruption.

Along with cultural and technological trends in the global business environment, the economic crisis became a catalyst for the development of a new person-centered perspective on business and education. This perspective is based on positive psychology,[1] spiritual aspects of individuals, and a fascination of scholarly management with the human brain and intelligence. It is clear that universities throughout the world cannot ignore this trend.

Inspiration for exploring academic ethos management also comes from an awareness that, while integrity "is at the heart of what effective business and education is all about," future business leaders seem to have a problem with the challenge of managing their businesses with integrity. Related to this is the fact that we know very little about how universities prepare managers and professionals for those challenges. There is also a more popular thesis that the best way to develop the moral character of future business leaders and to encourage them to behave with integrity is by giving students the opportunity to study and work in an organization with integrity: the university itself.[2] That is why the challenge now is to search for answers to questions about the causes of academic ethos erosion on the one hand, and for the ways of creating and developing integrity at higher school on the other hand.

Third, in today's world of local society, where an organization's borders become more and more transparent, as well as in times of global crisis, a deep understanding of academic ethos core values and the best practices of managing them is especially important; such studies may show how individuals, groups, organizations, and whole societies can pro-mote a sense of purposefulness, direction, meaning, and appropriate ways of creating moral frameworks for ethical conduct in a world of constant change.

Fourth, the fascination with the theme of integrity, which is clearly visible in the academic world as well as in business, is connected with the intensified interest in core values. Since the launch of Porras and Collins's book *Built to Last,*[3] this fascination has been confirmed by numerous research and scientific elaborations. The authors focus on the importance and crucial role of values in managing contemporary organizations,[4] emphasizing the fact that the oldest organizations managed by core val-ues are not Sony, American Express, Disneyland, DuPont, or Marriot but churches, armies, and universities. Numerous higher schools are proud of their core values and present them to their employees, students, and stakeholders. Walls in many campuses are adorned with placards express-ing those core values, which are also frequently included in the first pages of many academic publications. Though, the role and influence of these core values can appear restricted to these superficial actions. True core values seem dead, covered with the dust of time, forgotten. They provoke cynicism and laughter among students and employees as they are not transferrable to the real day-to-day activity of a higher school. Conse-quently, decisions made by a university's authorities do not fit declared core values; they do not create a culture of internal integrity at a school as much as they foster a culture of cynicism and a lack of trust in interper-sonal relations. This, in turn, causes the atrophy of organizational bonds and the decrease of social capital inside a university.

It is time for a change.

Fifth, core values of academic ethos are the core of cultural identity, which plays a crucial role in the development of today's universities. Cultural integrity is a particular logic of transferring academic ethos core values into a university's development behaviors; it is the university's indi-vidual paradigm, typical for a given higher school.

We should be aware that university does not simple exist; rather it happens, becomes, and transforms. For a contemporary university, it is the consciousness and stability of its academic ethos core values that condition the way it evolves.

With these motivations in mind, I have designed this book to achieve the following goals:

1. to develop the conceptual framework of academic integrity based on positive academic ethos;
2. to present a new, holistic approach involving developing academic integrity based on human fulfillment and development of man's virtuous nature;
3. to provide empirically grounded, theoretical insights for redefining academic ethos as a result of the last economic crisis stemming from the unethical behavior of contemporary organizations and their leaders;
4. to formulate the assumptions (guidelines) for integrity development at the higher school through the process of managing core values of academic ethos;
5. to formulate recommendations for developing academic integrity through the process of managing core values of academic ethos, based on conducted qualitative research (case study) in deliberately chosen universities from different parts of the world (North America, South America, Europe);
6. to describe the process of academic ethos management and identify its particular phases and their components;
7. to provide particular methods and tools for managing the core values of academic ethos as the attitude for the construction of academic integrity.

I have organized these goals in 10 chapters.

Chapter 1, "The Erosion of Academic Ethos—*Quo Vadis* Higher Education?" focuses on the definition of academic ethos and the core values that constitute it for management of the contemporary university. The chapter also examines sources of academic ethos erosion and the steps that should be taken for its redefinition in the twenty-first century.

Chapter 2, "Discovering and Developing the Core Values of Academic Ethos," offers detailed description of the first phase of the process of academic ethos management. We may learn not only how to discover the values of academic ethos and how to define them in terms of desirable behavior but also which type of conduct threatens the particular values of academic ethos. This chapter is replete with examples of core value defini-tions extracted from higher schools throughout the world.

Chapter 3, "Enacting the Core Values of Academic Ethos," provides specific guidelines for enacting the core values of academic ethos through reflecting and supporting the core values of a university's goals, objec-tives, measures, and through familiarization with a university's policies, procedures, and codes. By doing this, a university forms a dialogue at the institutional, classroom, and individual levels around fundamental values of academic ethos and enhances the conduct of academic community in performing their duties in pursuit of academic ethos.

Chapter 4, "Communicating Core Values of Academic Ethos," pre-sents examples from around the world showing the spectrum of tools used in the process of communicating values of academic ethos, ranging from age-old traditions and cultural models to academic publicity, archi-tectural, physical, and prestige symbols, and beyond to contemporary instruments based on information technologies such as chatterbots.

Chapter 5, "Maintaining Core Values of Academic Ethos," uses con-crete examples to describe elements of maintaining core values of aca-demic ethos through recruitment, core values explanation, training on core values in and out of the classroom for students, and consistent, updated training for employees. The goal is to study the importance of instilling core values of academic ethos over simple behavioral compli-ance of academic community members with the behaviors ascribed to core values.

The subsequent chapters present a section devoted to the descrip-tion of the process of managing academic ethos in deliberately chosen higher schools from the North America (United States), South America (Argentina), and Europe (Iceland, Poland). Each case study lists the main facts about a particular higher school and presents a brief history; then, based on direct research (interviews) and internal documentation analy-sis, the core values of academic ethos are characterized and their specific implementations within a particular school are enumerated.

Chapter 6, "Core Values Management at the University—Insights from USA," highlights the process of academic ethos management at two American universities (DePaul University and Wright State University) that are different in terms of its form of ownership, age, and the phase of development as well as the core ideologies constituting their values of academic ethos.

Chapter 7, "Core Values Management at the University—Insights from International Case Studies," describes the process of academic ethos management coming from the merger of universities (Reykjavik University and Technical University of Iceland) as well as a relatively young Argentinean higher school (IAE Business School at Austral University), which is placed among world's top business schools in many prestigious rankings.

Chapter 8, "Core Values Management at the World's Oldest Universities," is devoted to descriptions of academic ethos management at higher schools that are proud of their long-standing traditions. This chapter looks at academic ethos management at one of the oldest European universities (Jagiellonian University) and at the oldest 200-year-old university in Minnesota (Hamline University).

The next chapter, "Recommendations from Cases—Toward the Concept of Academic Integrity Development by Academic Ethos Management," presents guidelines for the construction and development of academic integrity by managing the core values of academic ethos based on the conclusions and recommendations of research (case studies).

The last chapter, "Positive Academic Ethos—the Frame for Integrity in Managerial Education," is a synthesis of the considerations about the role of managing the core values of academic ethos for the construction and development of academic integrity. Previous considerations of the author as well as conclusions and recommendations from research enable the identification of the phases of academic ethos management process, including the indication of components constituting each particular phase. This chapter presents alternatives to current attitudes, examining theories of higher school management toward the creation of academic integrity based on Positive Organizational Scholarship and virtue ethics. The conceptual framework on integrity based on positive academic ethos is also presented.

The author believes that the university as an institution and the scholars and academic teachers are responsible not only for discovering the truth and delivering knowledge but also for educating citizens who will make this world a better place. Such visionary aspiration cannot be achieved without integrity within academic world.

CHAPTER 1

The Erosion of Academic Ethos

Quo Vadis Higher Education?

The Crisis of Academic Ethos—Fact or Hype?

The university is one of the oldest institutions in the world. Even a commercial enterprise with a bold 500-year history pales by comparison. The first university was founded in 849 AD in Constantinople. Two of the oldest universities in the Western world, Bologna University and the University of Paris, are steeped in more than 1,000 years of tradition.

The success of a university that has existed for many centuries and is still developing without any noticeable constraints is recognized as a luxury available to only a few enterprises. It is an extraordinary phenomenon that, when it occurs, is recognized with respect, and its sources, origin, and history are scrutinized with attention. We are so sure that a university's longevity and development are a result of exceptional talent, leadership, or even unexpected luck, and we do not ask basic questions: What made, makes, and will make universities the great ones? What determines their existence and development? What becomes autonomic in a higher school, what separates from the particular persons and outlives them? Why do the aged universities exist despite the turbulent changes in their environments?

First of all, universities are highly organized groups. This organization is one of the most persistent attributes of a university.[1] However, a much more important attribute not only of the persistence, but also of its development are the known and codified core values in the form of academic ethos. These values define a university's identity and express particular modes of its conduct. The university not only exists but also evolves.

The awareness and stability of universities' identities and their academic ethos were a security for their existence in the past and also were conditions for their happening and becoming in the future.

In my opinion, centuries-old tradition and the organizational and cultural heritage of a university still influences its social recognition as the respected and reliable institution. Many countries and large social communities treat the national scientific heritage with a recognizable esteem as they observe the key role of higher education in shaping the potential of not only regions but entire nations as well.[2] Universities have always been leaders in developing paradigms for how to live well; in general, society views the university in its ideal form as a haven for truth, knowledge, democratic principles, and the development of students as positive, productive citizens of the world.

Provocative issues arise as to whether or not contemporary higher education[3] complies with these obligations well and whether the academic environment truly shapes the moral attitudes of young people and creates the appropriate exemplars for them. Does academic ethos and core values that constitute it (that are included in some declarative documents, such as mission statements, codes of ethics, and core values statements) really shape the behavior of the academic community (students, staff members, and university officials)? Has higher education, and especially business school, forgotten about its prime objective: not only promoting the discovery and exchange of knowledge ideas, but also educating wise people who will be equipped with knowledge and integrity?

As I argue, an educated person of the twenty-first century is not only an expert, but he or she can also be a rather wise person, who is not only mentally efficient but who is also able to distinguish between good and bad solutions, since wisdom is highly connected with the ability to perform an accurate appraisal of what is possible, desirable, and what is not appropriate. Hence, it may concluded that wisdom as an individual characteristic is the capability to accurately recognize correct values and to conduct, in accordance with them, the process of searching for the best solutions.[4] The most important skills for our collective sustainable well-being are moral competency skills, skills that allow us to honor the moral principles of integrity, responsibility, compassion, and forgiveness.[5]

In itself, capitalism is not necessarily immoral or degrading. It can help vast populations not only survive but thrive in unimaginable ways. The key is for people utilizing capitalism to abide in simple precepts put forth by economist and philosopher Adam Smith: "Tell the truth. Keep your promises. Be responsible for your actions. Treat other as you would like to be treated—with compassion and forgiveness."[6] And be wise.

The beginning of the current decade was abound with numerous financial crises and corruption scandals involving global corporations such as Enron, WorldCom, Xerox, Tyco, Dynergy, Arthur Andersen, Global Crossing, Adelphia, ImClone, and AOL. The scandals revealed that many people and corporations making their business worldwide do not have a sense of responsibility toward the societies, cultures, or entities they encounter while carrying out their international ventures.[7] Table 1.1 summarizes many of these most egregious cases of corporate scandals during the past decade.

However, as Wankel and I have noted, much unethical behavior can be ascribed not only to particular corporations but also to their very leaders such as Kenneth Lay (founder and CEO of Enron Corporation), Jeffrey Skilling (CEO of Enron), Bernard Ebbers (CEO of WorldCom), Leo Hindery (CEO of Global Crossing Limited), Richard Scrushy (CEO of Healthsouth), and Dennis Kozlowski (CEO of Tyco Corporation). On the basis of these facts, we may come to the conclusion that the business world seems to be ethically disoriented. If we are right, we need to consider the possibility that the root cause of this is the inattention of higher education, especially business schools, toward ethical education. The code of ethics does not guarantee cultivating an understanding of moral principles in the world of business. It is necessary, therefore, to develop virtuous characters of future business leaders.

During the past decade, the educational system in general and the business education in particular were immersed in a wave of criticism as being responsible for moral ignorance in the business world and for their failure to inculcate in students the standards of good conduct and even as having weakened the moral character of students.[8] Wankel, Tamtana, and I observed that if current trends continue, incidences of ethical misconduct in business practice along with negative public perception will continue to increase.[9] To promote more ethical reasoning within the field

Table 1.1. A Summary of Ethical Lapses in Business Practice

Company	Ethical Issues	Outcomes
Enron	• Engaged in network capacity "swaps" with other carriers to inflate revenue • Accounting loopholes used to hide billions in debt • Shredded documents related to accounting practices	• Company filed Chapter 11—largest US corporate bankruptcy at that time • Shareholders lost nearly $11 billion • Spinning off various assets • Kenneth Lay, CEO, resigned (later died) • Congress is examining the role played by company's accounting firms in its bankruptcy • Investigations of governmental connections in the US and Great Britain
WorldCom	• Overstated cash flow by booking $3.8 billion in operating expenses as capital expenses • False accounting to inflate revenue • Gave founder Bernard Ebbers $400 million in off-the-books loans	• One of the biggest accounting frauds in US history • Barnard Ebbers found guilty of fraud, conspiracy, and filing false documents with regulators • Sentenced to 25 years in prison • Other executives, for example, Scott Sullivan and David Myers, plead guilty to securities fraud
Adelphia Communications	• Members of Rigas family hid $2.3 billion in debt, backed by Adelphia	• Two of the Rigas family were convicted of conspiracy, bank fraud, and securities fraud
	• Deceived investors about condition of the company, pocketed money, lived lavish lifestyles	• Company now operating under bankruptcy protection • Spawned more than 50 lawsuits, 17,000 claims • Adelphia under new management; separating themselves from Rigas family
Tyco	• $600 million pilfered from the company (Over $170 million in undisclosed loans; $400 million in undisclosed stock transactions) • Lived lavish lifestyles	• Kozlowski, Swartz convicted of multiple counts of grand larceny, falsifying business records, securities fraud, conspiracy • Sentenced to 25 years in prison • Ordered to pay $134 million in restitution
Madoff	• Ponzi scheme money from new investors is used to pay off early investors, giving the appearance of returns • Investor experienced false gains of 12–15%	• Global in scope • Estimated $50 billion in losses • Bernard Madoff sentenced to 150 years in prison • Investigations into how Madoff scheme avoided detection for over a decade

Source: Heisler, W., Westfall, F., & Kitahara, R. (2012). Chapter 29: Technological approaches to maintaining academic integrity in management education. In: Handbook of research on teaching ethics in business and management education, Ch. Wankel, A., & Stachowicz-Stanusch (Eds.), (p. 510). US: IGI Global.
Reprinted by permission of the publisher.

of business, business education programs must better develop students' abilities to confront moral and ethical dilemmas with knowledge, sensitivity, and conviction.[10] Ghoshal provides one of the most discussed critiques of business school education.[11] His primary thesis is that today's business education, with its foundations in agency theory and economic liberalism, contributed significantly to the recent stream of unethical business practices.[12]

On the basis of the data extracted from AACSB International for the year 2008/2009, only "1% out of the 604 schools reporting MBA programs is devoted to business ethics, while other fields such as general business or management receive attention from 69.5% and 34.9% of the business schools, respectively."[13] Critics of today's educational system (and business education particularly) became the subject not only of newspapers and popular science publications, but also of the scientific literature. More and more often, the academic environment sees the destruction of academic ethos. Moreover, from behind university walls appear examples of unethical conduct, such as: cases of plagiarism,[14] master theses written on request,[15] or the unreliability of conducted research,[16] cheating,[17] and academic dishonesty (such as fabricating or falsifying a bibliography). According to a report for the United Nations Educational, Scientific, and Cultural Organization (UNESCO), bribery and corruption damage universities and schools throughout the world. Koichiro Matsuura, director general of UNESCO, states, "Such widespread corruption not only costs societies billions of dollars, it also seriously undermines the vital effort to provide education for all." Authors Jacques Hallak and Muriel Poisson paint a bleak picture of world education. Their report says: "In most societies—rich and poor—the education sector is facing severe difficulties and crisis; financial constraints, weak management, low efficiency, wastage of resources, low quality of service delivery, and lack of relevance as illustrated by high unemployment of graduates, among others."[18]

Searching for Sources of Academic Ethos Erosion

Academic ethos is understood as a group of core values shared by the majority of people in an academic environment, namely tutors, students, administrators, and employees, and is recognized by all parties as a foundation for a university's endurance and development. The fact is that ethical erosion has occurred at all levels, from the foundation up, and redefinition is in order.

The first step toward redefinition of academic ethos is to become aware of the causes of the current state. Those causes may be defined (in the easiest and most logic way) as a consequence and continuum of pathological phenomena and behaviors happening outside the university, such as the global problem of corruption or the moral crisis of business world. However, adopting this view seems to be insufficient or even unacceptable if taking into account a feature that constitutes a higher school—its autonomy.[19] Causes of the erosion of the university's core values can be traced to the "marketization of education," which resulted in mass and commercialized academic education.[20] Despite the adopted model of a university (Kant's model, model of Humboldt, model of Napoleon, or the British model), its traditional vision faces the market reality, ICT development, the external pressure to be more competitive and open for requirements of labor market and needs of society.[21] According to Ramaley, these pressures include "financial constraints, demands for accountability and enhanced productivity, concerns about student learning and values, student and family concerns about employability of jobs, demands from policymakers for responsiveness to societal problems and a trend toward seeking private answers to public questions (e.g. privatization, contacting for services, reinventing government high tuition/high aid proposals)."[22] The university transformed from a "temple of wisdom" into a "higher school" or even into a "professional service firm" as it adopted many rules of organizational culture of a corporate world making the same mistakes.[23] These mistakes of managing the university made by authorities of higher schools may be perceived as the next cause of erosion of academic ethos.

In recent years, such initiatives as defining vision, mission, or core values are very popular not only among entrepreneurs, but also among authorities of higher schools.[24] Numerous higher schools are proud of their core values and present them to their employees, students, and stakeholders. Walls in many campuses are adorned with placards expressing those core values as well as including them in the first pages of many academic publications. In contrast, though, the role and influence of these core values appear restricted to these superficial actions. True core values seem dead, covered with the dust of time, and forgotten. They provoke cynicism and laughter among students and employees as they are not transferrable to the real day-to-day activity of a higher school.[25] Consequently, decisions made by a university's authorities do not fit declared core values; they do not create a culture of internal integrity at a school as much as they foster a culture of cynicism and a lack of trust in interpersonal relations. This, in turn, causes the atrophy of organizational bonds and the decrease of social capital inside a university.

Fortunately, the current crisis of academic ethos has inspired colleges and universities to be more introspective and to draw lessons from very public mistakes; in this way, they will redefine their ethos in order to better educate honest and responsible future leaders in the world. A *sine qua non* condition for this process is the return of higher schools to their fundamentals—to the core values that consolidate an academic community. A fundamental academic value is the truth. This value permeates all three basic spheres of academic activity: scientific research, educating, and social servicing. The ethos of truth is supported with other values that are characteristic of academic life, such as reliability and responsibility.[26] The academic community is obliged to search for truth during scientific research in a reliable and responsible way, educating in a manner that results in creating a wise, usable, engaged, and responsible human being; thus, truth nourishes the individual at school and fortifies society at large.

The basic constitutive feature of a university is a community of educators and educated. Values that are characteristic for the community are truth and goodness, including the common good. In their book, Harland and Pickening present a list of concepts that have embodied the Western university traditions: Freedom of speech, Critical thinking, Tolerance, Respect, Knowledge, Truth, Creativity, and Democracy.[27]

In *Campus Life—In Search of Community*, published by the Carnegie Foundation for the Advancement of Teaching, we find six principles that, taken together, define the kind of community that every college and university should strive to become:[28]

- *A college or university is an educationally purposeful community, a place where faculty and students share academic goals and work together to strengthen teaching and learning on the campus.*

- *A college or university is an open community, a place where freedom of expressions is uncompromisingly protected and where civility is powerfully affirmed.*
- *A college or university is a just community, a place where the sacredness of the person is honored and where diversity is aggressively pursued.*
- *A college or university is a disciplined community, a place where individuals accept their obligations to the group and where well-defined governance procedures guide behavior for the common good.*
- *A college or university is a caring community, a place where the well-being of each member is sensitively supported and where service to others is encouraged.*
- *A college or university is a celebratory community, one in which the heritage of the institution is remembered and where rituals affirming both tradition and change are widely shared.*

On the other hand, the European University Association declares:[29] "The development of European universities is based on a set of core values like: equity and access; research and scholarship in all disciplines as an integral part of higher education; high academic quality; cultural and linguistic diversity."

Intense scientific discussion and public debate on core values creating, consolidating, and developing the academic community initiated by the moral crisis of recent years has resulted in a focus on the topic of integrity within higher education and the necessity to reconstruct academic integrity, called the "culture of integrity," or the culture of university's character.[30,31] Leaders of higher schools as well as society as a whole expect that higher education will reconstruct a culture of integrity that will "provide the foundation for a vibrant academic life, promote scientific progress, and prepare students for responsible citizenship."[32]

On the basis of reports from the world of science and the world of higher schools' managing practice, we may state that various values are defined as those that constitute academic integrity. According to The Center for Academic Integrity (CAI), "academic integrity is based on the five fundamental values: honesty, trust, fairness, respect, and responsibility. From these values flow principles of behavior that enable academic communities to translate ideals into action. An academic community flourishes when its members are committed to those five fundamental values."[33] Respect, Trust, Honesty, Responsibility, and Effort are considered by School of Ethical Education to be the core of the academic integrity.[34] Turknett and Turknett provide this definition of a company with character: "Like people with character, they get results, but they do it with integrity and a respect for people. Like people with character, companies with character are able to balance accountability and courage with humility and respect" (p. 2).[35] At the same time, Paine defines organizational integrity in a broad sense as "honesty, self-governance, fair dealing, responsibility, moral soundness, adherence to principle, and consistency of purpose."[36]

However, it is not so important which values are perceived to constitute the academic integrity (whether they are enumerated as truth, trust, honesty, or responsibility). The most important issue within the process of constructing academic integrity is to enliven and cultivate it in an ethical way. If there exist enterprises such as Sony, which in its set of core values does not include "leading customer value" and is still the example of market orientation, or Nordstrom, which does not include "teamwork" and is an example of employees' cooperation, then the higher school does not necessarily need to include in a set of values constituting its academic ethos terms such as integrity, responsibility, or respect. The only requirement here is to manage core values of a university in a confident and consistent way. We need to manage the academic ethos of a university.

Academic Ethos Management is a process of managing the university identity and transferring the university's core values from one management generation to another by taking over responsibilities resulting from core values and their protection in the name of and for the benefit of the university and its members through their institutionalization in a morally positive manner. It is the awareness, loyalty, and respect of core values in everyday activity that lead to the flourishing of an academic community and are fundamental to fulfilling its social and educational mission. This mission essentially is to foster sound judgment and ethical behavior in youth, thus creating an entire foundation for a better society in the future; this is coupled with an awareness of environmental imperatives and a need to harmoniously coexist in all aspects of human interaction.[37] *Human interaction* encompasses mind, body, and soul, developing an individual's intelligence, sense of responsibility, sensitivity to the needs of others, awareness of the environment, aesthetics, and spirituality.[38]

How to Understand Core Values Constituting Academic Ethos and Why are they Important?

In the area of management of organizations, in 1939, Barnard noticed that commonly shared values appear to be useful in solving problems of creating and managing compound organizations.[39] Over the past decades, the term "core values" has been very popular among researchers examining organizations as well as among the employees of organizations. The existence of "core values" or "common values" that can be identified is a characteristic of an organization that has achieved success.[40] Such are the key elements of organizational management, as well as the source of a high level of organizational involvement and individuals' morality.[41,42]

Table 1.2 presents examples of scientific research results that indicate the beneficial effect of an organization's core values.

Table 1.2. Beneficial Effect of an Organization's Core Values—Research Results

	Year	Authors	Results
1	1997	Arie de Geus	Core values as a source of organization's persistence and development.
2	1985	B. Posner, J. Kouzes, W. Schmidt	The existence of identified core values: 1. promotes a high level of organizational loyalty, 2. enables the consensus on the main organizational objectives, 3. provokes ethical behaviors, 4. promotes strong norms on hardworking and care giving, 5. reduces the level of stress and pressures in work, 6. enhances the understanding of expectations connected with work,
			7. develops strong conviction about personal effectiveness, 8. develops soul and honor or participating within organization, and 9. develops team work.

(Continued)

Table 1.2. (*Continued*)

	Year	Authors	Results
3	1997	J. Collins, J. Porras	Relationship between the awareness of core values of an organization and its development in the long run as well as with its stock value
4	1996	A. Kristof	Relationship between the awareness of core values of an organization and the increase in organizational engagement of individuals
5	1989	B. M. Meglino, E. C. Ravlin C.L. Adkins	Relationship between the awareness of core values of an organization and the increase in job satisfaction
6	1991	C. A. O' Reilly, J. Chatmann, D. F. Caldwell	Relationship between the awareness of core values of an organization and the decrease in the absence and fluctuation of employees
7	1991	D. E. Bowen, G. E. Ledford, B. R. Nathan	Relationship between the awareness of core values of an organization and the increase in work results
8	1996	D. Turnipseed	Relationship between the awareness of core values of an organization and the increase in citizenship behaviors measured with subordination, altruism, and attendance
9	1982	T. E. Deal, A. A. Kennedy	Importance of common values in creating a strong organizational culture
10	1980	W. G. Ouchi	Importance of common values in creating a strong organizational culture
11	1982	T. J. Peters, R. H. Waterman, Jr.	Importance of common values in management practice and leadership within organizations
12	1997	C. Anderson	Importance of common values for the pace of organizational development
13	2000	Ch. A. O'Reilly	Positive relationship between identified core values and organization's development
14	1999	J. Pfeffer, R.I. Sutton	Positive relationship between identified core values and organization's development
15	2005	Darrol, S.	Organizational culture is a potential source of excellent financial results
16	2007	Maznevski, M., Steger, U., Amann, W.	Organizations dealing best with complexity have never defined more than 3–4 core values complied with their business idea

Source: Based on Stachowicz-Stanusch A. (2004). Zarządzanie Poprzez Wartości. Perspektywa rozwoju współczesnego przedsiębiorstwa. Gliwice: Wydawnictwo Politechniki Śląskiej, p. 36.

But what precisely are the core values of an organization and how should they be understood?

Webster defines the notion "core" as "a central and often foundational part usually distinct from the enveloping part by a difference in nature," and a "value" as "principles, objectives or social standards shared and accepted by the human entity, social class or society." Core values are the most intrinsic standards, shared and accepted by members of an organization.[43] According to J. Porras and J. Collins (2003: 89), core values, next to the mission statement, are the component of the leading ideology.[44] It was discovered quite early that people need to feel that they are a part of a sublime vision. Defining core values is thus necessary to help people make their everyday decisions. The mission is very abstract. Vision has an impact in the long run. People need a lodestar for navigating.[45] Core values are also defined as the principles that are permanent, fundamental, and inviolable. They are what we believe in, and they do not change.[46] They are also understood as fundamental ethical, moral, or professional beliefs of an organization, and they are leading in a process of decision making.[47] In the turbulent and changeable world, core values remain constant. They are not a description of a work or of strategies chosen by an organization in order to fulfill its mission. Values are the basis for work, our cooperation with others; they determine the course of a strategy that helps to fulfill the mission. They are the practices used by an organization every single day in everything it does.[48] Senge states that the leading idea answers three questions: what, why, and how. A vision answers the question "What?" by giving an image of the future we want to create. An objective or a mission answers the question "Why?" by showing why we exist. Core values answer the question "How?" by showing how we need to act in accordance with our mission in order to approach our vision. The term core values relates to a particular group of publicly expressed values or concepts that are shared for the majority of organization's members and that are considered to be the most central and most important for organization's continued development.[49] In many cases, those values are formalized and expressed in writing for all the organizational members. They are also often shared by other key units from the organization's environment.[50]

Research conducted by me and my team in 2009 that analyzed core values declared by higher schools included on their websites, which construct academic ethos in the context of different national cultures (according to G. Hofstede), enabled to distinguish the most frequently declared core values of higher schools with regard to the dominant dimension of Hofstede's national culture. Having analyzed the results of this research, it was noticed that the universities from countries with a dominant Power Distance Index (PDI), such as Indonesia, China, or Ecuador, most often declared innovativeness and academic excellence as their core values. Quite opposite were the results for countries with a dominant Uncertainty Avoidance Index (UAI), such as Argentina or Israel, as the most often preferred values, there were social engagement, progress, and the quality of educating and research. The core values that create academic ethos most often appearing on the websites of the analyzed higher schools with regard to a dominant dimension of national culture (G. Hofstede) are presented in Table 1.3.

The most popular values appearing on websites of analyzed universities (taking the number of indicated values in all national culture dimensions into account) are presented in Figure 1.1.

Core values of a university may comprise team work, reliability, or justice. The examples of higher schools from different parts of the world and their core values are presented in Table 1.4.

In my opinion, values of university members that are fully accepted and made real in their behaviors create academic ethos. Those values

Table 1.3. Core Values Most Often Occurring on Websites of Analyzed Higher Schools with Regard to the Dominance of National Culture Index (Hosftede)

Without Dominance	PDI Dominance	IDV Dominance	UAI Dominance
Examples			
Innovativeness	Innovativeness	Creativity	Social engagement
Quality	Excellence	Independence	Progress
Freedom	Truth	Excellence	Quality
Equality	Integrity	Cooperation	Excellence
Responsibility	Freedom	Respect	Respect
Cooperation	Engagement	Responsibility	Spirit of cooperation
Excellence	Cooperation	Honesty	Innovativeness
Truth	Tolerance	Quality	Freedom

Source: Based on Stachowicz-Stanusch A. (Ed.) (2009). Główne wartości uczelni wyższych w kontekście różnych kultur narodowych. Koncepcja badań i wyniki badań sondażowych. Gliwice: Wydawnictwo Politechniki Śląskiej.

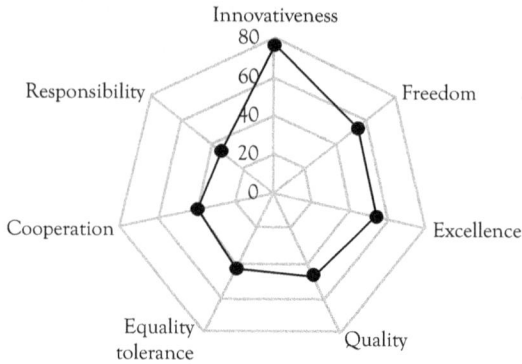

Figure 1.1. **Core values appearing most often on websites of analyzed universities in total.**

Source: Based on Stachowicz-Stanusch A. (Ed.) (2009). *The Core Values of Universities in the Context of Different National Cultures. The Concept of Research and Survey Findings.* Gliwice: Wydawnictwo Politechniki Śląskiej.

permeate all dimensions of academic life; they are a justification of adopted objectives and ways of their realization. It is not a partial implementation and respecting the values just in particular situations or toward particular partners. Academic ethos is connected with the whole academic environment as it is a set of values and principles that lead a life of academic community and serve as a guide for a higher school's authorities.[84]

Core values, which are fundamentals of academic ethos, are realized by all higher schools—however to the different extent—and connections between them may be classified in the following three groups.

Within the first group there exist academic values connected with fundamental objectives of science and education as well as with university obligations toward its social environment. It includes values such as: truth, reliability, or social and global responsibility.

The second group consists of values connected between a higher school institution and academic community of a university. Those values guarantee basic academic liberty. It includes values such as: autonomy, freedom, liberty (of research, teaching, and views dissemination), courage, responsibility, and tolerance or common good.

The third group includes values that are dominant inside a community and which are correlated: a master–a pupil, understood as the

Table 1.4. Examples of Universities from Different Parts of the World and Their Core Values

North America

University	Core Values
Texas A&M University[51] (United States)	Excellence, Integrity, Leadership, Loyalty, Respect, Selfless Service
Michigan State University[52] (United States)	Quality, Inclusiveness, Connectivity
University of California[53] (United States)	Integrity, Excellence, Accountability, Respect
University of Central Arkansas[54] (United States)	Intellectual Excellence, Community, Diversity, Integrity
University of Washington[55] (United States)	Integrity, Diversity, Excellence, Collaboration, Innovation, Respect
St. John's University[56] (United States)	Truth, Love, Respect, Opportunity, Excellence, Service
Canadian University College[57] (Canada)	Excellence, Service, Spirituality, Integrity, Community
Northern Caribbean University[58] (Jamaica)	Christ-centeredness, Affirmation, Respect, Excellence, Stewardship

Latin America

University	Core Values
Universidad EAFIT[59] (Colombia)	Excellence, Tolerance, Responsibility, Integrity, Boldness
Escuela Agrícola Panamericana Zamorano[60] (Honduras)	Academic Excellence, Learning-by-Doing, Character Formation and Leadership, Pan-Americanism, Entrepreneurship
Pontifical Catholic University of Peru[61] (Peru)	Pursuit of truth, Respect for human dignity, Pluralism, Social responsibility and commitment to development, Honesty, Solidarity, Justice

(Continued)

Table 1.4. (Continued)

ASIA	
University	Core Values
Peking University[62] (China)	Patriotism, Progress, Democracy, Science, Diligence, Precision, Factualism, Innovation, Pursuing truth, Pursuing excellence, Cultivating talent, Cultivating academic prosperity, Serving the people and society
Effat University[63] (Kingdom of Saudi Arabia)	Ibhath—undertake life-long research [cf. albahth: "life-long research"], Qiyam—ethical social and educational values, Riyada—responsible and creative leadership, At-tawasul—effective communication and reaching out to others
National Taipei University[64] (Taiwan)	Hope, Opportunity, Life & Liberty, Integrity, Service, Truth, Ingenuity, Competence
Singapore Institute of Management University[65] (Singapore)	Trust and Respect for the Individual, Teamwork, Open and Timely Communication, Performance Excellence, Spirit of Innovative Adventure
City University of Hong Kong[66] (Hong Kong)	Excellence, Honesty, Freedom of Enquiry, Accountability, Civility and Collegiality
Manipal University[67] (India)	Integrity, Transparency, Quality, Team Work, Execution with passion, Humane touch
Universiti Teknologi Malaysia[68] (Malaysia)	Commitment, Communicativeness, Creativity, Consistence, Competency
Lahore University of Management Sciences[69] (Iran)	Merit-Based Approach, Hard Work, Value Addition, Intellectual Rigor, Character Building

Africa	
University	Core Values
University of Nairobi[70] (Kenya)	Freedom of thought and expression, Innovativeness and creativity, Good corporate governance, Team spirit and teamwork, Professionalism, Quality customer service, Responsible corporate citizenship and strong social responsibility, Respect for and conservation of the environment
Covenant University[71] (Nigeria)	Spirituality, Possibility Mentality, Capacity Building, Integrity, Responsibility, Diligence, Sacrifice

University	Core Values
Mogadishu University[72] (Somalia)	Committed to high work ethics, Dedicated to the national cultural values, Devoted to excellence and professionalism
Central University of Technology[73] (South Africa)	Institutional Core Values, Customer service, Integrity, Diversity, Innovation, Excellence
Kwame Nkrumah University of Science and Technology[74] (Ghana)	Leadership in Innovation and Technology, Culture of Excellence, Diversity and Equal Opportunity for All, Integrity and Stewardship of Resources
Nile University[75] (Egypt)	Excellence, Integrity, Service to the community, Commitment to diversity, Respect for the individual

Europe

University	Core Values
University of Cambridge[76] (United Kingdom)	Freedom of thought and expression, Freedom from discrimination
Maastricht University. School of Business and Economics[77] (The Netherlands)	Forward thinking, Value exchange, Inspiring
Tampere University of Technology[78] (Finland)	Responsibility, Courage, Culture, Wisdom
Freie Universität Berlin[79] (Germany)	Veritas—truth, Justitia—justice, Libertas—freedom
Alexandru Ioan Cuza University[80] (Romania)	Prestige, Innovation, Excellence
Uniwersytet Slaski w Katowicach[81] (Poland)	Truth, Knowledge

Australia and Oceania

University	Core Values
Macquarie University[82] (Australia)	Ethics, Be enquire, Creativity, Be Inclusiveness, Agility, Excellence
University of Otago[83] (New Zealand)	Intellectual Independence and Academic Freedom, Excellence, Partnership, Leadership, Collegiality and Collaboration, Knowledge, Equity and Ethical Standards, Consultation, Stewardship

Source: Our own study based on the analyzed websites.

respect of dignity and subjectivity of each community member, care for student's personal and professional development, supporting research curiosity, lack of discrimination, tolerance, kindness, fairness, reliability, and honesty—there are just a few of values that are realized inside a community.[85]

The awareness of core values and even writing them does not cause their persistence and university's development. An organization does not simply exist—it also develops and transforms. During its development and transformation, a university's members may easily forget the values that have been a source of success for their organization. Time, success, and other factors blur human memory about the reasons for success. Moreover, the new, unfamiliar values that are identified by higher schools' management or that were considered to be better and more competitive are often imposed on a university's participants. In such a case, the university develops a strong and centralized organizational culture that hinders initiatives and innovation—a culture supporting bureaucracy and egocentric behaviors. There are two primary reasons for this:

First, it is often forgotten that core values are not something that may be "bought or borrowed." Core values are an internal element of an organization; they are those values that are shared by its members in a deepest and strongest way.

Secondly, core values as the core of culture and integrity have not been passed from one generation of management to the next.

What causes the persistence and development of an organization and is a fundamental of integrity at university is not just awareness of its core values but also a consequent management of them and implementing them into organizational life in a morally positive manner.[86]

How to manage core values that create academic ethos? The answer may be found in the following chapters of this book.

CHAPTER 2

Discovering and Developing the Core Values of Academic Ethos

How Should the Values of Academic Ethos be Discovered? Who Should do This? And How Should it be Done?

The first step toward academic ethos management is to discover the core values that constitute it. Collins said: "You can only discover them. Nor can you 'install' new core values into people. Core values are not something people 'buy into'. People must be predisposed to holding them."[1]

Core values exist as an internal element that is strongly independent from the external environment. They are a small set of timeless values that do not require external explanation; they are of recognizable worth and importance for organizational members. They are inspiring for them but do not necessarily make a similar impression on people from the outside of an organization[2]. Thus, the most important issue is that core values are not a result of trends in management, competition, or market requirements. Core values are those values that are shared by an academic community in the deepest and strongest way; they are not those values that are required or declared as core values by the management of a university. Those values are shared but are not preferred or declared. Core values do not have roots in imitating the values of other colleges or universities, and they cannot be imposed by someone from the outside. They also cannot be articulated after reading some books on management, and they do not come from sterile intellectual exercise connected with indicating those values that are the most pragmatic, popular, and profitable. Values cannot be a forgery. They also cannot be "intellectualized." We should not ask: Which core values *should* we possess? Instead, we should ask: Which core values *do* we actually possess? Thus, it is obvious that there does not exist a universal and appropriate set of core values, but it is important that they are authentic, shared, and inspire passion. The key matter is not which core values a particular university have, but the fact that a higher school does possess them, is aware of them, and that those values are the most shared within an organization.[3]

A question emerges: How many core values should be discovered? Using the word "core" suggests that they should not be numerous. In their book *Build to Last,* Jim Collins and Jerry Porras argue that visionary firms seem to have a tendency to share just a few values, usually from three to six. If more than five or six values are indicated, they may be omitted from the list of those that are truly core. A particular institution not only defines its own core values, but also sets a limit to the number of them applicable to the institution at a given point in time. If a college or university thinks that three values are sufficient in defining its authentic core values, the number should be limited to 3. But if it identifies 10 core values and each of them is seen as authentic and gripping, there should be 10 values taken into account. A set of core values is not a closed set during the life of a university; there occur some moments when extending this set becomes necessary.[4]

The next question becomes: Who should be involved in the process of discovering core values of academic ethos? In the process of discovering core values, representatives of all the groups constituting an academic community should be involved, for example, managers (presidents, deans, or heads of departments), researchers, teachers, staff, and, of course, students. The difficulty in discovering core values depends on many factors, such as an organization's age, its size, or geographical dispersion. However, despite the size and dispersion of a higher school, each group that constitutes an academic community needs to feel like a participant of this important process and needs to be convinced that its opinion is important and meaningful for the ultimate shape of a university's core values. When having any opinion about the core values of one's organization, academic community members need to be aware of their own personal core values that are crucial in the place of work or education. Thus, the process of core value identification should be provided on an individual level (What is important for me in my work or educational environment?), as well as on an organizational level (What are the core values of my university?). We should remember that wherever values occur, there should be involvement and trust. It is difficult to require involvement from an academic community in the realization of values that have been imposed and that are not believed in. Such a procedure can lead to cynicism and profound doubt. Truth is a fundamental academic value. This value penetrates all three basic spheres of academic activity: scientific research, education, and social service. The ethos of truth is supported by other values that are specific to academic life—mostly reliability and responsibility.[5] The academic community is obliged to search for truth in a reliable and responsible way in scientific research.[6] The main responsibility for initiating and conducting a study of a university's core value lies with the top management. That is why, in most cases, the academic community expects advice and definitions from its leaders of what is important to them, what is important for the university, and how everyone should act.[7]

How could we discover the values that constitute academic ethos? In the subject literature and on websites of many consulting firms, we find examples of numerous methods enabling to realize this task. Following are three examples that will illuminate these points. One way to identify academic authentic core values is to form what Collins calls "the Mars Group."[8] He described the idea of this approach in the following way: "Please, imagine you've been asked to re-create the very best attributes of your organization on another planet, but you only have seats on the rocketship for five to seven people. Who would you send? They are the people who probably have a gut-level understanding of your core values, have the highest level of credibility with their peers, and demonstrate the highest levels of competence. The Mars group should wrestle with certain basic questions: What core values do you bring to your work—values you hold to be so fundamental that you would hold them regardless of whether or not they are rewarded? How would you describe to your loved ones the core values you stand for in your work and that you hope they stand for in their working lives? If you awoke tomorrow morning with enough money to retire for the rest of your life, would you continue to hold on to these core values? And perhaps most important: can you envision these values being as valid 100 years from now as they are today? Would you want the organization to continue to hold these values, even if at some point one or more of them became a competitive disadvantage? If you were to start a new organization tomorrow in a different line of work, what core values would you build into the new organization regardless of its activities? The last three questions are key because they help groups make a crucial distinction: core values are timeless and do not change, while practices and strategies should be changing all the time."[9]

The next method has been suggested by Hultman and Gellerman. It is connected with the identification of core values with the use of a table of values. The members of an organization get it in a written form or as an electronic online survey. Participants are asked to indicate from 5 to 10 the most important values that lead the organization's activity (from their point of view). This method enables to:

- identify current values of an organization, a group, or an individual;
- establish desired values of an individual, team, or an organization;
- make the following comparisons within values:
  1. comparison between values of an individual and current values of an organization (or of a team);
  2. make comparisons between current and desired values of an organization (or of a team);
  3. make comparisons between current values of a team and desired values of a team;
  4. make comparisons between current values of an organization and values that are declared by it.

- indicate the most important values of the values that are verbally declared as the core ones:
  1. within a team;
  2. within an organization.

After such research, all answers should be summed up and presented with a list of those indicated most often.[10,11]

Another method of discovering core values was proposed by Lebow and Simon.[12] This method starts with a session for the top management. Managers prepare their own list of core values. Each participant gets a set of 10 to 15 paper sheets and each one writes down a simple phrase consisting of one to five words. This phrase represents one idea of a core value. This single statement is called a "cept" as it is just a part of the concept that should be included in the value expression of an organization. For instance: "Hiring of scientists that are outstanding and righteous (in ethical way)" will be written on two paper sheets: "Outstanding Scientists" and "Righteous (ethical) People." When everyone finishes (after 15 minutes), each person chooses the seven best ideas and ranks them according to their priority. Then each person partners another, and these both choose the best ideas and rank them again. In this way, a group reaches a consensus and formulates the first version of declared core values.[13]

One of the general principles of organizational psychology is a statement that people are more willing to comply with particular declarations, policies, or codes if they are actively involved in the process of their creation and development. That is why the essence of success of this and other methods of discovering a university's core values is to ensure that representatives of each group that constitutes academic community (students, faculty, staff, administration, and so on) are active participants in discovering and developing core values. Understanding and trusting academic community participants in core values may be achieved through their involvement in the discovery process, granting them a right to object as well as giving them opportunities to study core values and relate them to their own lives.

Development of Core Value Through Description and Definition in Behavioral Terms

The next step of this phase is the description of core values. Defining the core values of an organization starts with the answer to the basic question: What does a particular value mean for our organization? Values such as excellence, integrity, or diversity are just general statements that may have a different meaning for various universities.

On the basis of her research analyzing core values in American organizations, Rose Ann Stephenson argued that the same value (such as integrity) was defined in 185 ways.[14] Without a common agreement on the actual meaning of a value for a higher school in practice, the value that is even known and widely communicated will never result in its development. Giving a clear answer to the question "What does a particular value mean to our university?" is a base for effective implementation of those values.

Core values may be described in different ways. The most crucial is to use a simple and understandable description. The main responsibility of value description lies with management as managers initiate the process of defining values. A university's authorities should make the core values clear and understandable for its academic community. Effectiveness and efficiency of defining values depend on the cascade approach to this process. Top management of a university shows its basic understanding through core values descriptions, but each organizational unit, each faculty member, and each employee should define a particular value for taking one's work specifically into account.[15]

Examples of descriptions of higher school core values are presented in Table 2.1.

Description of a particular value that explains its general meaning is not enough to make it viable. It is just the beginning of the route whose destination is to directing the effort of the whole academic community toward the realization of a particular objective in a specific way. A university should aspire to define values in behavioral terms.

Defining Academic Ethos Core Values in Behavioral Terms

Definitions of Desirable Behaviors

Practice of higher school management gives us two ways of defining core values in behavioral terms. The first is connected with defining desired behavior regarding particular core values for the whole academic community (without distinctions of students or teachers). An example of this approach is defining desired behavior as described by Boston College for values such as honesty and integrity, excellence, and mutual respect. Table 2.2 expands on this method.

The second approach for defining behavior coupled with core values is connected to indicating particular behavior for a particular value

Table 2.1. Examples of Descriptions of Higher School Core Values

University	Value Definitions
	Integrity
University of Technology (Jamaica, North America)	As a University community we value ethical behavior in all our endeavors whether scholarly, cultural or intellectual and expect all conduct to be grounded in integrity, mutual respect and civility.[16]
Saint Xavier University (United States, North America)	Integrity gives us the ability to realize the greater good in our actions and programs, and challenges us to look at our work and ourselves holistically and as one united with others across the globe.

Integrity, whether personal or institutional, implies coherence between words and acts. It calls each member of the Saint Xavier community to live in accord with what the University professes to be as an educational institution with a Catholic and Mercy character. Integrity suggests both a certain wholeness in the University itself and connections between the University and the larger educational, religious, and social worlds in which it functions.[17] |
Al-Ahliyya Amman University (Hashemite Kingdom of Jordan, Middle East)	Honesty and mutual trust between the University and related bodies.[18]
Korea Aerospace University (Korea, Asia)	We will work as a team for the good of the whole. We will promote an environment of openness, honesty, and fairness, while holding ourselves and each other to the highest standards of professional and ethical conduct.[19]
	Diversity
Ferris State University (United States, North America)	By providing a campus which is supportive, safe, and welcoming, Ferris embraces a diversity of ideas, beliefs, and cultures.[20]
Loma Linda University (United States, North America)	The quality of living a unified life in which one's convictions are well-considered and match one's actions. Integrity encompasses honesty, authenticity, and trustworthiness.[21]

(Continued)

Table 2.1. (*Continued*)

	Diversity
Saint Xavier University (United States, North America)	Diversity builds a community that fosters a climate that is open and welcoming to diverse people, ideas, and perspectives; that promotes a constructive discourse on the nature of diversity; and that engages faculty, staff, and students in activities that promote the University's core values.
	Saint Xavier's founding sisters were Irish, American, German, and French. Its first students included Native Americans and "Yankees," as well as Midwesterners; Protestants and Jews, as well as Catholics. Today's diverse student body has expanded such early diversity, and the University continues its efforts to enrich the diversity of its faculty and staff. Such diversity strengthens Saint Xavier's academic program and educational environment, preparing students to live and work in an international society and global economy.[22]
Webster University (United States, North America)	By creating an environment accessible to individuals of diverse cultures, ages and socioeconomic backgrounds, and instilling in students a respect for diversity and an understanding of their own and others values.[23]
	Excellence
Saint Xavier University (United States, North America)	Excellence commits us to challenge ourselves to utilize our God-given gifts—intellectual, social, physical, spiritual, and ethical.
	Saint Xavier's commitment to excellence impels both individuals and the University itself to consistently strive for outcomes that are exemplary rather than simply satisfactory. Such striving for excellence touches all aspects of University life from academic programs to sports, from student services to campus environment, from recruitment to publications, from special occasions to daily business. This value also inspires the University community to recognize its members' significant achievements and contributions to the welfare of others.[24]
Ferris State University (United States, North America)	Committed to innovation and creativity, Ferris strives to produce the highest quality outcomes in all its endeavors.[25]
Loma Linda University (United States, North America)	The commitment to exceed minimum standards and expectations.[26]

	Dignity
University of Wisconsin (US, North America)	The CCP values the intrinsic dignity and worth of all human beings and seeks to involve diverse populations by maximizing access to all our efforts.[27]
College of Education (US, North America)	**Ethics and Dignity** We are committed to the highest standards of honesty, fairness, respect, and professional and scholarly ethics. We demonstrate our value of the dignity and worth of all people. We expect all conduct to be based on integrity, mutual respect, and civility, and that conduct is driven by the highest ethical standards.[28]
Humboldt State University (US, North America)	We believe in the dignity of all individuals, in fair and equitable treatment, and in equal opportunity. We value the richness and interplay of differences. We value the inclusiveness of diversity, and we respect alternative paradigms of thought.[29]
	Dignity
Youngstown State University (US, North America)	As a campus community, we expect all conduct to be rooted in integrity, mutual respect, and civility. We value ethical behavior in scholarly and other endeavors; believe in the dignity and worth of all people; strive to foster an appreciation of, and respect for, differences among the human race; and celebrate the diversity that enriches the University and the world.[30]
Manuel S. Enverga University (Philippines, Asia)	Respect for basic freedoms/human rights Exercise of rights with responsibility Moral sensitivity Recognition of cultural differences[31]
	Truth
St. John's University (US, North America)	Knowledge in accord with reality, behavior faithful to ethical standards. St. John's affirms the threefold mission of a university to seek truth through research, to disseminate it through teaching and to act on it. The University values and utilizes the perspectives of different cultures to assist its members in seeking truth and developing ethical standards, while affirming the Judaeo-Christian tradition.[32]

(Continued)

Table 2.1. (Continued)

Freie Universität Berlin (Germany, Europe)	*Veritas*—truth—is the highest aim of the research and teaching activities pursued at Freie Universität. In the modern sense, this focus on truth means outlining a clear interest in new findings and insight for the university's academic activities, protecting those activities from the risk of arbitrariness, and observing the standards of good academic practice. It is in the quest for truth that academia finds the core of its intellectual self-image, its methodological sustainability, and its internal drive and dynamism.[33]
Lipscomb University (US, North America)	Truth is sought in each class and should be lived out in the behavior and speech of each employee and student.[34]
Bethel University (US, North America)	At the same time, we are **truth-seekers**, recognizing that all truth—scientific, artistic, philosophical, or theological—has its source in God.[35]
University of Bagamoyo (Tanzania, Africa)	**Truth** is a core value that makes UB candidate a socially conscious person committed to service of the community through leadership and governance skills attained for the time to be spent in the University system.[36]
Respect	
University of Central Arkansas (US, North America)	We support a community and climate of respect and thoughtfulness among students, faculty, staff, and the people of our community, state, nation, and the world.[37]
University of California (US, North America)	We will respect the rights and dignity of others.[38]
University of Illinois (US, North America)	Treating every individual with respect as we would like to be treated ourselves. We are committed to diversity.[39]
Korea Aerospace University (Korea, Asia)	We will recognize and appreciate differences among ourselves and we will value the unique strengths of each individual, which will contribute to the University's advancement. We will support each other to excel personally and professionally, fostering a strong positive energy on campus.[40]

Source: Author's own study based on analyzed websites.

Table 2.2. Examples of Defining Desired Behavior Regarding Particular Core Values

Value	Description	Behavior
Honesty and Integrity	We are committed to promoting the highest standards of honesty and integrity to ensure that all members of the community recognize the inherent benefits of living these ideals and to guarantee that academic performance is evaluated reliably and rewarded fairly.	– Written work is original – Citations are used appropriately in all written work – Oral statements are presented candidly – Resume is presented truthfully – Assignments and examinations are completed honestly – Credit for group work represents the personal contribution of the individual
Mutual Respect	We are committed to fostering an environment in which every member of the community nurtures the spirit of trust, teamwork, openness and respect that is necessary to embrace and fully capitalize on our professional community.	– Abstaining from harassing behavior – Listening to and respecting the opinions of all members of the community – Focusing attention on what is happening in class, events, or meetings only when authorized – Appropriate attire for special events and guest appearances
Excellence	We are committed to creating an environment where all members of the community pursue the highest possible level of academic performance and personal development for themselves and other members of the community.	– Personal commitment to academic excellence in course work and assignment – Personal commitment to developing technical and nontechnical skills, including dealing with ambiguity and operating outside of one's comfort zone

(Continued)

Table 2.2. (Continued)

Value	Description	Behavior
		– Personal commitment to performing at a high level
		– Personal commitment to developing as a management professional
Personal Accountability	We are committed to fostering an environment where every member of the community understands and accepts responsibility for upholding and reinforcing our values.	– Being proactive in acquiring material that was missed due to an absence
		– Arriving at class, events, and appointments on time
		– Active participation in class discussions and other meetings
		– Active participation in group activities
		– Being fully prepared for classes, events, and appointment

Source: Based on http://www.bc.edu/content/dam/files/schools/csom_sites/mba/pdf/Core_values.pdf

separately for students, academic teachers, scientists, administration staff, and even for students' parents or guardians. An example of such an approach is ascribing the responsibility for the value of "integrity" that may be found on websites of The School of Ethical Education or in the Code of Conduct for the University of Connecticut.

Table 2.3 presents definitions of "integrity" in behavioral terms for particular groups of academic community.

The second approach seems to guarantee a greater understanding of requirements for a particular value regarding particular participants of academic community. Similar to a core values description, there should be a cascade approach when defining in actual behavioral terms.

Definitions of Unacceptable Behavior

A crucial step of this phase of core value management is to define behavior that may threaten our core values (that have a destructive influence on academic ethos values). Having analyzed websites of higher schools from throughout the world as well as having conducted interviews and research at chosen universities, it appears that, in most cases, universities define particular behaviors for their core values (e.g., integrity), their "basic standards of academic integrity." They formulate a set of unacceptable behaviors such as cheating, plagiarism, fabrication, or any research misconduct. Defining base academic ethos core values is, foremost, a matter of defining desired (positive) behaviors and not the negative ones. This is because only positive behavior may be a catalyst for moral character development of an individual and an organization; this, in turn, can lead to the development of overall academic integrity. In general, human beings want to act on behalf of goodness, peace, and integrity, not for evil, war, or corruption. The fundamental aspect of humanity is goodness, constructed by individuals.

Of course, it does not mean that we should not indicate negative behavior as a threat for core values, but this practice should not be the priority in a process of constructing academic integrity. Such destructive behavior should be not only defined by types of behavior, but also evaluated in terms of specific examples and values that this type of behavior threatens. The necessity of defining behavior that threatens core values is

Table 2.3. *Definitions of "Integrity" in Behavioral Terms For Particular Groups of Academic Community*

Value	Student	Academic Teacher	Scientist	Administration Staff	Parent/Guardian
Integrity	Completing all assigned work, activities and tests in an honorable way that avoids all cheating, lying, and stealing.	Support the school's core values that prioritizes student learning over letter grades.	Properly collect, record, and maintain research data.	Support publication of the Honor Code and Pledge in the student and faculty handbooks and the Honor Policy on the school's website.	Review and understand the Honor Code and honor uidelines for individual teachers' classes.
	Maintain records of research notes, outlines, rough drafts, and reference works to validate individual effort.	Collaborate with other teachers and departments to avoid multiple large projects coming due at the same time.	Take responsibility for all publications and presentations of which we are author or co-author.	Facilitate ongoing conversations and reflection about the Honor Policy and Honor Code.	Communicate your support for the school's core values and Honor Code and discuss with your student their opinion of academic integrity and its relevance to their education.
	Seek supplemental assistance from teachers, parents, or peers to understand lessons and assignment.	Check student papers for plagiarism.	Appropriately acknowledge, in publications and presentations, those who have contributed to our research.	Support the Academic Honor Committee with annual budget.	Support the imposition of consequences if the Honor Code is violated and discuss with your student the value of maintaining academic integrity.

Source: Based on http://www.ethicsed.org. Example of an Honor Policy; The University of Connecticut Code of Conduct. Available at: http://www.audit.uconn.edu/doc/codeof conduct.pdf

caused by the need to fully interpret appropriate behavior by students, academic teachers, or even administrators.[41] The subsequent enforcement of desired behaviors and possible punishment for behavior that are reprehensible will be impossible without a clear definition of what is acceptable and what is not.

It also results from cultural differences: "students from certain Middle Eastern, Asian, and African cultures are baffled by the notion that one can 'own' ideas, since their cultures regard words and ideas as the property of all rather than as individual property."[42] So, those students do not perceive plagiarism as unethical or morally reprehensible behavior.

Table 2.4 presents types of behaviors that are destructive for academic ethos core values, particularly examples of behaviors threatening academic ethos, and it indicates core values that may be threatened by those behaviors.

Similar to defining desired behaviors, defining behaviors that threaten core values is a cascade process. It not only should be initiated at the top management level of a university, but also should be conducted for each faculty member, institute, or department.

Discovering and developing academic ethos core values as described above produces a consensus within an academic community on core values that are authentic, shared, constant, limited in number, fascinating, clear, written, defined, and transformed into positive behavior. Within the process of core values discovering and development, an organization may be forced to face various axiological complexities that are results of a relationship among *current*, *declared*, and *core* values.

It is worth recalling that declared values are those that are said to be core. Current values are those that comply with organization's actions and that lead its everyday activity.

- In the first case, an organization acts in accordance with what it says, and the values that lead its activity meet the criteria of core values. This is a perfect example of Academic Ethos Management.
- In the second case, an organization does not comply with what it declares, and the declared values are the core ones. It is not "walking the talk."

Table 2.4. Example of Behaviors Threatening Core Values of Academic Ethos

Types of Behaviors Threatening Core Values	Core Values Threatened by a Particular Behavior Type	Examples of Behaviors Threatening Core Values
Abuse (physical, mental, or verbal)	Community, respect, and integrity	Harm to another or aid in commission of an act that causes physical or emotional harm to others.
Research misconduct	Honesty, excellence, respect, and integrity	Fabrication of data, plagiarism, data-dredging, selective data reporting, "salami-science"
Cheating	Honesty, excellence, respect, and integrity	Using crib notes during an exam, arranging with another student to copy answers during an exam, writing a paper in English and having someone else to translate into the required foreign language.
Plagiarism	Honesty, excellence, respect, and and integrity	Copying someone else's term paper, buying a term paper, using a paper for more than one class without the teacher's permission.
Fabrication	Honesty, excellence, respect, and integrity	Making up sources for a bibliography, changing data so they look better in a lab report, writing a lab report without doing the experiment.
Felicitation/academic dishonesty	Honesty, excellence, respect, and integrity	Writing a paper for someone else, selling a term paper.
Misrepresentation	Honesty, excellence, respect, and integrity	Giving a false excuse for missing an exam or deadline.
Sabotage	Honesty, excellence, respect, and integrity	Removing items from a reserved reading file so that others cannot use them.
Cyber-plagiarism	Honesty, excellence, respect, and integrity	Copy ideas found on the Web without giving proper attribution to the source.
Cyber-cheating	Honesty, excellence, respect, and integrity	Download research papers from the Web, in whole or part, and submit the paper as original work.

Obtaining an unfair advantage	Honesty, excellence, respect, and integrity	Stealing, reproducing, circulating, or otherwise gaining access to examination materials prior to the time authorized by the instructor. Intentionally obstructing or interfering with another student's academic work.
Unauthorized access to computerized academic or administrative records or systems	Honesty, respect, and integrity	Teoing or altering computer records, modifying computer programs or systems.
Alcohol	Community, respect, personal development, and integrity	Excessive drinking and intoxication. Drinking games designed for the purpose of the irresponsible consumption of alcohol.
Computer and other electronic device misuse	Excellence, community, respect, and integrity	Unauthorized transfer of a file. Use of computing facilities to interfere with the work of another student, faculty, member, or University Official.
Damage to property	Community, respect, responsible stewardship, and integrity	Damage and vandalism to personal property of others or University.
Discrimination and harassment	Community, respect, and integrity	Discrimination because of race, color, religion, gender, sexual orientation, national origin, age, handicap, or military service.
Disruptive behavior	Excellence, community, respect, and integrity	Disruption or obstruction of teaching, research, administration, and disciplinary proceedings.
Falsification	Excellence, respect, personal development, and integrity	Providing false information to any campus official or providing false, altered, or forged academic records.
Fire safety	Community, respect, and integrity	Failing to evacuate a building or failing to cooperate with authorities during a fire alarm or drill.
Fireworks, explosives, weapons, and other dangerous items	Community, personal development, and integrity	Possession, use, or sale of weapons, ammunition, combustibles, fireworks, explosive devices, or any other substance or devices designed to harm or incapacitate.

(Continued)

Table 2.4. (*Continued*)

Types of Behaviors Threatening Core Values	Core Values Threatened by a Particular Behavior Type	Examples of Behaviors Threatening Core Values
Hazing	Community, respect, responsible stewardship, and integrity	Whipping, beating, branding, forced calisthenics, exposure to the elements, forced consumption of food, liquor, drug, or other substance, or any other forced physical activity that could subject the individual to extreme mental stress.
Solicitation	Excellence, community, respect, responsible stewardship, and integrity	Solicitation, sales, or door-to-door canvassing by students or nonstudents on University property except with permission.
Theft or unauthorized possession	Excellence, respect, integrity, community, responsible stewardship, and personal development	Taking, sale, or possession of property without the expressed consent of the owner.
Use of university name or symbols	Excellence, and integrity	Use University name, seal, symbols, logos, slogans, or songs without the written authorization.

Source: Based on Whitley, B. E. and Keith-Spiegel, P. (2002). Academic Dishonesty. An Educator's Guide. US: Lawrence Erlbaum Associates, Mahwah, NJ, pp. 37–40; https://guides.library.ualberta.ca/content.php?pid=62200&sid=457651; http://www.saintleo.edu/Campus-Life/Code-of-Conduct; http://www.northwestern.edu/provost/students/integrity/principles.html;http://www.saintleo.edu/Campus-Life/Code-of-Conduct; http://nfaetyka.wordpress.com/2011/12/22/klasyfikacja-naduzyc-naukowych/

- In the third case, an organization does not comply with declared values, but its current values (in accordance with the way in which an organization acts) are its core values. It is a situation that may be a consequence of imposing external values to organization's employees. In such a situation, it is recommended to transform current values into declared ones.
- In the fourth case, an organization does not comply with what it declares and current values are not core ones. It is preferable to check if declared values are the core ones. If so, a process of their implementation should be initiated. If not, preferable core values should be discovered initially and then transformed into core values.
- In the fifth case, an organization complies with declared values but does not meet the criteria of core values. In such a case, core values should be redefined.
- In the sixth case, an organization does not comply with declared values, and those declared values do not meet core values criteria. In this case, it should be verified whether current values meet core values criteria. If so, they should be transformed into core values. If not, there arises a necessity to discover preferable values and then transform them into core values.
- In the seventh case, an organization does not possess declared values, and the current values do not meet core values criteria. It is highly recommended then to develop current values into values that are declared.
- Finally, in the eighth case, an organization does not possess declared values and the current ones are not the core values. In such a situation there is a necessity to discover preferred values and transform them into the core ones.[43]

Once the proper core values have been discovered and documented, they must be implemented in a sound, strategic manner that has lasting effect on the school of higher learning. This strategy for success will be analyzed in Chapter 3.

Chapter 3

Enacting the Core Values of Academic Ethos

Toward Enacting Academic Ethos Values

By discovering and defining academic ethos, a school of higher learning makes general statements about its central characteristics (core values). These characteristics constitute the set of meaning that management wants the academic community to use in viewing, describing, and relating to a university. The key differences among higher schools lie not in the general core values statement (many universities have very similar or nearly the same core values), but in the effectiveness of transmitting the chosen academic ethos to the academic community and other stakeholders. The instrument of core values of academic ethos transmission to participants of an academic community is the next phase of the academic ethos management process. This phase is called *enacting academic ethos*.

Core values declared by universities, which may be beautifully defined, are just words until the school starts to comply with them. Core values resist their continuity mostly through their implementation into the organizational framework, through including them into particular goals and objectives, policies, procedures, and practices, and through each organizational act adapted to them—namely through their institutionalization.[1] Based on the words of Whitley and Keith-Spiegel from their book *Academic Dishonesty. An Educator's Guide*, we may state that unless the leadership and representatives of the university enforce core values in all areas of the institution's functioning, public statements, business affairs, athletics, research, and so forth, neither the faculty and students nor the general public will believe that the university has a valid commitment to core values of academic ethos.[2]

So, the next phase of academic ethos management process is enacting academic ethos core values through

1. reflecting and supporting core values of academic ethos in university's goals, objectives, and measures;
2. formalizing a university's policies, procedures, and codes, which
   - form a dialogue at the institutional, classroom and individual level around fundamental values of academic ethos;
   - guide and enhance the conduct of academic community in performing their duties in pursuit of academic ethos;
3. communicating core values of academic ethos.

Reflecting and Supporting Core Values in a University's Goals, Objectives, and Measures

As a guidepost in a university's life, core values should not merely be defined in behavioral terms (in a positive or a negative way). The most important points are to define and communicate to members of the academic community: What should be done for their implementation (goals)? How should this be implemented (what particular actions should be taken for activating, that is, objectives)? How should the effects of core values implementation be measured? What should be the deadline for objectives achievement (measures)? If values of academic ethos of a particular university are reflected in its goals along with associated objectives, strategies, and plans, then they send a clear message to students, staff members, faculty members, and university officials that the values of academic ethos are substantial. Research has shown that the most successful organizations are those that have core values and goals that are clearly defined, consistent, and shared among their members.[3] To ensure that a particular value has been understood in an appropriate way by all the members of academic community and with the aim of providing clear guidelines that are the criteria of work executing, values should be defined in a form of simple, measurable, and attainable objectives and tasks.

Each core value of academic ethos may be expressed by a university though a particular objective, tasks for its realization, and measures to enable assessment of the effectiveness of its activity.

Table 3.1 presents examples of core values, their description as well as objectives, tasks, and measures for their enlivening.

Formalizing a University's Policies, Procedures, and Codes

Schools of higher education can set forth various policies supported by executive instruments in the form of procedures and codes in order to create a base of examples for patterns of conduct, to outline basic principles of academic ethics, and to give opportunities for fulfilling the objectives connected with the values of academic ethos. The bases for those documents are obviously the values of academic ethos. Formalizing of policies with the use of their instruments such as procedures and codes is a crucial step on the way to enacting an academic ethos.

University policies regarding academic ethos are needed to make sure that expectations are clear in every situation[4] and to help reduce uncertainty about acceptable and unacceptable behavior.[5] University policies based on academic core values have symbolic overtones in representing and communicating their core values. However, much of their impact on core values enacting stems from their application and use of concrete procedures and codes.

There are great numbers of policies and codes that are created to guarantee the integrity of a university. It is hard to find a university that does not boast on its websites of its integrity policy, honesty policy, or more detailed policies against unethical behavior among members of academic community, such as university policy on cheating, plagiarism, or research misconduct, not to mention other codes of conduct that are present at nearly every good university. This is all because critics of higher education, and business education especially, as well as numerous cases of unethical behavior ascribed to members of academic community (misconduct in research, cheating, corruption inside university, etc.) became a cause for universities to develop their internal infrastructure of ethics in a form of integrity policies supported by executive instruments such as procedures and codes. They are designed to guarantee ethical behavior of academic

Table 3.1. Examples of Core Values, Their Description as well as Objectives, Tasks, and Measures for Their Enlivening

Values	Value Description	Example of an Objective Aimed at Enacting a Value	An Example of a Task for Objective Realization	Measure of Task Realization
Excellence*	– Excellence in all we do: academic, research, and service excellence and managerial and service excellence from ourselves	To achieve the highest-quality faculty and faculty life.	– To expand our research activities by hiring the best scholars in their fields. – To create and refine structures and mechanisms that encourage and support interdisciplinary work.	– Quadruple the number of faculty who are members of the National Academy of Science, the National Academy of Engineering, or fellows in academic and professional societies.
		To increase the size and quality of the graduate population.	– To recruit top students. – Postdoctoral study should be increased for graduates of Texas A&M University as well as for those from peer institutions.	– Recruit 75% of graduate students from institutions other than Texas A&M University and from outside Texas. – Double the number of postdoctoral fellows.
		To strengthen the letters, arts, and sciences.	– To generate a range of programs that compares favorably with the nation's best public universities.	– Establish doctoral-level faculties in appropriate arts, humanities, and social sciences disciplines.
Direction-finding**	– Being innovative, respected, and visible.	To be the preferred partner of choice among academic environments and industrial partners.	– To establish and hold conferences about innovations. – To create dynamic research environments, including by means of external research funds. – To keep actively in touch with the press and private sector.	– Organize Computer Games and Digital Textualities. – Increase gained research funds by 50%. – Increase the number of private sector representatives participating in join research projects.

Forthcoming**	– Being inquisitive, holistically oriented, and willing to see beyond its own demarcation lines and domains.	To be open and unprejudiced and to conduct a mutually respectful dialogue.	– Welcome new employees in an open and outreaching manner. – The teachers develop courses and teach together. – Listen and try to understand those who contact us. If we cannot perform the task for them, we provide them with guidance about where it can be performed.	– Reduce the number of new employees reporting problem with atmosphere at work to zero – Increase number of interdisciplinary and interfaculty programs by 30% – E-mail response within 24 hours
Diversity*		To lead in diversity.	– To create an environment that respects and nurtures all members of the student, faculty, and staff community.	– Reduce the number of students, faculty, or staff who leave because of a perception of a less-than-welcoming environment to zero.

Source:
* Examples of core values, objectives, tasks and measures for values "excellence" and "diversity" based on Vision 2020: Creating a Culture of Excellence, Texas A&M University (http://vision2020.tamu.edu).
** Examples of core values, objectives, tasks and measures for values "direction-finding" and "forthcoming" based on The IT University of Copenhagen's Value Statement, August 27, 2003, Version 1.3.

community participants and to reinforce academic ethos. However, we should remember that the name of a particular policy or code is not so important. The important issue is that the instruments for enacting academic ethos should be a result of previous phases of academic ethos management. It should be a subsequent step of the consistent and deliberate process of academic ethos management.

Cases from business reveal that despite the best elaborated codes of ethics and ethical policies (such as those of Enron), the process of academic ethos management may be ineffective as the base for their elaboration if they were not actually shared organizational values or if those documents were not an element of the whole managerial process. Elaborated policies should be a reflection of academic ethos values, leading ideology, and an organization's history. The implementation varies considerably from institution to institution, but most policies related to academic ethos include policy or goal statements, core values statements, definitions of communal responsibility and rights, definitions and consequences of prohibited behaviors, and tips for preventing academic misconduct. Those policies should also describe reporting and adjudication process as well as procedures for sanctions and appeals.

Communicating Core Values of Academic Ethos

The spectrum of tools viable in core values of academic ethos communication process is broad; Chapter 4 discusses this process in detail.

How to Make Academic Ethos Values
Alive—Few Guidelines

Considering that elaborating the policy and its executive instruments in a form of procedures and codes should be a reflection of academic ethos values of a particular university, it is not necessary at this point to define model policies, procedures, or codes. However, if there is such a need, it is recommended visiting the website of Center for Academic Integrity or The School of Ethical Education—Integrity Work.[6]

However, the following is a description of some fundamental elements and assumptions that may help to transform instruments such as policies and procedures for academic ethos values enacting into effective tools that create academic integrity.

Coparticipation of Academic Community Representatives in the Developmental Process of Policies, Procedures, and Codes for Enacting Academic Ethos Values

One of the fundamental principles of creating policies, procedures, and academic codes is connected with the broadest possible participation of academic community representatives in this process. Formulated and defined principles of conduct included in those documents regard students, staff members, faculty members, and university officials as well. Providing coparticipation in the work on those documents may become a precondition for the success of creating an academic community that is based on values.

Process of Policy Statement and Core Values Statement Formulation

Using a policy or a goal statement and core values statement as a preface of documents such as a university's policy on academic ethos is significant from a psychological point of view. They may be published as separate documents such as policy statements:

> "Academic honesty is essential to the development of personal integrity and the fulfillment of the second goal of striving to have students grow in the knowledge and the practice of Gospel values. In the Rule of St. Benedict, the dignity of work is an important tenet and offers a strong connection to the SEHS goal to respect and honor a person's work, including intellectual property. In the fulfillment of this goal, the Academic Council has established the following Honor Policy."[7]

and core value statements:

> "Saint Leo University offers a practical, effective model for life and leadership in a challenging world. As such our community has

adopted six steadfast moral Guidelines to help us recognize the dignity, value, and gifts of all people. We encourage all members of our community to use and embrace the following values in their day-to-day lives in order to strengthen our commitment to each other, our University, and to God."[8]

They also may include both of these elements in a one statement, as for example in the Policy on Academic Honor from Hillsdale College:

Virtue, courage, and wisdom, goods of the highest order being the aim of a liberal education, it is necessarily the policy of Hillsdale College to act firmly and decisively to promote the academic integrity and honor of this institution. Honesty in academics, as in all walks of life, is a matter of personal honor for which each individual must ultimately take responsibility. It is the primary purpose of this policy, by its very existence and application, to increase and ensure academic honesty within the Hillsdale College community.[9]

Despite the fact that the mentioned element seems to be hardly significant, people are more likely to comply with the regulations when they identify the reasons for them.[10] Moreover, it is good to communicate and recall core values at every opportunity. Furthermore, the preface in the form of a core values statement helps to illustrate to its receivers what is the core and basis of their creation.

Formulating of Academic Community Responsibility

Policies and codes of a university, which support values of academic ethos, are an essential force in the academic life of a university. So it is, without reservation, a responsibility of all members of the academic community to actively promote the contents. To make effective tools of those documents, all the members need to clearly indicate a responsibility of the academic community as a whole and of its participants—students, academic staff, school's administrators, and even the students' parents or guardians.

Responsibility of academic community as a whole is to[11]

- *share the responsibility to ensure that the Academic Ethos Policy is upheld;*
- *advance and disseminate knowledge and understanding, and thus they strive for excellence in research, scholarship, practice, and teaching as well as should be consistent with the responsible use of academic freedom;*
- *perform their duties in a fair and ethical manner in accordance with established policies, procedures, and regulations based on core values of academic ethos;*
- *carry out their duties with professionalism;*
- *treat other persons equitably, irrespective of gender, sexual orientation, race, disability or medical condition, cultural background, religion, marital status, age, or political conviction;*
- *treat each other with consideration and respect. Managers and supervisors have an elevated responsibility to demonstrate these behaviors and support their expressions in the workplace;*
- *be responsible for complying with all workplace safety and health regulations and report unsafe conditions, equipment, or practices to appropriate University officials, as required by law;*
- *report any behaviors that threaten values of academic ethos, behaviors that are against preferred policies, procedures and codes, to one's supervisor, head of department, or dean who should consult immediately with designated offer regarding the nature of the concern.*

To formulate a more detailed responsibility of particular members of the academic community, it is recommended to consider it for students as well as for academic staff, with specification for its particular academic roles, for example, teacher and supervisor, consultant and practitioner, manager, employee, or colleague in relations with other staff as well as at the administration level.

A student's responsibility is to[12]

- *Share to ensure that others, as well as themselves, uphold the spirit and letter of the Policy of Academic Ethos. Various methods of encouraging behavior related to university core values exist, such as setting an example for new students, education through student organizations, and student-to-student moral suasion.*

- *Avoid acts of dishonesty; students, for example, should not give or receive aid for an examination; that they will not give or receive unpermitted aid in class work, in the preparation of reports, or in any other work that is to be used by the instructor as the basis of grading; that they will not copy or paraphrase without proper acknowledgment; that they will not forge an instructor's or an administrator's signature (cf. Jordan High School Academic Honor Policy).*
- *Clarifying with the instructor anything that may be unclear about an assignment, with respect to how the Honor Policy/Code may apply to it.*
- *Participating in the further development in the Honor Policy/ Code during the student's high school career.*

A teacher's responsibility

As in the case of the student's responsibility, members of academic staff, such as teachers and supervisors of students, should take proactive steps (actions) to promote academic core values, policies, and codes. Teachers should therefore "treat students with respect at all times and encourage students to think independently and to exchange ideas freely."[13] All syllabi should contain a statement concerning academic ethos core values and refer students to the university policies, procedures, and rules, which, for example, may be found on the web. Teachers should have an open discussion about academic ethos with students at the beginning of their courses. They are also responsible for "developing assessment procedures that are fair and effective and that contribute to student learning, and administering them in a fair and efficient manner, and providing timely and constructive feedback to students; continual seeking to improve their teaching effectiveness on the basis of all available information about their performance and its impact on students; where appropriate, providing suitable advice and assistance to former students in their academic and professional development"[14] as well as "they share in the responsibility and authority to challenge and make known acts that violate it."[15]

Academic staff's responsibility

The academic staff is additionally responsible for matters connected with the role it plays at a university. For example, in a document entitled "Code of Ethics for Academic Staff," from the University of Waikato,[16] this responsibility is listed as follows

> Academic staff as researchers and scholars should, for instance, scrupulously acknowledge the contributions that others have made toward their research and scholarship, especially colleagues and students, and comply with the standards and ethics of their own professional societies, and with nationally and internationally accepted standards.
> Academic staff as consultants and practitioners should refrain from engaging in any work that would compromise their integrity and independence as academic staff and avoid representing themselves as acting for, or on behalf of, the university when undertaking private consulting work.
> Academic staff as managers should manage their unit in a way that will help staff to teach and research effectively, encourage appropriate discussion among colleagues on major policy matters including new staff appointments and should not allow personal relationships with staff to affect or appear to affect the managerial relationship between them.
> Academic staff as employees should acknowledge and contribute to the achievement of the university's objectives, participate appropriately in the institutional life of the university, as well as accept a responsibility as stewards of university property.

Academic administrators' responsibility

Beyond the responsibility of the whole academic community, academic administrators are also obliged to manage the university in a manner that reflects a conduct in accordance with the values of academic ethos and act categorically in situations of value violation by students, faculty, or academic administrators. "Nothing better demonstrates commitment than taking action at some cost to oneself."[17] Based on "Example of an Honor Policy. The School for Ethical Education–Integrity Works!"[18] administrators should also support publication of all policies supporting academic ethos in the student and faculty handbooks and in the Academic Ethos Policy on the school's website and maintain confidential records of academic ethos violations.[19]

Students' parents and guardians are also responsible for enlivening the values of academic ethos, which is connected with their role in understanding and actively supporting the enacting of academic policies for core values.

Academic Pledge

Students, staff, faculty, and administrators should be required to read and understand the university's policy regarding academic ethos and sign a statement saying they understand and agree to abide by the policy. A popular practice of higher schools is the formulation of declarations from members of the academic community that confirm not only their awareness of academic ethos values but also their obligation to obey policies and codes. There are various forms of declaration, starting from the general pledge with responsibility for others:

> As a member of the Mainland community, I maintain a high level of respect and integrity. I uphold the Honor Code in letter and spirit. I do not lie, cheat, steal, vandalize, or commit forgery. I encourage fellow students who commit honors offenses to acknowledge such offenses. I inform the Honor Council of my own and others infractions. I make this pledge in the spirit of honor and trust[20]

through student pledge:

> Students in the Carroll Graduate School of Management are expected to adhere to the highest standards of professional conduct as outlined in the Core Values. A student who accepts and adheres to the standards will remain in good standing within the Carroll Graduate School of Management.

> For additional information on the Core Values and the disciplinary process please refer to the Graduate Management Student Handbook.

I acknowledge that I have received, read, and understand the Graduate School Core Values and disciplinary process.[21]

ending with faculty member pledge:

I promise to actively promote student honesty by explaining the importance of academic honesty, maintaining vigilance, keeping test materials secure and varied, and assessing penalties as prescribed in the Honor Policy.[22]

or parent pledge:

I will support St. Elizabeth High School in its goal of helping students to grow in moral values by encouraging academic honesty in my child. I have read the Honor Policy and understand the penalties for violations. I understand and accept the consequences for failure to abide by the provisions of the policy.[23]

Reporting and Adjudication

A very important element of each policy for values of academic ethos enactment is a specification of procedures that enables reporting cases of misconduct in the academic community working against core values and that offers precise reporting procedures, hearing procedures, and particular sanctions for unacceptable actions. It is necessary for procedures to offer precise ways of appeal against a disciplinary decision as well as to define rights of such a person in the whole process of reporting behavior inconsistent with applicable standards. Grabeski's analogy illuminates methods for enhancing a social system in order to detect a wrong-doing in the academic community:[24]

When there were not so many cars, there was enough to announce that a driver has to behave cautiously and properly, in accordance with principles of ethics or Ten Commandments. However, when traffic increased, these general rules are no longer enough. There occurred a need to implement a traffic code including precisely defined do's and don'ts, procedures for its efficiency and sanctions as the plausibility of accidents (including those with the participation of cautious people) could be threatening for traffic at all.

Specified procedures of reporting cases of behavior against values of academic ethos for university's employees

Procedures of reporting and judging behaviors against values of academic ethos that are based on a university's policy (honor policy, integrity policy, etc.) should specify the steps (options of conduct) that should be taken by students and teachers as well. For instance:

In Carroll Graduate School of Management, faculty members and directors have the responsibility to report all incidents to the Associate Dean for graduate Programs in writing (see attached form). If the incident is deemed to be of a minor nature, the faculty member or director may handle the matter themselves and communicate the repercussions appropriate o the violation. If the incident is deemed to be serious, the Committee on Professional Standards will be convened. The Committee on Professional Standards will conduct a hearing on the matter and, if the student is found responsible, shall recommend a sanction to the Associate Dean for Graduate Programs, who may accept or reduce the recommended sanction, but not increase it. The report of the Committee on Professional Standards shall remain in the offending student's file for up to five years beyond the date of his/her graduation.[25]

A procedure of Texas A&M University or Florida State University is quite similar:

Instructors have two options for adjudication of cases: they can refer the case to the Honor Council for further investigation and decision-making, or they can adjudicate the case themselves, if it is a first offense, following the instructor procedures for adjudication specified by the AHSO.[26]

When instructor believes that a student has violated the Academic Honor Policy in one of the instructor's classes, the instructor must first contact the Office of the Dean of the Faculties to discover whether the student has a prior record of academic dishonesty.[27]

Instructors can adjudicate the case themselves, if it is a first offense, following the special instructor procedure for adjudication, which should be specified by the correct department. If the student is found to have a prior record of academic dishonesty or the serious nature of the allegations merits a formal hearing, the instructor must refer the case to a specially organizational unit as, for example, an Honor Council (Texas A&M University)[28] or Academic Honor Policy Hearing Referral (Florida State University).[29] With either option, the instructor shall complete a Violation Report Form and submit it to the appropriate organizational unit, provide a copy to the student and the instructor's department head as soon as practicable, preferably within five university business days of discovery of the alleged incident.

At Texas A&M University,[30] there are following three additional methods of reporting honor code violations.

- General reporting constitutes submission of a report in which the reporting party is willing to fully identify himself or herself to all involved in the case. This is the preferred reporting format and will ensure that all facts are obtainable.
- Confidential reporting constitutes submission of a report in which the reporting party is willing to provide his or her name to the instructor and the AHSO, but wishes to have his or her name remain confidential through the proceedings of the case. Confidential reporting allows the instructor and the AHSO to contact the reporting party to gather further information when necessary.
- Anonymous reporting constitutes a submission of a report in which the reporting party desires to remain anonymous. This report will be considered a tip and handled as such. The reporting party will not be identifiable and cannot becontacted for further information on the case. An anonymous tip is not a sufficient ground to initiate a charge; however, the tip can initiate an investigation.

Specified procedures for reporting cases of behaviors against values of academic ethos for a university's students

As in the case of teachers, a similar procedure should specify options of conduct in reporting provided by students. In the example of Texas A&M University,[31] this procedure is as follows:

Students have two options when reporting an alleged violation. They may report alleged violations to either the AHSO or the instructor of the course in which the alleged violation occurred. Initiating formal procedures is a necessary and obligatory remedy when other methods are inappropriate or have failed (i.e., drawing attention to a suspected violation, moral suasion, etc.).

If a student is alleged to have violated the Honor Code but the class, department, and instructor cannot be identified, charges may be brought by any instructor or student who has knowledge of the violation.

Each member of the academic community should also have the option of anonymous violation reporting with the use of an appropriate hotline (this line should have no caller identification or number recognition) or a website (see, e.g., "Procedures for Reporting Violations or Concerns" from Washington University in St. Louis).

Whistleblowers' Protection

When describing procedures connected with reporting inappropriate behavior, it is necessary to consider the problem of whistleblowers' protection. Of course, at universities in the United States, United Kingdom, or Germany, certain rules are in place to offer such protection and are handled through internal committees such as, for example, the Honor Council or Academic Standards Committee. There is still a question: To what extent are those committees functioning in universities or institutions actually prepared for doing their duties? Nonetheless, this approach seems to be better than the attitude of certain places in the world where the outstanding honesty of scientists and the existence of a "self-cleaning mechanism" of science are taken for granted. In those places, the issue of whistleblowers protection is usually underestimated.

Slightly modified principles of those adopted by American universities were implemented in Germany in order to increase the efficiency of whistleblower protection. They created a position of ombudsman, who is a third part in this process. People who have noticed examples of unreliable behavior in the academic community may report to an ombudsman with complete trust and ask for advice and help. If an ombudsman recognizes the case as the serious one, he or she requests the initiation of proceedings personally. This conduct provides a whistleblower with protection. Ombudspersons are a separate organization (Ombudspersons Office) aimed at representing members of the academic community, resolving conflicts, and verifying university's compliance with its core values or with Academic Ethos Policy. The main feature of their work is confidentiality. An employee or a student who reports may be sure the ombudsman will maintain privacy and confidentiality of the information. That is why ombudsmen should use an independent electronic mail system and an external hotline, and their offices should be equipped with soundproof rooms. They also should be free from managerial pressures and be responsible only to the university president. Moreover, the budget for their activity needs to be separate from the budget of a whole university (in some cases, it may be paid by an independent foundation).

Employees and students should be able to come to an ombudsman with various problems they cannot resolve on their own or if they notice that other employees do act in accordance with established principles. An ombudsman may use a vast array of actions and rights (from giving advice to conducting internal investigation). The Ombudspersons office should be open to all the members of the academic community (including part-time employees). Ombudspersons also have their own code of ethics that emphasizes characteristics such as neutrality, confidentiality, and a duty of protecting possessed information (even from a university's management).

There also exists a simple instruction for employees and students who need to make an ethically difficult decision. In such cases, members of the academic community should ask key questions:[32]

- If, by making a particular decision, do I compromise with my own system of values?
- Would I like my action to become a commonly accepted practice?

- How would I feel like if my action was described on the front page of a local newspaper?
- Would I feel good if I told my partner, parents, or children about my decision?

Specification of Hearing Process Principles and Employees' and Students' Rights During Both Formal and Informal Resolutions

The section of the policy statement dealing with procedures for reporting violations should also specify the principles of hearing process as well as the rights of students or the another member of academic community during the whole investigation connected with suspicion of behavior incompliant with academic ethos. At a minimum, these rights include:[33]

- *to be informed of all alleged violation(s), receive the complaint in writing and be given access to all relevant materials pertaining to the case;*
- *privacy, confidentiality, and personal security;*
- *to choose not to answer any question that might be incriminating;*
- *the assistance of a faculty member, staff member, administrator or other advisor in preparing and presenting their cases.*

The student has the right to continue in the course in question during the entire process.[34]

A feature of hearing process is that it is "an academic process where evidence is put forth before a panel of faculty and student members to allow them to make a decision on whether there was sufficient proof of an academic misconduct violation having occurred and if so, to assign an appropriate sanction."[35]

The minimal standards that should be fulfilled during the hearing procedures are (among others):[36]

- a panel representation should include: *a faculty member appointed by the dean from the unit in which the academic work is conducted; one faculty member appointed by the Dean of the Faculties who is not from that unit; and two students appointed through procedures established by the Dean of Students Department;*

- *an opportunity for the student to examine the evidence to be presented;*
- *tape recording or transcription of the hearing proceeding;*
- *the panel is required to provide a clear written justification for imposing a sanction;*
- *all records from the hearing and follow-up meeting are securely and confidentially stored with other Honor Council files with the school administration.*

Detailed descriptions of hearing procedures may be found, for example, at links presented in Table 3.2.

Specification of Consequences of Violating Policies and Procedures: Sanctions and Appeals

An effective policy should not only specify the procedures of reporting and judging of actions incompliant with university's values, but it also

Table 3.2. Links to Descriptions of Hearing Procedures

	University	Link
Hearing procedures	National University	http://www.nu.edu/OurPrograms /StudentServices/AcademicPolicies andP/HearingProcedures.html
	Towson University	http://www.towson.edu/student affairs/judicialaffairs/hearing procedures.asp
	Purdue University Calumet	http://webs.purduecal.edu/integrity /honor-council/honor-hearing/
	Bradley University	http://www.bradley.edu/campuslife /studenthandbook/policies/ procedures/
	DePaul University	http://sr.depaul.edu/catalog/catalog files/current/undergraduate%20 student%20handbook/pg135.html
	Michigan State University	http://www.inclusion.msu.edu /Equity/Interim%20ADP%20 Student%20Disciplinary%20 Hearing%20Procedures.pdf

Source: Author's own study.

should indicate sanctions such as reduction in a grade for an assignment or course, a letter of reprimand, probation, reduction or revocation of a scholarship award, suspension, or expulsion for a particular violation (e.g., Boston College, Carroll School of Management).

The essence of sanctions for behaviors threatening core values of academic ethos should be an aspiration to a balance between the role of sanctions connected with sending a clear message to academic community

Table 3.3. Links to Examples of Sanctions for Behaviors that are not Compliant with Academic Ethos

	University	Link
Sanctions	University of Southern California	http://www-bcf.usc.edu/~bpeter/203/sanctns.htm
	Penn State University	http://www.psu.edu/dept/oue/aappm/G-9.pdf
	The University of New Mexico	http://dos.unm.edu/student-conduct/academic-integrityhonesty.html
	Arizona State University	https://provost.asu.edu/files/AcademicIntegrityPolicyPDF.pdf
	University of Notre Dame	http://nd.edu/~hnrcode/docs/Guidelinesfor Sanctions.pdf
	Saint Leo University	http://info.saintleo.edu/COL/Advising/HonorCode.cfm
Appeals	Aston University	http://www1.aston.ac.uk/registry/for-staff/regsandpolicies/academic-appeals-procedure/
	University of Sussex	http://www.sussex.ac.uk/governance/1-2-1.html
	University of East Anglia	http://www.uea.ac.uk/calendar/Academic+Appeals+Procedure
	University of Edinburgh	http://www.docs.sasg.ed.ac.uk/AcademicServices/Appeals/Students/University%20of%20Edinburgh%20Academic%20Appeal%20Procedure%20-%20Information%20for%20Students.pdf
	University of South Australia	http://www.unisa.edu.au/celusa/formsand policies/A011%20Academic%20Appeals%20PROCEDURE.pdf
	Victoria's School for Business Technology	http://www.qcollege.ca/prospective-students/school-policies/student-academic-appeals-procedures

Source: Author's own study.

about the lack of acceptance of particular behaviors and the role of sanctions connected with moral and mental development of an individual.

Examples of sanctions for behaviors that are not compliant with academic ethos may be found at the websites given in Table 3.3.

Components of the phase named enacting the core values of academic ethos do not include all the actions that should be taken by a higher school on this stage of academic ethos management. There still remains a very substantial element: communicating of academic ethos core values. The spectrum of possible tools for communicating values is broad and will be fully addressed in the following chapter.

CHAPTER 4

Communicating Core Values of Academic Ethos

Involvement of Top Management of Higher School in the Process of Academic Ethos Management

As a leader, a college or university president may define the core values of a university and write them in the form of core values statements, but until he or she starts the communication process concerning those values and makes an effort to inculcate them into an academic community, implementation of those values will be a very hard or unfeasible task.

Many tools for core values communication exist, but the most significant and effective is through an example, a way of conduct that top management exhibits. If punctuality is the main feature of an organization, it is unacceptable for top management to be late. If treating others with equal respect is the core value of a university, top management cannot have reserved parking spaces, top floor offices, a special elevator, and an executive dining room. In a particular organization we may broadly communicate the core values, but unless its leaders are the exemplars and demonstrate those values with their own lives, those values will promote cynicism and discouragement.[1] The president, as leader, is accountable for all that happens within the institution and assumes the obligation to provide ethical and academic guidance. Leadership is a moral act infused with a vision and commitment to action. Leaders can serve as symbols of moral unity for their institutions.[2]

Clearly, the academic ethos of an institution of higher learning must be communicated, promulgated, and protected by all its members, but the main responsibility for dissemination of academic ethos regardless the model of campus governance—the dual-organizational model, the academic community model, the political model, or the organized anarchy model[3]—lies with its leader (the university president). Every action taken—or not taken—conveys information about the values of leadership. Top management's obligation to conduct in accordance with its core values is the first step to making such an obligation applicable to all the employees.[4] Institutions with a strong positive ethos are led by managers who explicitly articulate the values and development of both character and intellect in a caring community.[5] We should remember that we assess ourselves by taking our intentions into account, but others judge us by our actions. People not only hear what we say, but they also see what we do, and they believe what they see.[6]

Making decisions about implementing the next value and then resisting getting involved for better and for worse is a serious venture. This decision influences others; to gain others' cooperation requires support in the form of real personal involvement in order to achieve all what has been planned. The leader must live and breathe the academic values. As Harvey and Lucia state: "Words to live by are just words, unless you live by them. You have to walk the talk."[7]

It is not important how leaders demonstrate their involvement in managing academic ethos. What is really important in the process of academic ethos management goes beyond particular techniques or approaches, as it does not matter how the involvement is demonstrated if it is visible. If the involvement is visible, the lesson about being concerned about values is being diffused to the next levels of a university and can be passed from one generation of managers to the next.

Top management should demonstrate their involvement in core values not only by what they do, but they should also take each opportunity to discuss those values. The message about core values should be repeated and forwarded during favorable organizational moments. Carvenka, CEO and general director of Philips Plastics Corporation, often talks about a need to communicate (even exaggerate) values in different ways.[8] Each opportunity, each speech, every celebration, or business meeting should be used for core values communicating.

Declarations of Core Values of Academic Ethos

The next tool for core values propagation is writing them in the form of declarations. The process of developing core values of academic ethos offers a number of benefits. First, it helps the academic community distinguish between activities that reinforce the institutional imperatives and those that do not. Second, a clear core value statement has the ability to inspire and motivate those within a university and to communicate its characteristics and history to key external constituents.[9] Morphew wrote, "An organization such as university succeeds when anyone inside and outside the organization agrees that it is a university! According to this theory, colleges and universities would develop core values statements so that those within the organization (students, faculty) and outside (accreditors, regents, prospective students) see that such a statement exists, in proper form and verbiage".[10]

If the values of academic ethos are clearly articulated and well written, they are ready to be communicated. It is a specific test of well-prepared declaration. If values are significant enough to be published, they are significant enough to be complied with.[11] People who have core values and their definitions available in a written form may be better able to cause their enactment and may be more willing to remember them in everyday work.[12] Eric Harvey also assumes that the core value statement not only directs the organizational members' behavior, but also affects the organization's decisions. It is obviously impossible for all decisions to be fully compliant with organization's core values, but through core values statements, a university may avoid decisions that do not comply with those values.

Methods for resolving of ethical dilemmas may be also used for verifying a particular decision compliance with our core values.

Language As a Tool of Core Value Articulation

The successful tool for core values communication is its clear, precise, unambiguous language. A language distinguishes a group of people who use it from those who communicate in other languages. A language is a means of identification and integration[13] and is defined as a particular form or manner in which members of a group use vocal sounds and written signs to convey meanings to each other.[14] Implementing new values (such as quality, for instance) in an organization is connected with including new vocabulary regarding those values. Moreover, Bernard Harvey Levi says, "People (who) are talking are talking nonstop, and they will not stop talking with the language of their teachers."[15]

Tradition and academic ethos at Cambridge University[16] are enshrined in terminology that we still persist in using. "Kitchens are called 'gyp rooms,' two-part degree courses are called 'triposes,' the student common room is the 'combination room,' and all manner of people and practices have strange Latinate names that nobody knows the origin of. So students returning home after a term here can sometimes appear to their friends to be speaking a foreign language."[17]

Academic Publicity

Academic publicity, such as a student and faculty handbook, college or university catalogue, brochures, and so forth, should be used in a communication (promoting) process of core values. Placing the core values of academic ethos in the catalogue or university's website makes it available not only to currently enrolled students but also to prospective students and their parents, thereby emphasizing the importance the institution places on academic ethos.

University Tradition

The most plentiful and important set of tools for communicating academic ethos are the university's traditions. Universities and colleges, of course, are not the only organizations steeped in tradition; religions, governments, and military bodies, to name a few, take pride in their rich traditions that reflect values that are built into their specific DNA codes, as it were. These traditions and rituals, ceremonies, myths, folk lore, or symbols are the most durable carriers and communicators of academic ethos values. They create a sense of community, distinction, and membership as well as feelings of pride.

This holds true for higher learning. Despite the fact many traditions have disappeared through time, most of them have survived, and today they are a substantial symbol of academic values for students and for their alma maters as well. "From solemn graduation ceremonies rooted in the Middle Ages to silly but enduring student rituals like food fights and pumpkin tossing, campus life is big on traditions."[18]

This process may be perfectly described in words that we may find on Princeton University's websites:[19]

> Traditions are things that you can't buy. It's like a reputation, you can't buy a reputation, you have to earn it. But traditions have to keep growing, and they have to keep fresh. I like to describe tradition as a river, not a wall. A wall is a rigid thing—firm, you can never move it. But a river, although the course stays the same, the water is always new. If it isn't, it's stagnant, and then the tradition becomes a burden. (…)

> In days of old, when this country and this University were still young, many of the Princeton traditions we now take for granted did not exist. Indeed, the history of this University and its many customs, rituals, and traditions has been ever-evolving throughout our history.

> Through more than 250 years of its history, Princeton has enjoyed a remarkable number of endearing and enduring traditions. But as the following will indicate, many of these traditions are not chiseled in stone, but rather, they are initiated, perpetuated and modified by succeeding generations.

However, "every trustee, faculty member, administrator, student, alumnus, and groundskeeper is a guardian of our traditions."

Myths and Folk Tales

Important tools for values of academic ethos communication are myths and folk tales. Myths are anecdotes that become established and have an aim at socializing. They emphasize what is accepted, practiced, and intolerable within a particular culture. Myths are the link between present and past and serve as an explanation of some of today's practices. There are reasonable arguments confirming that folk tales also have a great impact on people's beliefs and values. First of all, it has been proven that legends and stories are more likely to be remembered than bare facts and statistics. Second, stories and "urban legends" keep organizational values alive. Research has confirmed that employees who identify with an organization to a great extent and who are likely to demonstrate their loyalty know many tales that have been flowing within organization for years.[20]

Each member of Auburn University[21] community surely knows the tale of "War Eagle":

> "War Eagle" is Auburn's battle cry, not a mascot or nickname. The most popular story about the battle cry dates back to the first time Auburn met Georgia on the football field in 1892 and centers around a spectator who was a veteran of the Civil War. In the stands with him that day was an eagle the old soldier had found on a battlefield during the war. He had kept it as a pet for almost 30 years. According to witnesses, the eagle suddenly broke free and began majestically circling the playing field. As the eagle soared, Auburn began a steady march toward the Georgia end zone for a thrilling victory. Elated at their team's play and taking the bird's presence as an omen of success, Auburn students and fans began to yell "War Eagle" to spur on their team. At the game's end, the eagle took a sudden dive, crashed into the ground, and died. But the battle cry "War Eagle" lived on to become a symbol of the proud Auburn spirit.

At Princeton University,[22] the Office of Communications in conjunction with the Annual Giving Office has produced a series of little books that focus on particular aspects of Princeton's history and campus. These include legends and lore description of Princeton's presidents or chronologies of campus buildings. Probably every member of the academic community of Princeton knows the story connected with "Theft of the Clapper":[23]

> One of the more peculiar traditions at Princeton pertains to theft of the clapper by members of the Freshman Class from the bell in the tower atop Nassau Hall. One of the oldest customs of the

college is the ringing of the bell to signal curfew at 9:00 p.m. at night. For more than one hundred years Freshmen were not to be seen after the bell had stopped ringing. Thus, according to the legend, if the bell did not ring, they would be permitted to stay out later.

The tradition of stealing the clapper dates began in 1863. (…)

Through time, it became one of the challenging "duties" of the Freshmen Class to steal the clapper. At some point, the reward was shifted from evening curfew to the beginning of classes in the morning. According to legend, successful theft would result in cancellation of 8:30 morning classes.

Capturing the clapper became a point of Class pride, and in some instances, the iron from the clapper was melted down and used to make miniature examples of the prize, such as those sold to the Class of 1887 for $1.00. Examples of these pins exist in the Seeley Mudd Archive Collections.

However, university leaders should not rely solely on legends and stories from the past in order to cultivate core values. They should also participate in the process of furthering the university's traditions. They should not only talk but also listen, as it is highly recommended to hear what academic community members are talking about, what jokes and tales they are telling, and choose those that reflect organizational values in the best way. Then, those stories should become commonly known.[24]

Rituals and Ceremonies

Rituals and ceremonies that are strongly rooted in the values of academic ethos also communicate what is important for the community and what are the elements that constitute it:

Founded in 1666, Lund University has a number of traditions and rituals which continue to be passed on to each new generation of students at Lund. One of them, the doctoral conferment ceremony, is the major academic event of the year at Lund University, accompanied by all the usual pomp and circumstance. It is a tradition which dates back as far as 1670 with ceremonies taking place at the end of May or early June, in Lund Cathedral. At the ceremony, the University bestows its highest honor on those who have completed a doctoral degree and defended their thesis. Canon salutes ring around the city to celebrate the new doctors, who are dressed in black and wear special hats or laurel wreathes. The tradition of this ceremony has even featured in an Ingmar Bergman film.[25]

Hey Day. On January 29, 1985, Auburn reinstated an annual tradition of the Fifties and Sixties called "Hey Day," a day on which all students wear name tags and say "hey" to everyone they pass. Leaders on campus join forces and pass out name tags to support this tradition and prove that Auburn University has the friendliest campus around.[26]

Every Polish student of the Mining Faculties[27] knows and celebrates the Miner's Day:

The Miners' Day (Barbórka) has been celebrated by Polish mining students since at least 1878. The program of celebrations at the University usually includes a holy Mass, an official meeting, the jumping over an apron—a tradition that symbolises that mining "apprentices" or "foxes" are admitted to the miners' community. These traditions were observed in several mining academies and schools: Scheimnitz, Banska Stiavnics (from the late eighteenth century), Loeben (after 1849) and Pribram (after 1849). These traditions were then brought to Poland by Polish students gathered in the Polish Students' Mining Library in Leoben from 1878. The jumping over the apron is a custom brought by Polish students of mining from Loeben. The candidates to the mining profession (i.e., foxes) are admitted to the miners' community during a ceremony reviving all traditional customs cultivated by the miners' professional associations (gwarki) and by the students. By jumping and being bound with the apron (a piece of hide) a candidate becomes a full member of the miners' family. During the same ceremony the University banner and a torch are handed over to the younger generations, which is an impressive symbol. The parade of 'foxes' means the march of uniformed students through the city, each carrying the torch, accompanied by the orchestra. The parade is led by the mounted Lis (Fox)-Major, followed by the Rector and professors in hansom cabs or sleighs. A huge barrel of beer is transported on the platform. They leave the University grounds and march to the Main Square in the town, adding color to the city and becoming a great attraction for passers-by.

Ceremonies and rituals are also strongly connected with a university's songs, such as "Dear Bucknell" (Bucknell University), "Boomer Sooner" (University of Oklahoma), "Greek Sing" (Auburn University), "Purdue Hymn" (Purdue University), or many traditional Princeton songs that express a pride of participation in a unique community. At the University of Manitoba,[28] the official theme song of the U of M Students' Union was written in 1940 and is still sung today. Entitled "The Brown and Gold," it urges, "Forward to success, wisdom, happiness." One of the oldest academic songs is "*Gaudeamus*," which is a popular academic commercium song in many European countries, mainly sung or performed at university graduation ceremonies. Despite its use as a formal graduation hymn, it is a jocular, light-hearted composition that pokes fun at university life. The song dates to the early eighteenth century, based on a Latin manuscript from 1287. It is in the tradition of *carpe diem* ("seize the day") with its exhortations to enjoy life.

Cultural Models

Exemplars and cultural models are another tool for core values communication. Exemplars are an integral part of a system of values; as they embody a set of values, they become symbols. In the Middle Ages, for example, knights and saints served as exemplars of the ideal human being;

in the seventeenth century, it was a nobleman. In the eighteenth century, it was a philosopher; in the United Kingdom of the nineteenth century, it was the gentleman, while in France it was the townsman.[29] Such models exist on many levels: there may be model human beings, model teams, or organizational models.

Fred Fox[30] for Princeton University may serve as an example of a cultural model:

> Over the years, Fox enlarged his role at Princeton, lecturing to a generation of first-year students and staff about Princeton's legends, myths, colors, artifacts, sons, stories, and people. In 1976 Fox became Keeper of Princetoniana, moving to Nassau Hall where he increased his work with alumni, friends of Princeton, and the public at large. Fox's contribution to Princeton is best enunciated in President William G. Bowen's memorial remarks {hot link} about this 'colorful, delightful person' who was described as 'a cross between a curator, a ringmaster, and a storyteller.' (...)

> He also had a much more subtle sense of tradition than all the orange and black trappings might have suggested to some. His symbol of tradition, of continuity, was the river, because it was never stagnant, never still, always moving. He believed so deeply in the core values of Princeton that he became incensed when people mistook the trappings for the real thing and tried to preserve the form at the expense of the substance.

Symbols

Symbols may also be used as a tool for values of academic ethos communication. Architecture symbols such as the external architecture of campus buildings, monuments, logos, seals, or colors, or the physical symbols such as a dress code (ceremonial gowns), rings, mascots or symbols of prestige, symbols of hierarchy or social position such as a presidential costume, chain, or mace may be a manifestation of a university's values.

Architectural symbols

For example:

- Constructed in 1894, Gibson Hall of Tulane University is the oldest building on the uptown campus. It symbolizes the traditions and history of Tulane.[31]
- Clemson University[32] has a proud tradition of military excellence. Founded as a military school in 1889, Clemson built its reputation by consistently graduating well-prepared officers. Clemson's military spirit is commemorated through sites such as the Clemson Military Heritage Plaza, which overlooks Bowman Field and features an array of ribbons and honors, the footprints of brave service men, and inscriptions from a variety of alumni classes.
- On St. Patrick's Day in 1939 Texas Tech University[33] unveiled that they had discovered a piece of the Blarney Stone. According to the legend the stone was discovered by a group of petroleum engineers while they were on a field trip. After doing tests it was discovered that the stone was a piece of the original Blarney Stone. The stone now lies on a stand in front of the old Electrical Engineering Building. It is said that seniors that kiss the Blarney Stone upon graduation will receive the gift of eloquent speech.

The care for traditions and heritage of particular higher school may also take a form such as at Tulane University.[34] The oak trees on the Newcomb Quad were transplanted from the original campus of Newcomb on Washington Avenue when the school moved to Broadway in 1918.

Another example of architecture symbols that reflect university's values is a seal:

- Three years after the founding of the Bucknell University[35] in 1846, trustees approved a resolution calling for a committee "to report the form and devise of a seal for the University at Lewisburg." On April 17, 1849, the seal was approved. The seal shows the sun, an open book, and waves, symbolizing the light of knowledge and education surmounting the storms of life.

- The official seal of New York University[36] combines a silver ceremonial "torch of learning," which is carried in formal academic processions, with a group of four running figures symbolizing effort or striving in the pursuit of learning. The seal carries the Latin motto "*Perstare et Praestare*," which is generally translated as "to persevere and to excel," together with the name of the University and the roman numerals for 1831, the year of the founding of the institution. When reproduced, the darker portions of the seal are usually printed in violet, the official color of the University.
- The Texas Tech[37] Seal was designed by the campus' master planner, William Ward Watkin, in 1924, the Tech Seal's symbols are the lamp, which represents "school," the key for "home," the book for "church," and the star for "state." Cotton bolls represent the area's strong cotton industry and the eagle is suggestive of our country.
- At the University of Oklahoma[38] the idea for seal came from a chapel talk he made on the parable of the man sowing seeds. George Bucklin drew the design, a sketch of a sower with his bag of seeds. The Latin motto, "*Civi et Reipublicae*," furnished by Professor Paxton translated to "For the citizen and the state."

Physical symbols

Physical symbols rooted in academic tradition also take different forms. One of them is the gown—a classic style for many university students. At Cambridge University,[39] for instance, "Until the mid-1960s, students could be fined if they were not wearing a gown when in the street after dark. The undergraduate gown is still worn on the odd occasion; rather scarily, on the first couple of days at Corpus, especially for the Matriculation Ceremony—which in practice means walking to the front of the hall and signing student's name (with a biro, no less) on a form. After that, the only occasions when new Cambridge students might wear a gown are if they go to services in Chapel, and for Formal Hall."

Another case comes from Trinity College.[40] "There was a time when Trinity College students had to wear their gowns, not only on campus but also whenever they ventured into the city," said Sylvia Lassam, the Rolph-Bell Archivist at the U of T Federated College. (They were fined 25 cents if caught un-gowned). Gown-wearing endures to this day, but only for the 6:30 p.m. serving of the Wednesday evening dinner. The so-called "high table dinner" generally attracts about 50 people, including a "high table" of college officials. It's also a tradition to wear robes to chapel." Similarly, at Bucknell University,[41] the university's official colors, orange and blue, "were chosen in 1887 by a student committee. The official resolution of the faculty and students followed and the colors were approved by the board of trustees in January 1888."

Another symbol of academic tradition and symbol of esprit de corps to graduates of a university are rings. There are engraved with a university's symbols and inscriptions on them. A ring from Clemson University[42] offers a bold question that reads more as a challenge: "Who shall separate us now?"

Symbols of prestige

To the last group of university symbols—symbols of prestige—we may include an academic mace, presidential chain, and presidential costume. Use of the mace dates back to the University of Vienna in 1385.[43] It was the weapon for a bishop in battle, protecting the clergy, who were forbidden to fight themselves. Through time, the mace became the symbol of power in civil ceremonies. In the sixteenth century, Oxford University[44] used a decorated mace in ceremonies to represent academic strength (excellence and independence); the mace as symbol of distinction and tradition is used to this very day.

A dignitary at official events sometimes wields a mace or a staff to showcase the power and prestige of an institution. For example, at commencement and at other George Washington University ceremonies, a marshal brandishes a ceremonial mace, representing the high standing of the University and the elevated status of higher education overall as a force for good. The mace was created at George Washington University[45] by Harry Irving Gates, associate professor of sculpture, and was presented by the Faculty Women's Club of The George Washington University. Its flanges bear a profile of George Washington.

Using New Technology for Communicating
Core Values of Academic Ethos

The process of communicating core values of an organization such as a higher school may be, or even should be, supported by using modern technologies. The aim of the communicating process of core values should be to reach the target group consisting of an organization's employees (such as academic teachers, scientists, administrators, and service staff), the university's partners (e.g., suppliers of services or materials), and students. The application of modern media may be the most appropriate way to communicate, especially with the last of the mentioned groups. It is widely known that students do not have any objections to use new technologies. Moreover, the resistance against tradition and traditional communication media is palpable, as they are perceived as obsolete, fossilized, or "for adults" and they are a generational barrier that hampers the process of information diffusion. The unwillingness to use traditional ways of communication may become a crucial factor that makes core values communication quite difficult. Young people prefer to send SMS or to chat than to have a conversation. They also prefer to read the content of a website than from a printed brochure, and they prefer to search for interesting information via Google than to ask a professor. From such a perspective, the use of the newest information, communications, and technology (ICT)s seems to be perceived better by this group of the young receivers. This will enable the process of communicating core values of a university to be more effective.

What can a university do in order to enhance its communication process? What media may be used? What technologies should be used? There is a wide spectrum: from those commonly used in the business world like contact centers, social media, to dialog systems based on artificial intelligence. The last one especially may be very interesting. Using hotlines, tweets, or listings on Facebook has become an integral part of the communication process in various organizations. The use of dialog systems based on artificial intelligence is in its initial stage. Nevertheless, the use of hotlines, Facebook[46] profiles, or writing a microblog on Twitter involves valuable resources: it requires a lot of human, time, and financial resources. As a result, such processes of core values communication become costly.

How can organizations tackle such problems? One of the solutions is resorting to modern technologies that use methods and techniques of artificial intelligence. They are by now effective enough to be successfully put into practice. Such technological advances use so-called chatbots, also known as avatars, virtual advisers, or lingubots. Chatbots are computer programs using artificial intelligence, enabling a conversation with a user by means of natural language. Such systems are placed on Internet websites. Their task is to dispense information to users. They are also frequently used for entertainment purposes (e.g., video games), or for advisory purposes (e.g., a virtual credit adviser or a physician).

A chatbot can talk about almost anything; once it is provided with a knowledge base specific to a given firm or organization, it becomes an authentic virtual adviser. Chatbots provide a unique, interactive, and personal way for users to get answers and assistance on websites, 24/7. A user simply chats online with the chatbot, and it acts as a human contact center, providing answers and solving users' problems. Some chatbots support text-to-text, text-to-speech, speech-to-text, and speech-to-speech interactions, and are also available on popular mobile devices. Chatbots are available 24/7, 365 days a year, and they are less expensive for the college or university than other methods. The chatbots handle repeat questions that human service tires of answering, as well as queries of low-to-medium complexity.[47] Students often prefer media like chat and SMS to personal or phone conversations; chatbots not only meet that preference but also make the conversation interesting with an avatar front-end.

The first prototype for all chatterbots was ELIZA, devised by Joseph Weizenbaum back in the 1960s. ELIZA mimicked a psychotherapist and enabled simple dialogue with a user. The mechanics behind ELIZA was simple; it had little to do with artificial intelligence, relying on several rules of English grammar. In point of fact, ELIZA did not have its own database, and its responses and questions were generated as simple transformations of the user's input. It should be admitted, however, that despite its simplicity it managed to deceive many human interlocutors unaware of the fact that it was a computer they were talking to.

In the 1980s to 1990s, chatterbot technology boomed. The modern chatterbots are furnished with gigantic knowledge bases, and they are able to associate pieces of information and to learn using their user's responses. In the case of specialist knowledge, six out of ten of them pass the Turing's test, a universal measure of a machine's ability to demonstrate intelligence, proposed by Alan Turing more than 50 years ago.

How can an organization use the technology? The uses that chatbots can be put to are solely dependent on the decision makers' imagination. A chatbot can be furnished with any kind of knowledge and it can be used as, for example, a virtual spokesperson of the university, serviceperson, virtual teacher (e.g., part of an e-learning system), virtual adviser, or simply a navigator leading one around the university's website. The possibilities are practically unlimited.

The technology can have numerous applications, including:

- relieving congestion on overburdened call centers, taking over part of user service inquiries;
- enhancing the university's website;
- setting up interactive support;
- providing information resource systems for employees, lecturers, and students or partners.

Benefits for Organizations

Universities willing to implement such services can certainly expect many benefits, including:

- reducing user service costs through relieving congestion on overburdened call centers and other traditional communication channels;
- increasing user satisfaction levels through enhanced 24/7 user service availability, with no negative emotions, health leaves, holidays, training courses, and so forth;
- avoiding the "shy user/student effect," eliminating the need to contact the call center through the phone number given on the website;
- increasing the popularity of the website;
- enhancing the university's image in the eyes of students as an innovative organization.

Admittedly, however, the present solutions are far from ideal. As a rule, they are limited to a singular scope of use. Once you go beyond the scope, the computer starts behaving like a baby and is completely lost in the "other world." It simply cannot function in a different context because it lacks sufficient general knowledge of the world. This is the main reason why a computer labeled artificial intelligence software may sometimes seem "stupid." This will soon be over. There are many projects underway in the world, which aim at creating gigantic "common sense" term databases, including pieces of information such as, for example, "grass is green," "organisms need water to survive," "humans live 75 years on average," and so forth. The most famous of such projects is the American CYC project, which boasts a huge database consisting of more than 10 million terms. For a computer, however, to have a knowledge comparable with that of a human being, it needs to amass about 100 million terms. This may be only a matter of time and money.

Chatterbots at the Universities

Chatterbots began appearing at universities at the beginning of the twenty-first century. Among the higher schools that implemented such solutions are: Pontificia Universidad Católica Argentina, Leeds Metropolitan University, Basque Country University—Universidad del Pais Vasco, University of Nebraska-Lincoln Libraries, Szkoła Wyższa Psychologii Społecznej, University of Wolverhampton Library, Faculty of Economics and Business Administration, University of Maastricht, University of Granada, Kingston University, Gonzaga University, and Wyższa Szkoła Zarządzania Personelem, Wyższa Szkoła Handlu i Finansów Międzynarodowych.

The following are select implementations in the segment of higher schools:[48]

Mariana, a Virtual Agent developed by BotGenes, who works as a university advisor of Universidad Católica Argentina, one of the most prestigious universities in Argentina, which offers more than 50 degree titles and numbers some 50,000 graduated students. Mariana has studies in Advertising and Institutional Communication and enjoys orienting the applicants with the peculiarities of income and characteristics of every career. Mariana uses the more advanced "brain" developed by BotGenes, with more than 400,000 decision rules, allowing her to handle thousands of regionalisms, typos, spelling, and grammar errors; she can also contextualize answers. She integrates natural language processing (NLP) technologies with text to speech (TTS), also offering chat, audio streaming, and an animated avatar from BotGenes's servers.[49]

Unai is a virtual assistant for the Basque Country University. Its goal is to help students know how to join the university, prices, grants, entrance exams, and so forth. Because it is a "fifth generation" virtual assistant, it can understand natural language, show emotions, and even comprehend ambiguous phrases. It can also engage in a social dialogue or correct spelling mistakes.[50]

Elvira is a virtual assistant, which can tell you everything about the University of Granada. You can write the question down or choose to click on any of the options showed to the right of Elvira. You can also send any suggestions you have about Elvira's work by clicking on the white envelope icon.[51]

There are many tools for core values communication. This chapter has just touched the tip of the communications iceberg, as the only limitation for creating new communication methods is the brain and abilities of creative thinking of organizational leaders. Thus, leaders who want to call themselves the "custodians of values" should constantly search for new, more effective core value communication tools.[52]

CHAPTER 5

Maintaining Core Values of Academic Ethos

Elements of Maintaining Core Values of Academic Ethos

The subsequent phase of core values of the academic ethos managerial process refers to their maintenance. Discovering and defining core values by an academic community, writing those values in the form of declarations, establishing policies, procedures and codes, or even communicating them throughout the world is not enough to manage core values of academic ethos in an effective and conscientious way. A school of higher education does not only exist; rather, it happens, becomes, and transforms.

During such "happening" of higher schools, ways of conduct inside it may maintain and protect core values of academic ethos or, quite the opposite, they may cause hindering, forgetting, and eroding of those values.

An important role in maintaining core values of academic ethos is ensured by the following actions:

1. Protection of core values of academic ethos ensured by:

   - recruitment—the way of choosing employees;
   - actions taken in order to explain core values;
   - trainings on core values for members of academic community;
   - the way of awarding and promotion system.

2. Control over of behavior compliance of academic community members with the behaviors ascribed to core values of academic ethos (systems of control and power).
3. Redefinition of core values of academic ethos.

Protection of Core Values of Academic Ethos

Recruitment

Recruitment is understood as employing people with necessary personality traits and fundamental abilities required for implementing core values. Recruitment has always been perceived by organizational executives as the main success determinant. However, the emphasis was put on professional qualifications of applicants while those requirements usually may be fulfilled by more than one person. A higher school that wants to protect its core values of academic ethos should pay attention to the so-called cultural adequacy of an applicant. It means that the school should ensure that the core values of a prospective employee are the same as that of the school; it should employ people who believe in similar values (substantially compliant with organizational core values) and exhibit most, if not all, of these values. Beyond particular abilities connected with a particular post, a university's attention should also be focused on the personal traits of applicants, their personal value scale, and similar factors. Those actions should be taken in order to find people who fit a university's culture and image.[1]

The business world (e.g., American Express, Disney Corporation, Microsoft, and Procter & Gamble) as well as the science world provide us with many examples of approaches to the recruitment process. The chain of Ritz-Carlton hotels is an exemplar for many companies, especially in the areas of service quality and treating clients with attention and respect. The chain uses the following criteria of prospective employees selection: ethics in work, self-respect, persuasiveness, ability to establish interpersonal contacts, team work ability, recognition of the term "service," empathy, health, and precision.[2]

One of the core values of Texas A&M University is defined as follows: "We seek excellence in all we do." To protect this value in the recruitment process, Texas A&M University formulates the following statement:

> Recruiting processes should be focused on excellence. An excellent sabbatical program is also required. Job opportunities for spouses, given the dual-career nature of today's families, must be enhanced on and off of the campus. Lose no faculty to other institutions for reasons that do not involve sound professional decision making.[3]

It also clearly states that the university should quadruple the number of faculty who are members of the National Academy of Science, the National Academy of Engineering, or fellows in academic and professional societies. It is one of the main objectives: realizing the values of excellence in Texas A&M University.

A similar approach is evident with Northern Kentucky University.[4] One of its core values is described as "the high standards of excellence in every dimension of our work." They understand that great universities depend on outstanding faculty and staff committed to the full breadth of the institution's mission and core values. That is why it was decided to develop recruitment, performance planning, and evaluation procedures based on the university's mission, core values, and strategic priorities.

The process of recruit selection also provides additional information about a university. Those applicants who notice a conflict between their own personal values and the values of a higher school may withdraw from the recruitment process on their own. In this way, a recruitment process is realized in two directions as it enables both employer and applicant to withdraw before establishing a formal relation when they realize their values are not compatible. The recruitment process maintains organizational culture by eliminating those applicants who potentially could attack or question fundamental values of an organization.[5]

Explaining Core Values

Explaining core values of academic ethos is the next action aimed at particular values protection. Through such explanations, systemic actions are directed toward current and new participants of academic community; they are aimed at providing information about what are the values of academic ethos, why they are so important for a higher school, and what conduct is expected from an academic community. Lack of understanding what academic ethos really is may cause nonconformist behavior that sometimes results in one's exclusion from the community. A college or university should strive for a systematic renewal of knowledge about core values among its employees and students through meetings, academic events, or university publications.

Each public appearance of a university's authorities, such as at an inauguration of the academic year, graduation (or diploma) day, or other celebrations should serve as pretexts for explaining and underscoring the core values of a particular academic institution. It is especially important that the explanation of those values be a part of events such as new student conferences, first meetings for every course, new faculty orientation, graduate teaching assistant training, or faculty/staff in-service training.

Detailed explanations of values of academic ethos as well as desired or reprehensible behavior connected with them should be constantly present in basic organizational documents of a university, such as faculty/staff job application materials, the faculty/staff handbook, catalog, admissions application material, student rules and handbook, schedule of classes and course syllabi as well as Advisor's Handbooks, the institution's website, student calendars, welcome letters to new students, posters, and bookmarks.[6]

Including the message explaining academic values in the documents and aforementioned events should be aimed at creating and increasing the level of awareness about the values of academic ethos in the academic community. The awareness of academic ethos values is not just a matter of organizational visibility, but it is also an adoption by participants regarding the level of core values (acceptance by particular groups constituting the academic community). Core values of a higher school will gain the status of Durkheim's cultural facts only if they are organizationally visible (exposed inside and outside organization) and shared by the organization's participants.[7] Those values become separate from those who had formalized them and are something external to the individual awareness. This awareness (through core values articulation and their transparency) creates a sense of order, predictability, regularity, and safety. It results in a common trust at the school. Chaotic, poorly articulated core values, on the contrary, can result in accidental, unpredictable actions by an organization. It creates a sense of anarchy, uncertainty, or even threat.[8]

Training on Core Values of Academic Ethos

A higher school not only should explain the essence of its core values but should also educate its employees (the new ones as well as the current ones) and students to help them understand the importance of values and how to develop them through proper training. Such training helps the employees recognize ethical dilemmas, broadens their knowledge of ethical issues determining their actions, and confirms an organization's expectations on ethical conduct from its members.[9] It is not enough if an organization means well and formulates clear standards and excellent policies or procedures. Without appropriate capabilities, success is not possible. Competent employees will not maintain their abilities on the same level forever. Those abilities can weaken and may become outdated. Higher schools should equip new employees and students with abilities to behave in compliance with the core values of a particular university. An exemplar for such trainings is the program of U.S. Marines, which includes an obligatory recruit training camp during which every recruit reveals his or her involvement. Another example is a practice at Disneyland: during the first 2 days of work, employees watch films and attend lectures on what appearance and conduct is expected of Disney's employees.

Higher schools may be also proud of their exemplar solutions of trainings shaping the capabilities to act in accordance with a particular core values. Texas A&M University not only declares "diversity" as one of its core values, but also has founded the Diversity Training Institute:

> DTI is a dynamic and interactive 3-day training program that combines theory and practice to give participants the essential tools necessary to design, promote and present a variety of diversity education activities. The Institute is designed for people interested in the development, management or training components of diversity education initiatives. Facilitators will share methods designed to promote general cultural awareness, as well as ways to facilitate effective dialogue.[10]

Higher schools should not forget about cyclic trainings on values of academic ethos for their current employees. There also should be a standard to attend obligatory trainings for new employees in this field (e.g., within 30 days of a person's date of employment).

Furthermore, training on values of academic ethos for students is very important. Although we assume that the members of academic community are familiar with core values, as well as its policies, procedures that support those values (such as faculty/student handbook, catalogues, or other documents) and actions aimed at explaining those values, we should not conclude it in advance that they acquired the knowledge on those values. We should be aware that both employees and students may have not necessarily read those documents describing policies, procedures, or codes that are tools for core values enacting. It is worth mentioning here that, according to Kibler's study,[11] few higher schools that were analyzed used a proactive way to inform and train on a value such as integrity. Only 22% of schools required including information on "integrity" in syllabi and 36% organized seminars and discussions on this matter. Even if the values of academic ethos are explained to the members of academic community, we should be aware of the fact that human memory is volatile and they may simply forget about those values. The additional threat is visible when we talk about students as even if they read the materials explaining the values of academic ethos, they may not understand them thoroughly as data collected on two campuses reveal that only one student in 20 believed he or she had a working knowledge of their school's academic honesty policy.[12]

Colleges and universities should not forget that the values of academic ethos are heritages that live, evolve, and work in harmony with the world around them. That is why it is so important to organize trainings for employees in a form of cyclic seminars, discussions, and dedicated correspondence, including information not only about all the actions aimed at implementing values of academic ethos, but also about the suggestions for enhancing the current policies and procedures. Similarly, the training for students is crucial to the same extent. Effort for enacting and maintaining core values with the appropriate strategies should also be directed toward those two groups of university stakeholders. Carnegie Mellon University, for example, characterizes those strategies in the following way:

1. for students[13]
    - understand the expectations;
    - get organized and stay organized;
    - manage your time;
    - know your resources;
    - identify alternatives.

2. for instructors[14]
   - addressing cheating behaviors;
   - planning writing assignments;
   - communicating your expectations;
   - considering cultural variations.

Training on values of academic ethos that is dedicated to students is aimed at ensuring that students know and understand particular values as well as the expectations regarding those values. Such training may be divided into actions that can be realized during classes or out of it.

Fostering Values of Academic Ethos in the Classroom

The employees' involvement in enacting values of academic ethos is a result of top management's engagement (and its visibility) in this process (walk the talk). Quite similar to this, students' involvement is a result of behavioral patterns they acquire by interpreting their teachers' behavior. So, the first step of the teacher to train students in the values of academic ethos is establishing a positive classroom climate, which "is a term that refers to the social–psychological context of student–teacher interactions usually defined in terms of the students' perceptions of the teacher."[15] By interpreting a teacher's behavior, a student learns about values serving as a base for this behavior. So, if one of the university core values is integrity, it requires that a teacher show respect and treat students seriously by fulfilling the following minimal standards of conduct:[16]

- *come to class on time, and not leave early;*
- *not waste class time, but use it well to fulfill the objectives of the course;*
- *both encourage you and give you an equal opportunity, to participate in class discussions;*
- *respect the views you express and not make fun of you or of them;*
- *not allow others to ridicule you or your ideas, or you to do the same to them;*
- *tell the class a little about your personal and professional background;*
- *when you attend professional meetings, especially if you have to miss class, tell the students a little about what happened at the meeting;*

- *give students your e-mail address and encourage comments and questions. Reply promptly to the student and discuss selected messages with the class (keeping the sender anonymous, of course);*
- *be proactive about inviting students to visit during office hours.*

A teacher should also demonstrate care and concern for students by learning and using their names, conversing with them before and after class, thoughtfully responding to all germane questions with clear and thorough answers, and mentoring students who are struggling so that they can achieve higher academic goals. In addition, the teacher must hear out valid student complaints, sift out invalid complaints, and act on the needs of students when logically necessary.[17] The practical example of a concern for students is, for example, ATMentors:

ATMentors is an organization of faculty, staff, and administrators who volunteer extra office hours to make themselves available to students who just want to talk to someone. We have over 200 current mentors in almost every department on campus.

ATMentors have offices all over campus. To help students readily identify them, Mentors display ATMentors door plaques. Students can trust that faculty and staff members who display an ATMentors door plaque are willing to help students in need.[18]

A very important tool that may be used in a classroom in order to teach values of academic ethos and the behaviors that threaten them is and should be a syllabus. The syllabus serves as a contract between instructor and student, and it should not only offer precise information about objectives of a particular academic subject but also enumerate precise expectations and reprehensible behavior that could occur while learning a particular subject. The challenge for teachers should not only be teaching against academic dishonesty ("low academic values" like cheating or plagiarism), but also including in syllabi the declarations that explain to students that the teacher knows that academic dishonesty exists and that he or she will take these matters seriously. The teacher should be specific about what behaviors create academic dishonesty during the course and make it clear to students that: (a) academic dishonesty is ethically wrong;

and (b) that students are personally responsible for honesty.[19] Teachers should shape syllabi in order to be able to educate students in "high academic values," such as honesty, integrity, fairness, truth, and excellence.[20]

Taking the effectiveness of the educational process on values of academic ethos into account, it is recommended to include in syllabi at least the following elements:

- a brief, general statement about the importance of core values of academic ethos; a personal statement declaring instructor's commitment to academic ethos core values;
- a brief list of the types of behaviors that may support and destroy core values of academic ethos;
- a brief list of campus resources that may help to reduce the risk of unethical behaviors or behaviors that destroy academic ethos;
- a brief description of academic policy that is based on academic core values and is developed to support the process of their enacting (with reference to what the complete policy can be found).

The University of Central Florida (UCF) publishes on its websites an exemplar declaration that should be included at the beginning of every syllabus. Its short version is as follows:

As reflected in the UCF creed, integrity and scholarship are core values that should guide our conduct and decisions as members of the UCF community. Plagiarism and cheating contradict these values, and so are very serious academic offenses. Penalties can include a failing grade in an assignment or in the course, or suspension or expulsion from the university. Students are expected to familiarize themselves with and follow the University's Rules of Conduct (see http://www.osc.sdes.ucf.edu/).[21]

A similar syllabus statement can be found on Georgetown University websites:

Georgetown University—Georgetown allows each faculty member to describe his/her adherence to the overall academic integrity policy, and the Provost and Honor Council send a letter to all faculty every year, which includes the following statement that tells about the Honor System, general best practices, and encourages the inclusion in all syllabi of the piece in quotation marks/ blue text:

The goal of the Honor System is to achieve the highest level of integrity without need to invoke these procedures. To approach that goal, faculty must communicate forthrightly and persuasively to students the importance of academic honesty. Please plan to spend at least a few minutes of your first class meeting enunciating the basic principles you expect to see enacted, and please reinforce this message in your syllabus.[22]

Instructors should also train students on the values of academic ethos through discussion. As stated by Whitley and Keith-Spiegel, discussion means a complete explanation by the instructor plus input and feedback from students.[23] It is based on research that people are more likely to accept and comply with the policies and procedures when they understand their purpose even when they disagree with the statements included in those policies and procedures.[24] Aiken found that 55% of his respondents thought that discussing the problem of academic dishonesty would be an effective means to prevent dishonesty.[25] Through an open discussion with students, teachers may strengthen relations, creating alignment on interpretation of values of academic ethos, behaviors that determine them, and behaviors resulting in academic ethos erosion. In the educational process, it is very important to teach how to prevent behaviors not compliant with those values, especially behaviors that may be characterized as examples of academic dishonesty. It is not enough to say that plagiarism is bad. It is necessary to explain it is so, indicate possible situations in which it may occur during classes, and clearly communicate what the consequences are for inappropriate behavior. The essence of inappropriate behavior must be explained with the use of particular examples that equip students with appropriate abilities, enabling them to avoid unethical behavior. Teachers should not assume in advance that a student knows what plagiarism is and how to use data sources in order to avoid plagiarism.

Discussions with students (and employees) on the values of academic ethos may be conducted during classes as well as in residence halls, student organizations, and during new faculty/student member orientations. The side effect of such a discussion may be a new version of policies and procedures regarding enactment of academic ethos that occur on a university's website in the "FAQ" section, where the most frequent dilemmas of faculty members and students are presented with explanations. Those elements may also occur as extras in print versions of a university's policies and procedures.

Fostering values of academic ethos out of the classroom

In the process of explaining the values of academic ethos to students, a university and its teachers should use all their creativity and propose the newest educating methods that go beyond the course frameworks and classes. For many years we have known the maxim about the effectiveness of learning through play. We should do everything possible in order to teach them in the most intelligible, simplest, and most entertaining way. There are many examples of amusing ways for communicating information about core values of a university. One of the easiest mechanisms is organizing contests for the best T-shirt design that presents one of the values of academic ethos. Another possibility is to announce a contest for the best slogan, poster, or cartoon describing what may be called the university's DNA, namely its core values, and espousing the benefits of behavior that works in accordance with academic core values, for example, emphasizing the advantages of honesty and disadvantages of dishonesty. Examples of posters created for this purpose can be found on Clemson University websites.[26]

Today's technology provides us with other solutions in this area. Chatbot placed on the university's website may not only answer a question in a FAQ section but can also become a partner in a discussion on values of academic ethos. Another example may be a movie festival, including films concerning ethical dilemmas (e.g., *Quiz Show, Wall Street I, Wall Street II, The Firm,* and *Margin Call*) coupled with a discussion on issues that occurred in presented movies. Seminars, symposia, lectures of scientific personages, or discussion panels for both students and faculty are other ways of teaching values of academic ethos. Panels may address issues such as:[27]

- academic dishonesty in online courses: preventative strategies;
- grade inflation and its potential impact on academic integrity issues;
- techniques for students to avoid intentional and unintentional plagiarism and write better essays/papers;
- simplified procedure for reporting and appealing academic integrity violations, and discuss potential upcoming changes to the Academic Integrity Policy;
- the role of integrity while applying for jobs and graduate schools.[28]

Motivating and awarding

The last element of core values protection is combining formal and informal awards for actions compliant with the core values of academic ethos. University authorities should do everything in order to reward behavior compliant with core values and punish unethical behavior. The evaluation of employees' effectiveness should include not only the achieved success in their scientific, educational, or organizational activity but also the compliance of their actions and decisions with policies, procedures, and codes responsible for enacting the values of academic ethos. Members of an academic community that behave in accordance with the mentioned documents should be awarded for their behavior in a visible way (by gaining diplomas, verbal or written praise, awards, etc.). On the contrary, those who cause erosion of academic ethos should be punished in the way that attracts attention.

In East Chapel Hill High School:

"Members of the Student Academic Integrity and Leadership (S.A.I.L.) club instituted a new recognition of students, the Honor Scholars Award. The Integrity Committee along with S.A.I.L. asks each teacher to nominate one student who demonstrates values of honesty, integrity, and responsibility. Academic achievements are not part of the criteria for this nomination.

Everyone will have the opportunity to nominate students confidentially. Once the nominated students are approved through the cross-referencing process, they will be notified of their achievements. Seniors will be recognized in the graduation program. This award will be annual, and students will be able to cite this recognition."[29]

Bucknell University:

"...recognizes the exceptional contributions of faculty and staff with a number of honors. These include the Barry R. Maxwell Award for outstanding contributions to the Bucknell community, the John F. Zeller Award for support staff excellence, the Walter C. Geiger Award for administrative staff excellence, and the Burma-Bucknell Bowl for outstanding contributions to intercultural and international understanding within the Bucknell community. The Stephen W. Taylor Medal, the University's most significant award, honors those who render extraordinary service to the University. Annual awards presented during Reunion or Homecoming Weekend recognize alumni for loyalty, service to humanity, and outstanding professional achievement."[30]

Equally important as rewarding behavior compliant with core values and its public exposure is punishment for reprehensible behavior and reporting on violations of existing principles in academic community. All actions that threaten values of academic ethos and violate existing procedures and standards should be published in a university's bulletin, website, or in special brochures describing particular cases of core value violations.

The subsequent components of the phase of maintaining values of academic ethos are:

- control, understood as a systemic monitoring, supervision and evaluation of the compliance with core values of actions taken by employees, and
- core values redefinition.

Control of Core Values of Academic Ethos

Adapting particular policies and procedures by a university is connected with the necessity of constant monitoring. Monitoring is indispensable if the code has normative functions. Moreover, as noted by Schein, "If the president of an institution and faculty and student governance groups request periodic reports on academic integrity issues, then members of the institution will place more importance on academic integrity than in the absence of such interest."[31]

Universities have been conducting research on employees' and students' familiarity with basic documents elaborated for core values implementation as well as on cases of inappropriate behaviors and violations of adopted procedures and principles. The research is aimed not only at generating information about the current situation and progress of the core values implementation process, but also at taking actions of revising the current policies and procedures.

Recommendations for evaluating effectiveness of core values implementing became especially important after the year 2002 and a series of spectacular bankruptcies initiated by Enron. However, multiplication of controlling systems has also had negative results. As suggested by Stansbury and Barry, formalization regarding making ethical decisions may potentially have some harmful effects.[32] Forms of controlling, especially the compulsory ones that are assumed in policies and codes of ethics, may paradoxically limit their own effectiveness and, in extreme situations, they may cause the atrophy of employees' competency.

Redefining Core Values of Academic Ethos

Core values of an organization are its heritage, its past that exists in its present time. However, this past should not result in an organization's stagnation, its moving back. It should result in the organization's development. Core values are like lodestars, stable and unchangeable. However, their definitions should change in order to stay relevant. A definition of a core value is an element that links an organization's past with its future. In 1890, Sears defined its core value "Customer Service" as customer's satisfaction or the guarantee of money back.[33] But after years the guarantee of money back became a common behavior of many organizations. If Sears had not redefined its core value, this value would have resulted in its failure rather than in its present success.[34]

In the archives of many long-standing universities we may find a few different versions of their missions, visions, and core values. All of them express the same principles, but the words being used differ as they reflect various requirements of a particular time and conditions in which they existed. Definitions of core values that do not reflect current social expectations become stale, old, like a ball and chain that make organizations slow and make them fall into oblivion. Values are unchangeable, but words describing them need to change toward business reality. An organization's ability to develop is conditioned by its ability to redefine its core values and to maintain them as compliant with business reality. Hultman and Gellerman propose to check reality of core values by asking the following questions:[35]

- Is a particular value beneficial for both organization's and individual's increase?
- Is it clearly defined?
- Does it encourage people to achieve their potential for development?
- Is it based on trust?
- Does behavior ascribed to it bring positive results?
- Does it fulfill needs and desires?
- Does it take a long-term perspective into account?

It is hard to answer the question of how often a college or university should redefine its core values, but some warning signals may be identified. Those signals suggest a necessary facelift of core values. The first symptom is stagnation: an organization seems to be burned out and its main effort is focused on maintaining the status quo. The lack of effectiveness and failure to realize strategic objectives are subsequent signals. Bad communication between top management and employees causes the lack of trust, cynicism, and pessimism on organization's future, lack of confidence that a university has any future, and the lack of enthusiasm or involvement among employees, culminating in an attitude described as "I'll do what I have to do and nothing more."[36]

Values of academic ethos need to be continually redefined; sometimes the supplementing of a core values set is highly important, especially in instances such as a merger, a university's development, or changes in the university's environment. We have to remember that values of academic ethos are not given once and for all. Donnelly said, "Ethos then is not that which is formally stated or documented but is a process of social interaction; it is not independent from the organization but inherently bound up within it. It is a product of organizational interaction and will be produced and reproduced over time."[37]

As a result, academic ethos values management should be understood as the ongoing process of negotiating, during which an academic community tends to agree on who we are, what is important for us, and how should we behave in order to pass our identity (that constitutes our uniqueness) to the future generations.

Through actions such as recruitment or training, a school of higher learning protects its core values and effectively provides members of its academic community with new abilities required to achieve particular core values. It also creates a motivation system utilizing formal and informal awards for people who are the exemplars of conduct compliant with core values. Moreover, it establishes new information programs that explain the essence of core values. Those programs are for both current and prospective participants of academic ethos.

After many years of functioning formal systems of actions described in this chapter, values gradually become so rooted in people and organizations that external systems of execution become needless. There is an atmosphere of pressure from co-workers that guards core values on their own. Core values become a part of institutionalized environment. The following years result in a situation in which people in an organization (as they are willing to do this) automatically fulfill organizational expectations of deeply established core values. Such individuals internalize core values of an organization to the greatest extent and these values become their personal values as a whole; in effect, they become built into their own personality. Employees start to accept the importance of living in accordance with a university's values, even if there is no external pressure. Those people recognize such conduct as an element of good work. Individuals become great carriers and implementers of a university's core values. This implementation may be likened to the metaphor of the French political scientist of the second part of the nineteenth century, Alexis da Cacu Willa, who used the term "cardiac reflex."[38] However, such behavior is very rare—an ideal that may be approached by management of a higher school's identity through the use of the instruments of Academic Ethos Management.[39]

CHAPTER 6

Core Values Management at the University

Insights from USA

Case Study 1: DePaul University

Name: DePaul University[1]

Country: United States of America (Chicago, IL)

Date of foundation: 1898, by the Congregation of the Mission (or Vincentian) religious community

Motto: "Viam sapientiae monstrabo tibi" ("I will show you the way of wisdom." Proverbs, IV, 11)

Form: A private institution of higher education and research

Rector/President: The Rev. Dennis H. Holtschneider, C.M.

Structure

DePaul University includes ten schools and colleges: Driehaus College of Business, College of Communication, College of Computing and Digital Media, College of Education, College of Law, College of Liberal Arts and Social Sciences, College of Science and Health, School of Music, School for New Learning, The Theatre School, as well as six campuses: Lincoln Park, Loop, Naperville, Oak Forest, O'Hare, and Rolling Meadows.

University colors: blue and red

Enrollment: 25,398—including 16,384 undergraduates; 7,983 graduate students and 1,031 law students

Employees/Administrates: 3,927 faculty and staff members; of which, 2,636 were full-time and 1,291 were part-time employees

Alumni: More than 145,000 worldwide, living in 55 countries.

Notable alumni: Richard M. Daley, Richard J. Daley (Chicago mayors), Mary Dempsey (Chicago Library Commissioner), John Stroger (Cook County Board President), James Jenness (Former Kellogg Co. CEO), Frank Clark (ComEd CEO), Patrick J. Moore (Smurfit-Stone Container Corp. CEO), Richard Driehaus (Driehaus Capital Management CEO), Daniel Ustian (Navistar International Corp. Chief Executive), John C. Reilly (actor), George Perle (Pulitzer Prize-winning composer), Samuel Magad (Chicago Symphony Orchestra concertmaster), Josephine Lee (Chicago Children's Choir Artistic Director), Gillian Anderson (actress)

Brief history:

DePaul University was founded as a Catholic institution in 1898 by the Congregation of the Mission priests and brethren, known as the Vincentians. As followers of the seventeenth-century French priest Saint Vincent de Paul, the Vincentians valued philanthropy and access for everyone. Since its founding, and in keeping with its mission, DePaul has been widely known for welcoming students and employees from all ethnicities, religions, and backgrounds.

Student enrollment grew from 70 in 1898 to 200 in 1903 in what is now the Lincoln Park neighborhood of Chicago. In that year, James Quigley, Archbishop of Chicago, announced plans to create a preparatory seminary, now Archbishop Quigley Preparatory Seminary, for the archdiocese and allow the Jesuit Saint Ignatius College, now Loyola University Chicago, to move its collegiate programs to the north side, threatening St. Vincent College's survival. In response, the Vincentians rechartered in 1907 as DePaul University, expressly offering all of its courses of study to men and women of any religious background. DePaul began admitting women in 1911 and awarded degrees to its first female graduates in 1912. It was one of the first Catholic universities to admit female students in a coeducational setting.

With the entry of the United States into World War I in 1918, DePaul formed a unit of the US Army Reserve Officer Training Corps and converted its College Theatre into Army barracks.

The university continued to grow and build in the 1920s. In 1926, the university was first accredited by the North Central Association of Colleges and Universities.

DePaul mobilized for World War II, offering its facilities for war training and free courses to train people for industry work. The G.I. Bill, which paid the tuition of veterans enrolled in college, turned the financial tide for DePaul. Enrollment in 1945 skyrocketed to 8,857 students, twice as many as the previous year, and totaled more than 11,000 in 1948. Although a consulting firm recommended relocating from its deteriorating Lincoln Park neighborhood to the suburbs, trustees voted to remain and support revitalization of the neighborhood.

DePaul entered into a merger with Barat College in 2001, from which it withdrew in 2005 after continued low enrollment and rising maintenance costs made the campus unviable. The former Barat College had its final graduation on June 11, 2005 and was closed as of June 30, 2005. It sold the grounds of the 147-year-old college to a condominium developer Barat Woods LLC, who pledged to maintain the historic Old Main building, yet demolished the Thabor Wing with its Italianate style Sacred Heart Chapel. The remaining students, tenured and tenure-track faculty and some staff, were absorbed into DePaul's other campuses. Barat Woods LLC went into foreclosure and the property was auctioned, and the lender, Harris Bank, won. The former Barat College campus was donated by an anonymous donor to Woodlands Academy of the Sacred Heart.

Vision, Mission, and Core Values of Academic Ethos at DePaul University

At the beginning of document named as VISION twenty12 there is formulated the following vision declaration:

> "preparing women and men to be at the forefront of their chosen fields as ethical and socially engaged leaders."[2]

The declaration of the university's mission reads as follows:

> "This mission statement embodies the principal purposes of DePaul University. As such it is the nexus between past, present and future; the criterion against which plans are formulated and major decisions made; the bond which unites faculty, students, staff, alumni, and trustees as an academic community. As a university, DePaul pursues the preservation, enrichment, and transmission of knowledge and

culture across a broad scope of academic disciplines. It treasures its deep roots in the wisdom nourished in Catholic universities from medieval times. The principal distinguishing marks of the university are its Catholic, Vincentian, and urban character."[3]

According to the university's mission, its uniqueness is the combination of Catholic, Vincentian, and urban character that are created on the basis of the following core values:

The university states that it expresses its Catholic identity [(respect for a person and service to others)][4] by direct service to the poor and economically disenfranchised through such programs as actively engaging students, faculty and staff in volunteer and community service directed at impoverished areas.

Although it is a Roman Catholic school of higher education, DePaul's institutional uniqueness is related to a Vincentian identity (referring to the patron namesake of the school, St. Vincent dePaul) through respect for human dignity, diversity, and individual "personalism."

The urban identity of the University is expressed by connection and outreach to the community. Its connections include delivering quality education to locations in and immediately around the metropolitan area of the city of Chicago, IL, and to the global community.[5]

The extended organizational structure of DePaul University and its policy of diversity resulted in definition of free mission, vision, and core values by each particular organizational unit, but they all still need to be compliant with mission, vision, and core values of the whole school. For instance, the Office of Institutional Diversity defines those elements as:

Mission
The OIDE actualizes DePaul's Catholic, Vincentian, and Urban character by insuring respect, inclusion, and equity, for all members of our community.

Vision

Our vision is to achieve a truly diverse environment that reflects our collective values. Our work, programs, and initiatives will reflect this commitment to promoting change, equal opportunity, social justice, celebrating and fostering diversity, the recruitment and retention of diverse constituencies, and building a community that values and respects the differences and commonalities that each and every individual brings to DePaul. We will continue to strive to prepare our community to effectively navigate the opportunities and challenges of Chicago and beyond.

Core Values: Assist DePaul in achieving academic excellence, Embrace our Vincentian Heritage, Create understanding, Foster compassion, Promote equal opportunity, Foster respect, inclusion, and equity.[6]

Institutionalization of Academic Ethos Core Values at DePaul University

Having studied the internal documents of the university, having read the papers and book chapters about the identity of DePaul University as well as having spoken to its representatives, it is hard not to feel that core assumptions (central characteristics) in a form of values of academic ethos that constitute the identity of this higher school are deeply and broadly shared within the various groups of academic community (which was confirmed by the research described on the following pages of this book). In addition, the institutionalization of core values within the community has a systematic, formalized, and consequent form that resulted in a distinction within this university of a specific function of values management—values that constitute a university's identity. DePaul University is on its best way to make its core values to be—using a metaphor of the French political scientist Alexis de Cacu Willa from the nineteenth century—a "heart reflex" for the academic community.

I would like to return to some facts that explain my opinion presented earlier.

Core values of DePaul University not only are reflected in vision, mission, or in their declarations but also are implemented in the university's framework through the actions for their enactment. They are reflected in documents that create the strategy of the university's development and are transformed into central purposes, detailed objectives, and appropriate tasks:

DePaul, in common with all universities, is dedicated to teaching, research, and public service. However, in pursuing its own distinctive purposes, among these three fundamental responsibilities this university places highest priority on programs of instruction and learning. All curricula emphasize skills and attitudes that educate students to be lifelong, independent learners. DePaul provides sufficient diversity in curricular offerings, personal advisement, student services, and extracurricular activities to serve students who vary in age, ability, experience, and career interests. Full-time and part-time students are accorded equivalent service and are held to the same academic standards.

As a comprehensive university, DePaul offers degree programs at the undergraduate and graduate levels and a range of professional programs. The liberal arts and sciences are recognized not only for their intrinsic value in undergraduate and graduate degree programs, but also because they are foundational for all specialized undergraduate programs and supportive of all advanced professional programs. The university maintains that depth of scholarship to offer the doctorate in selected academic disciplines. Libraries, computer resources, and other academic support services match the levels and diversity of degree programs.

Research is supported both for its intrinsic merit and for the practical benefits it offers to faculty, students, and society. Broadly conceived, research at the university entails not only the discovery and dissemination of new knowledge but also the creation and interpretation of artistic works, application of expertise to enduring societal issues, and development of methodologies that improve inquiry, teaching and professional practice.

In meeting its public service responsibility, the university encourages faculty, staff and students to apply specialized expertise in ways that contribute to the societal, economic, cultural and ethical quality of life in the metropolitan area and beyond. When appropriate, DePaul develops service partnerships with other institutions and agencies.[7]

The leadership of the university is aware that all that is connected with values (all the plans, actions taken within this area) should be an effect of common decisions and common work. The involvement of academic community in the values implementation and acquisition of its trust for a given activity is possible only if there is wide access and coparticipation in all the works connected with values. It is confirmed by works on the document Vision twenty12 that supports the core values of academic ethos in DePaul University. A broad range of DePaul's faculty, staff, and students contributed to the document, providing a subtext of both DePaul traditions and contemporary directions.[8]

Vision twenty12:

is the product of a collective wisdom produced through countless committee meetings, brainstorming sessions and town hall gatherings attended by a broad cross-section of faculty, staff and students over the course of nearly 3 years. (…)

The process of creating a new, unified vision of DePaul's future began in the summer of 2003 at the President's Retreat. In October of 2003, 20 issue teams, the so-called red and blue teams, were appointed to explore 10 themes that emerged from the retreat. The process advanced when a university-wide committee was appointed in the spring of 2004 to distill the team reports into four overarching priorities and seven crosscutting themes. Planning took a major leap forward in April of 2005 when a 27-member Strategic Planning Committee was named to help drive the project toward conclusion.

A series of town hall meetings was convened in the fall of 2005 at which faculty, staff and students learned more about the latest draft and its associated metrics and costs. The meetings offered members of the university community yet another opportunity to weigh in with valuable feedback.

(…)

DePaul's Board of Trustees approved unanimously the plan at its March 4, 2006, meeting. After the vote, Board Chairman John Simon said, "This plan will improve upon what DePaul has done for 108 years. The trustees have embraced a plan that will further enhance the quality of a remarkable institution.[9]

Table 6.1 presents the core values of DePaul University and particular goals and objectives for their enacting.

However, DePaul University went farther beyond the process of core values enacting than what is presented in Table 6.1. It founded a separate organizational unit named the Office of Mission and Values, which aims at assisting the university community in achieving Goal VI of VISION twenty12, which states that responsibilities for the Catholic and Vincentian identity will be assumed by board, faculty, and staff.[11] The main purpose of this unit is reflected in its mission:

Guided by the university's strategic plan, VISION Twenty12, the Office of Mission and Values collaborates with university constituencies in ways that measurably enhance their understanding and support of DePaul University's Catholic, Vincentian, and urban identity. Together we provide the leadership that enables the university to fulfill its distinctive educational mission, serve its diverse student body and maximize its strategic capacities. As the premier international resource for Vincentian studies, the Office also serves a wide range of external constituencies who seek to deepen their engagement with Vincentian history, spirituality and service.[12]

The main areas of Office of Mission and Values may be divided into: Introducing and Orienting, Building Community, Educating and Enriching, Developing Leadership Capacity, Rewarding and Recognizing, Promoting Research and Scholarship, and Serving Community.

Table 6.1. Core Values of Depaul University and Particular Goals and Objectives for their Enacting

Core Values	Goal	Goal Description	Examples of Objectives
1 Catholic identity expressed by respect for person and services to others	Further institutionalize DePaul's Vincentian and Catholic identity	Charged with maintaining the university's Catholic and Vincentian identity, the board, faculty, and staff will foster a learning environment respected for its civic engagement. Business practices fulfilling the needs of faculty and staff will be employed.	– Increase opportunities for the study and exploration of Catholic intellectual and theological tradition and praxis through curricular and co-curricular initiatives. – The board, faculty, and staff will assume responsibility for the institution's Vincentian and Catholic identity. – Ensure that human resource functions, university business practices, and internal communication are responsive to the needs of staff and faculty. – Human Resources will coordinate, expand, and assess university-wide training efforts for staff. – Externally, be well known for civic and community engagement and a commitment to the common good as expressions of our Vincentian, Catholic, and urban identity.[10]
2 Vincentian identity expressed by respect for human dignity, diversity, and individual "personalism"	Be a model of diversity	Long known for its emphasis on the success of first generation, economically disadvantaged urban students, the university will attain leadership in recruiting and retaining a diverse body of students, faculty, and staff.	– Attain leadership in recruitment and support of diverse faculty, staff, and senior administrators. – Exceed national norms in recruiting, retaining, and graduating a diverse student body, with an emphasis on first generation, economically disadvantaged urban students. – Expand opportunities for the DePaul community to study and practice religious faiths in a pluralistic environment. – Create programming for all constituents of the DePaul community that affirms the central place of diversity in the university's mission and institutional culture.

(Continued)

Table 6.1. (*Continued*)

Core Values	Goal	Goal Description	Examples of Objectives
3 Urban identity expressed by delivering quality education, preparing women and men to be at the forefront of their chosen fields as ethical and socially engaged leaders in the Chicago area and beyond	Enrich academic quality Prepare students to be a socially responsible future leaders and engaged alumni' Selectively increase enrollment	Increased academic rigor, strategically enhanced curricula, and an intensified focus on ethical practices and Catholic theological tradition will drive student learning success as the university continues to tap the city of Chicago to extend classroom learning.	– Educate all students for an increasingly globalized world. – Provide opportunities for all students to learn ethical systems and demonstrate ethical practice. – Engage the City of Chicago to extend classroom learning. – Foster an academic advising environment that supports student learning success. – Raise DePaul's academic reputation. – Become a premier institution known for its student success programs. – Build strong alumni institutional affinity, pride and lifelong connections. – Expand and develop purposeful co-curricular activities to promote leadership, civic engagement, cultural awareness, and personal and spiritual development. – Raise the perception of quality attached to the university's brand.

Source: Author's own study based on http://www.president.depaul.edu/Downloads/VISIONtwenty12Brochure.pdf.

For each of these activities may be then distinguished particular actions for enacting and protecting core values. For example

- for Introducing and Orienting they are such as: new staff orientation, new trustee orientation, premiere DePaul parent orientation;
- for Rewarding and Recognizing they are such as: McHugh Quality of Staff Service Award, service awards, Spirit of DePaul Award, St. Vincent de Paul Award, Via Sapientiae Award and 21year club;
- for Educating and Enriching they are such as: annual Vincentian lectures, DePaul Reads Together, Vincentian Heritage Days;
- for Developing Leadership Capacity they are such as: international Vincentian scholars, Vincentian Endowment Fund, Vincentian Mission Institute.

The Office of Mission and Values annually prepares a strategic plan that includes detailed information on purposes, actions within a particular area of activity taken and to be taken for institutionalization of university's core values.

Table 6.2 presents examples of achievements within particular areas of activity of the Office of Mission and Core Values in 2008–2010 and the objectives formulated for 2010–2011 that are included in annual reports (executive summary of the Office of Mission and Values at DePaul University).

To create a base of examples for patterns of conduct and to outline basic principles of academic ethics, as well as giving an opportunity for fulfilling the objectives connected with core values, the Office of Institutional Compliance, along with members of the DePaul community, have developed a Code of Conduct, which highlights the policies most critical to working in higher education and at DePaul. Every action and decision of DePaul faculty, staff, and student workers, full-time, and part-time employees is guided by the instruction in this document. The main purpose of the Code of Conduct is to inform the academic community about the fundamental expectations DePaul University has for every one of its faculty and staff members, like, for example, to be

Table 6.2. Examples of Achievements of the Office of Mission and Core Values For Institutionalization of DePaul University's Core Values in 2008–2010

Area of Activity	Achievement	New Goal
Introducing and Orienting	– Last Year's Accomplishment: New Staff Orientation: All new staff members received a Mission and Values orientation as part of their Human Resources Orientation. 203 new staff members. – Last year's Accomplishment: Premiere DePaul Parent Orientation: 14% of parents/family members (448/3,280) attending Premiere DePaul Orientation chose to attend an optional Mission and Values orientation session entitled: Vincent) de) Paul: More) than) Old) Clothes.)	Create a new orientation DVD to replace dated version. Increase participation to 20%.
Building Community	– DePaul Emeritus Society: Increased philanthropy (24%). Continuation of Oral History project. Creation of Facebook page.	Work with History Department's Oral History class to conduct five in-depth oral history interviews in Fall Quarter.
Educating and Enriching	– Our office seeks to ensure that all new members of the university community: faculty, staff, students, administrators, and trustees begin their time at DePaul with an appropriate orientation experience highlighting the university's mission and values. These orientations are highly regarded by participants. – 38 new episodes produced (148 total in archive) 26,833 views and 91,447 downloads to portable devices. Increase of 68,300 hits over last year.	Increase total number of downloads.
Developing & Leadership Capacity	– Vincentian Heritage Tours: in August 2009, the fourth national Vincentian Family Heritage Tour to France attracted 34 participants.	August 6, 2010 Faculty/Staff Vincentian Heritage Tour; March 5, 2010 Senior Leadership Vincentian Heritage Tour.
Rewarding and Recognizing	– All of the reward and recognition programs sponsored by our office were administered successfully this year to the great appreciation of the university community.	
Promoting Research	– Vincentian Heritage Journal: Two issues of the Vincentian) Heritage) Journal appeared as scheduled.	Explore the feasibility and advisability of stopping the print edition of Vincentian) Heritage and moving instead to an "e version. Establish the capability of e-publishing."
Serving Community	– Website: This year saw the complete revamping of the management model, format, and content of the website.	Establish internal processes to facilitate real-time changes to content management. Establish metrics analysis of website use.

Source: Authoresses' own study based on: http://www.mission.depaul.edu/AboutUs/Documents/0910ExecSummary.pdf and http://mission.depaul.edu/AboutUs/Documents/0809ExecutiveSummary.pdf.

honest and responsible with the university's resources, to treat each other with dignity and in a collegial manner, and most importantly, to prepare DePaul's students for a fulfilling and successful life ahead. In addition to statements relating to certain conduct policies, the Code gives sample situations in which the policies apply. These samples serve as scenarios to clarify the university's stance on certain policies. All DePaul employees are responsible for knowing and adhering to the policies mentioned in the Code of Conduct, in addition to its sources, the Management Standards Handbook, the Faculty Handbook, and the University's Policies and Procedures website. The Code is updated and available online as well as the policies are often updated, and new policies are continually being considered. The faculty and staff of DePaul University are expected to handle properly and protect its financial resources, operations, strategies, and reputation. To fulfill this duty and goal the Office of Institutional Compliance was formed. Its main purpose is to foster a culture of compliance and accountability that is consistent with DePaul's mission. It has been stated clearly that

> Any concerns regarding compliance or alleged compliance violations should be addressed through managerial channels when appropriate. However, if there is an instance where a manager is part of the alleged noncompliance, or if an employee feels uncomfortable seeking resolution this way, he or she should report the concerns using one of the following methods

- A letter stating an alleged impropriety can be mailed to the Office of Institutional Compliance.
- The compliance department can be called directly regarding any questions or concerns.
- Other resources exist at the university, depending on the situation:
  - The Office of the University Ombudsperson (for confidential discussions or support).
  - Internal Audit.
  - Office of Institutional Diversity and Equity.
  - Human Resources.

- ○ Public Safety Office.
- ○ Misconduct Reporting Anonymous Hotline.

In addition, students in DePaul University are supported by the special codes and policies that have been designed especially for them. They are able to realize core values of the university in an active way by establishing behaviors that enact those values as well as by defining behaviors that threaten those values.

The Code of Student Responsibility serves as an example. The Code was developed by Student Affairs to give formal recognition to the rights and responsibilities of students at DePaul University and is based on the following principles: (a) the intrinsic value of the person stands above other values; (b) the student is respected as a responsible person; (c) the University is by definition a corporation; and (d) DePaul University recognizes that freedom to teach and freedom to learn depend on opportunities and conditions in the classroom, on the campus, and in the larger community. By voluntarily joining the DePaul community, a student assumes the responsibility for abiding by the standards that have been instituted by DePaul. However, students must take responsibility for confronting behaviors exhibited by their peers that negatively impact their experiences and violate established standards of behavior. It is imperative that students work in partnership with University faculty and staff members to protect the rights that have been afforded them. [13]

The policies and procedures established by DePaul University not only specify rights and responsibilities of academic community (faculty mentors, staff, students) for the compliance with the values of academic ethos, but they also define behaviors that are threatens to those values. In Academic Integrity Policy we may find the following note:

> Violations of academic integrity include but are not limited to the following categories: cheating; plagiarism; fabrication; falsification or sabotage of research data; destruction or misuse of the university's academic resources, alteration or falsification of academic records; academic misconduct; and complicity.[14]

The consequences of such a statement is a specified procedure that explains the incorporated aspects of the judicial review process that includes student's right to "bring one Advisor to an Administrative Hearing, a Judicial Board Hearing, or any other meeting included within this Judicial Review Process" as well as to "bring Witnesses to an Administrative Hearing or a Judicial Board Hearing to support their statements."[15] Members of the Judicial Board pool at DePaul University consist of: six current students with at least sophomore status nominated by the Student Government Association, six faculty members nominated by the Faculty Council, and six staff members nominated by the Staff Council.[16] Judicial hearings are described as follows.

- Administrative Hearing: An Administrative Hearing is a hearing in which the hearing officer is a University designee, such as the Dean of Students or another Student Affairs professional.
- Judicial Board Hearing: A Judicial Board Hearing is a hearing in which the hearing officers are selected from the Judicial Board pool of members.[17]

We may also find information about judicial sanctions; what is particularly important is that all the policies and procedures are easily available both for faculty members and for students. They are included in the Faculty Student Handbook that may be easily located and accessed at appropriate points on the University's website. Parents/guardians of students are also perceived by the University's authorities as active participants in the process of shaping the University's desired identity:

As parents and family members, you have an important role in supporting your student in all areas of the college experience—academically, socially and financially. The staff of DePaul's Office of Financial Aid is here to help you with the financial piece of that puzzle. (…)

[Parents] have several key responsibilities in helping your student apply for and receive financial aid. They fall in three areas: the aid application, completing the award process, and receiving funds.[18]

Regardless of the fact that the University elaborates and constantly updates appropriate policies, procedures, and codes in order to enact the core values, the members of the academic community may be supported by the independent unit of University ombudsmen in situations of ethical dilemmas:

> Established in 2001, the University Ombudsperson provides a confidential, neutral and independent resource for all of DePaul's faculty and staff. [This institution is] available to listen to and investigate issues or complaints, to explore informal resolution of conflict, clarify university policies and procedures or help you find the right person or department within the university to respond to your questions. The Ombudsperson offers an alternative informal, safe place to work with you in suggesting possible responses to any questions you might have-and if we don't know the answer, we will seek to find it for you. (…)
>
> The University Ombudsperson subscribes to The Ombudsman Association Code of Ethics and Standards of Practice.[19]

During 2008–2009, 282 clients received services from the ombudsperson.[20] Moreover, the interested person may find information about the history of the International Ombudsman Association, its mission, vision, and core values, code of ethics, and explanation of specific terminology.

Core values of DePaul University are not only reflected in strategic plans of the University but also used as a base for creating codes, policies, and procedures that enable their enactment; in fact, they are expressed in a dynamic assortment of academic programs, operational support services, and student services.[21] The main responsibility for core values protection is through the Office of Mission and Values. The main initiatives taken and realized by this organizational unit include an orientation program, divided into new employee orientation and student orientation.

> As a mission-driven institution it is very important for the university to ensure that all new students, faculty, adjunct faculty, staff, senior leadership, and trustees receive a thorough introduction to the university's history, mission, and values as they begin their relationship with the Institution.[22]

The orientation focuses on topics such as benefits, technology, university policies and procedures, and the mission and values of the university.

A representative from the Office of Mission and Values will present an overview of DePaul's mission and values, ensuring that each new member of the DePaul Community is introduced to the Vincentian, Catholic, and urban identity of the university.[23]

The Office of Mission and Values staff is available to any student group or class for a presentation of DePaul University's mission and values, or to facilitate a discussion on the history, mission and values of the University. The student presentations are well received whether they are given to first year students or to seasoned student leaders. In the past, students were impressed with "The connection to present times and Vincent DePaul's values" and they "enjoyed hearing about Vincent 'the man' rather than Vincent 'the ideal.'" Students also reported that "It was made very clear that being Catholic, or of a specific race, gender, orientation, etc., was not required. I felt very accepted."[24]

There are many courses, programs, minors, and majors in the Departments of Catholic Studies and Religious Studies that cover virtually every facet of DePaul's Catholic, Vincentian mission in a diverse and pluralistic environment. For example:

- Alternative Break Service Immersions that provide DePaul students the unique opportunity to work, live, and build relationships with over 12 marginalized communities throughout the United States and the Americas.
- University Ministry Community Service that provides students with service opportunities to communities in need, while encouraging students to develop their faith lives in light of their service involvement.[25]

DePaul University cares for not only current members of its academic community, but also its former employees. In 2007, the Emeritus

Professors' Society merged into the DePaul Emeritus Society, what strengthens ties between the university and its retirees, and fosters their continued participation in the DePaul University community.

Members of the academic community at DePaul University are being constantly motivated and rewarded for their behaviors that are compliant with core values supported in the process of creating a unique identity. Examples of those rewards are as follows:

The Spirit of DePaul Award was instituted during DePaul's Centennial celebration to highlight institutional Vincentian Values and their relation to the achievement of DePaul's mission. The award also seeks to personally honor and recognize diverse members of the DePaul Community for their leadership and service in the spirit of Saint Vincent de Paul.[26]

In order to recognize quality service provided by staff members to DePaul, the University and Staff Council introduced in 2003 the annual Ken McHugh Quality Service Award. Awards are presented to those individuals who have enhanced university initiatives by promoting collaboration and teamwork to support the institution's mission.[27]

Another example of action for the University's core values cultivating is "service to others" such as Tag Days during which volunteers at the Lincoln Park campus gather funds to benefit food pantries, local shelters, and those families and individuals who can benefit most from social outreach... "[In the year 2010] 22 volunteers collected $788.62."[28]

Vincentian Heritage Days, Vincentian Heritage Tours, and the faculty and staff Vincentian tour are the next examples of actions for institutionalization of values such as human dignity, diversity, and individual "personalism" expressing the Vincentian identity of DePaul University.

Vincentian Heritage Days [are] a series of community events that bring together faculty, staff, and students for discussions and celebrations in the spirit of St. Vincent de Paul.[29]

The Office of Mission and Values offers regular opportunities for members of the university community to deepen their understanding of the university's patron, by participating in guided Vincentian Heritage study tours to locations in Paris and throughout France associated with the life and works of St. Vincent de Paul.[30]

Participation in tours is open, on a competitive basis, to all full-time faculty and staff who have a demonstrated interest in the Vincentian heritage, mission, and values of the university. Applicants must provide a personal statement as to how they envision this trip helping to deepen their commitment to the university's mission as they live it out in their own departments. They also must provide a letter of endorsement from their supervisor.[31]

Another initiative taken in 2004 by the Office of Mission and Values is DePaul Reads Together, a program encouraging professors to join a book club that focuses on the DePaul missions and values. Small groups meet for robust discussion, followed with an overall panel gathering.[32]

Describing initiatives for core values implementation at DPU must include "The DePaul Leadership Project":

The work of the Project began in April 2002. Today the Project carries out the vision of the Hays to develop an awareness of Vincent-inspired leadership concepts and practices within the University community and Vincentian communities worldwide.

(...)

The de Paul Leadership Project is a concrete response to the increasingly urgent need for leadership succession planning. The initial stage of research (from April to August 2002) identified the needs and expectations for the research project.

- Assessment of existing Vincentian characteristics of leadership and management among lay and religious people at DePaul University and other Vincentian founded institutions.
- A timely response to leadership succession planning in religious and lay organizations, especially within the Vincentian family of higher education, social service and charitable service providers.

- Publication and delivery of educational materials, articles and training modules that advance Vincentian leadership concepts and practices.[33]

Such initiatives by members of academic community as those afore-mentioned create the base for identity, development, and communicating value-driven leadership practices inside university and at Vincentian organizations worldwide.

The variety of actions taken by DePaul University with the aim of implementing its core values is so great that for their description there should be created as a separate book or even some books. That is why I will describe just the one another example that proofs for complexity and model professionalism in managing values of academic ethos in DePaul University.

In 2002, Joseph Ferrari, PhD (LAS: Psychology Department) and the Office of Mission and Values developed "self-reporting" faculty, staff, and student assessments, gauging the perceptions of the university's Catholic, Vincentian, and Urban identity; the assessments also measured the university's success rate at exhibiting that identity.[34] Since then the monitoring research on the level of core values implementation are conducted regularly. The research also refers to the effectiveness of applied policies, procedures, and actions.

The actions described earlier aimed at core values institutionalization have a substantial purpose as they communicate the most important issue to academic community—values that create its identity. DePaul University utilizes a broad spectrum of tools for core values communication (materials and internal publications, writing about tradition, ceremonies and rituals used for promoting the university, trainings, seminars, and websites); what is most important is that every action taken by Office of Mission and Values and by the top management is undeniable evidence that core values at DePaul University are authentic, shared, constant, and alive.

Actions truly speak louder than words, especially in the presentation of core values. DePaul University clearly exhibits its core values in a multiplicity of ways: through its goals, objectives, the foundation of a special unit responsible for protecting those values, a new member orientation program, the Spirit of DePaul Award or Tag Days, and the Vincentian

Heritage Tours, to name a few. These methods communicate DEPAUL UNIVERSITY's core values of its academic community and present a model way for creating a message that DePaul University does really "walk the talk."

Case Study 2: Wright State University

Name: Wright State University[35]

Country: United States of America (Dayton, Ohio)

Date of foundation: founded in 1964 initially as the Dayton branch of both Miami University and Ohio State University, in 1965 transformed into a separate university

Motto: "Making a Living, Making a Life"

Form: It is a public research university

Rector/President: David R. Hopkins, P.E.D.

Structure:

Wright State University includes eight following colleges: Education and Human Services, Engineering and Computer Science, Liberal Arts; Nursing and Health, Raj Soin College of Business, Science and Mathematics, University College, and Lake Campus;

and three schools: Boonshoft School of Medicine, Graduate School, and Professional Psychology.

University colors: Green and gold

Enrollment: More than 19000 students

Employees/Administrates: 2385, including 860 faculty and 1525 staff

Alumni: 104,557

Notable alumni: Javed Abidi (disability rights activist), David Albright (founder of Institute for Science and International Security), Brian Anderson (professional baseball player, assistant coach), J. Todd Anderson (film storyboard artist), Jim Baldridge (local news anchor), Siva S. Banda (aerospace engineer), Michael R. Barratt (astronaut), Joyce Beatty (member of the Ohio House of Representatives), Andrea Bendewald (actress), David S. Brown (historian and professor at Elizabethtown College),

Iman Crosson (actor, Obama impersonator, Internet personality), Kevin DeWine (chairman of the Ohio Republican Party and former member of the Ohio House of Representatives), Chitra Banerjee Divakaruni (author), Christopher Easton (artist), Bill Edwards (professional basketball player), John B. Ellington, Jr. (Air National Guard general), Irene D. Long (Chief Medical Officer at the Kennedy Space Center), Steve Molla (author), Robert Pollard (singer and songwriter), Anthony Shaffer (U.S. Army intelligence officer), Brad Sherwood (actor and comedian), Joe Smith (professional baseball player), Chase Whiteside (journalist, documentary filmmaker, and founder of New Left Media), DaShaun Wood (professional basketball player)

Brief history:

Founded in 1964, Wright State University was originally the Dayton branch campus of both Miami University and Ohio State University. At that time it comprised only a single building, Allyn Hall (named for Stanley Allyn, then-president of National Cash Register and one of the University's founders).

A 1965 act of the Ohio General Assembly created the University. Several names were considered, including Dayton State University, Southwest Ohio State University, Shawnee University, Four Rivers University (after the four nearby rivers: the Great Miami, the Mad, the Stillwater, and Wolf Creek), and Mad River University. Wright State University was eventually chosen to honor the Wright brothers, residents of Dayton. On October 1, 1967, the university met enrollment criteria set by state legislature and Senate Bill 212 passed to actually create a new university. This led to the official charter of Wright State University.

Despite this, it has a Dayton address. Prior to current president David R. Hopkins' appointment, Wright State University had five other presidents: Brage Golding (1966–1973), Robert J. Kegerreis (1973–1985), Paige E. Mulhollan (1985–1994), Harley E. Flack (1994–1998), and Kim Goldenberg (1998–2006).

In 2007, Wright State University celebrated its fortieth anniversary in connection with the Presidential Inauguration of David R. Hopkins. To mark this milestone in university history, Wright State created a 40th Anniversary website to highlight the events, history, and vision of its community.

Vision, Mission, and Core Values of Academic Ethos at Wright State University

Studying the history and documentation of Wright State University, we may have an impression that the academic community at this university has always known why it exists and what is most important for its continued success. It is something that distinguishes this school from others. In other words, the axiological assumptions of this university from its beginning have been deeply rooted in the "spirit" of its academic community.

Despite this fact, the university's leaders have been fully aware that Wright State University's axiological assumptions, the fundamentals of its cultural identity, and its main principles need to stay constant but that certain ideologies should or even *must* change to ensure the university's development in the future. That is why, when in May 1996 the higher learning commission of the North Central Association (NCA) colleges and schools visited Wright State University, it observed that the university was "immersed in a lengthy, multileveled, long-range visioning process, later called Vision 2020: Shaping the Future, that included a reexamination of the university's mission and its governance processes."[36]

Wright State University has always been known for its innovation and flexibility, qualities that have helped us to develop and sustain our prominent position within the region, state, and throughout the country. We have many reasons for our pride but most importantly, we are proud of our faculty, staff, and students who have helped to build Wright State University into an eminent metropolitan university.

To remain competitive and to reach beyond what is known today, Vision 2020 was developed through an active dialogue regarding our future. Contained in the vision are the ideas, perspectives, opinions, and expertise of hundreds of faculty, staff and students, as well as community persons, who spent many hours engaged in that dialogue.[37]

Vision 2020 and subsequent related planning efforts culminated in a number of significant changes that have both focused the

university's energies and strengthened and transformed its governance processes. Among the most significant changes:

- the creation of new university "Aim" and mission statements,
  approved by the Board of Trustees in December 1996;
- the creation of a new university ethics statement, approved in
  1997;
- the development and implementation of two new 5-year
  strategic plans;

The creation in 1996 of the Office of Internal Controls and Audit
Services.[38]

The aforementioned changes have both sharpened and strengthened the
university's mission and governance structures.

Vision 2020 focused primarily on five strategic areas:

Students of the Future

Wright State University students of the year 2020 will be engaged
in learning communities that prepare them for success in life and
in work. As members of these learning communities, students will
be active participants in learning. Guided by faculty and staff and
assisted by their fellow students, they will be encouraged to become
service oriented, culturally sensitive, technically competent, knowl-
edgeable, civic minded, open, and poised for life-long learning.
Some students in the year 2020 will engage in learning simply for
seeking truth and knowledge, to fulfill their potential, and to realize their personal dreams. Others will aim to enhance employment
potential. Ultimately, through educational experiences that span
local and global boundaries, Wright State University students will be
prepared both to serve society and improve the human condition.[39]

Educational Programs of the Future

The strength of the Wright State University undergraduate experience will be ensured by supporting faculty as key contributors to
the learning community. Our vision for Wright State University

includes completion of the transformation of the learning process from traditional instruction to one that will free faculty
from the mechanics of knowledge transmission and enable
them to concentrate on their value as discoverers, interpreters,
mentors, and navigators. Programs in the learning communities
of the future will provide multiple points of entry and new ave-
nues of learning unrestricted by limits of time or space. Enrollment in the year 2020 will be increased as Wright State faculty
adapt to and take advantage of distance and distributed learning. Core values and skills will shape our programs and educational efforts. These values and skills will include: thinking
and reasoning; effective spoken and written communication;
quantitative analysis and scientific literacy; context awareness,
(i.e. the cultural/historical/global setting of the educational
enterprise); commitment to community service; ethics; and love
of learning.[40]

Excellent Faculty and Staff

Wright State University will continue to employ a highly qualified
and diverse faculty and staff who value student success and demonstrate a strong commitment to teaching, scholarship, research,
clinical practice, and professional service as the foundation of
our learning communities. We will obtain a work force that is
reflective of the ethnic, racial, gender, age, and disability composition of the region. We will enhance opportunities to achieve this
goal. We will reward and support units that develop a climate
that supports and values this diverse work force. Faculty and staff
will reflect changing enrollment and program priorities during the
next 25 years.

Excellent faculty will be the single most important factor in maintaining the reputation of Wright State University and fostering
the most effective learning environments for our students. We will
develop methods for acknowledging faculty workloads which take
into account their developing roles in learning communities of the
next century.[41]

Enhancing and Maintaining High Quality Facilities

We will remain committed to master planning to enhance our physical and environmental resources on the two campuses and the complexes throughout Dayton and the Miami Valley. Wright State will remain a national leader in its physical accessibility to all. New configurations of interactive living and learning communities will emerge. Facilities, programs and services will be provided to support the diverse needs of members of these communities.[42]

Securing Funding for the Future

The University's budget will continue to rely upon four major sources of income, including state subsidies, student tuition and fees-for-service, research and other sponsored programs, and private support. In keeping with Ohio's move toward a performance-based funding model, we will position ourselves to secure as many resources as possible by matching state mandates to our institutional mission. The mix of income sources will change from virtual dependence on the two former sources to a greater expectation of the latter two.[43]

On June 6, 1997, the University's Board of Trustees adopted "Vision 2020: Shaping the Future," which, according to then-President Harley Flack, "provide(s) the guidance needed by Wright State University to steer its course as the catalyst for educational excellence in the Miami Valley and beyond" (p.v.).[44]

Since then, the vision of Wright State University sounds as follows:

In the pioneering spirit of the Wright brothers, Wright State will be Ohio's most innovative university, known and admired for our diversity and for the transformative impact we have on the lives of our students and on the communities we serve.[45]

This commitment to the pioneering spirit of the Wright brothers led the university to change its logo to the Wright Brothers Biplane in 1998, thus embracing and celebrating their spirit of innovation and enterprise.

After being reaccredited by the NCA, Wright University clarified its purposes through a new mission statement that had emerged from its campus-wide visioning process. The statement, presented December 3, 1996, is as follows:

Wright State University will be a catalyst for educational excellence in the Miami Valley—

(the opening sentence of the new mission statement):

Wright State University will be a catalyst for educational excellence in the Miami Valley, meeting the need for an educated citizenry dedicated to lifelong learning and service. To those ends, as a metropolitan university, Wright State will provide: access to scholarship and learning; economic and technological development; leadership in health, education and human services; cultural enhancement; and international understanding while fostering collegial involvement and responsibility for continuous improvement of education and research (Approved by Board of Trustees on December 3, 1996).

The mission statement is built on eight tenets indicating that the university will

1. serve as a catalyst for educational excellence in Miami Valley;
2. promote a lifetime of learning and service;
3. offer complete access to higher learning and in-depth scholarship;
4. promote both economic and technological development to its fullest capacity;
5. provide fresh leadership in the areas of health, education, and human services;
6. foster an atmosphere of cultural enrichment;
7. cultivate international understanding and cooperation; and
8. support ongoing improvement of education and research.

These eight tenets can be found on the university's website and in its catalogs. They are in the mission statements of the individual colleges, schools, and divisions of the university and have shaped the development of two strategic plans evolving from Vision 2020.[46]

The integral parts of both documents are the core values with their definitions:

Commitment to people

We are committed to the success of students, faculty, and staff. We provide an inclusive academic environment for people with a diverse range of abilities and educational backgrounds; ethnic and cultural heritages; family experiences and economic means; physical and learning differences; geographically mobile and place bound circumstances; and career and life aspirations.[47]

Allow learning and its expression for all.

We are responsible for sharing a wealth of knowledge, enabling discovery, fostering innovation and supporting scholarship in its many forms to better serve our regional, national, and global communities. As a learning-centered university, we fulfill responsibilities most effectively when students are engaged throughout the process of discovery. Freedom of academic inquiry and expression are the foundations of knowledge and discovery.[48]

Continue to develop partnerships.

We are catalysts for transforming lives and the communities we serve. Through collaborations and partnerships with businesses, educators, agencies and organizations we will achieve our goals of regional development, cross-cultural cooperation, entrepreneurial advancement and improved global relations.[49]

Strengthen relationships.

The success of each individual strengthens our community. We promise to maintain high ethical standards in all of our relationships and operations through open communication, trust, professionalism, and a collaborative spirit. We recognize the inherent value and promise of each individual and welcome all who seek transform their lives.[50]

Sustainability for the long term.

The necessity of preserving our planet compels us to weigh the impact of our decisions, both short term and long term. Additionally, prudent financial management supports the sustainability of our operations. Furthermore, the pursuit of knowledge is sustainable, and our programs will maintain their relevance, only if we continually invest in the infrastructure to support research and creative endeavors.[51]

The process of redefining vision, mission, and core values does not need to stop at the university level. This university serves as a model for ensuring the participation of a wide spectrum of representatives from all groups constituting the academic community in the process of redefining both axiological assumptions and models for the cascade approach to this process. Each college, department, or division at Wright State University has redefined its mission, vision, or core values in order to make them reflect the current spirit of those administration units, taking into account the basic assumption that "[c]ollege, department, and division mission statements reflect the mission of the university, and, of course, it is primarily through these units, and the faculty, staff, and students within them, that the university carries out its mission."[52]

For example, Raj Soin College of Business defined its vision as:

To be a dynamic business leadership learning community, nurturing life-long education, creating positive impact on business and society.[53]

The College defined its mission as

The Raj Soin College of Business provides leadership and innovation to:

• develop students to be successful and ethical leaders capable of making valued contributions to organizations in the Miami Valley, the State of Ohio, and around the world;

- advance knowledge and business practices through research and other work;
- partner with individuals, businesses, government and other organizations to enhance professional, entrepreneurial, economic, and social progress;
- attract, develop, and retain committed, exceptional faculty.[54]

Raj Soin College of Business defined its core values as follows.

We embrace and practice

- exceptional teaching and learning, a focus on providing students with a high quality educational experience;
- ethics and character excellence, a desire to cultivate awareness of the attributes that enable excellence through personal and collective efforts;
- applied relevance, a focus on the practical implication of our work for the members of our stakeholder community;
- collaborative spirit, a desire and willingness to initiate work across boundaries in the way we conduct ourselves;
- imaginative thinking, a passion for creative, novel, innovative work across all areas of responsibility—service, research, and teaching;
- global perspective, an acknowledgment that all organizational activities take place in the context of an interconnected, global society;
- appreciation of differences, the willingness to embrace, leverage, and develop distinct perspectives, needs, and points of view;
- service and community engagement, a focus on creating regional economic and social impact.[55]

Annual reports from most colleges and divisions highlight benchmarks in the fulfillment of the university missions.

Institutionalization of Academic Ethos Core Values at Wright State University

Wright State University's current journey to fulfill its mission and to institutionalize the university's core values is guided by, among others, the University Strategic Plan, operational plans, and college/division plans, "which (are) annually updated in response to important societal and institutional changes, including priorities established by the state of Ohio to improve student access, transfer and articulation, and to strengthen the state's economy as expressed, respectively, in House Bill 95, in the report of Governor Taft's Commission on Higher Education and the Economy (CHEE), and by the Governor's Third Frontier Initiative."[56] These plans are interconnected, interdependent, and aligned with the university's mission and core values.

The university created two 5-year strategy plans pursuant to Vision 2020, the first implemented in 1998–2003, and the second in 2003–2008.[57] The first one focused on nine strategic goals that reflected the five overarching emphases of Vision 2020, for example: quality improvement, instructional and research equipment and library resources, faculty and staff development, or general education revisions. The second one, called "On the Horizon, Building Our Future," centered on three strategic goals.

- Enhance our distinctive learning experience to recruit and retain a diversity of students from the region and beyond.
- Expand our partnerships through external funding and collaborative scholarship both regionally and globally.
- Extend our engagement with government, business and nonprofits to focus on emerging areas of need.[58]

Table 6.3 presents examples of Wright State's core values, main goals in which they are reflected, objectives for their realization, and implementation results.

Annual campus reports on the implementation of the strategic plan make it clear that the university community has fully implemented the goals and strategies of the plan, thus continuing to carry out the university's mission.

Table 6.3. Examples of Wright State's Core Values, Main Goals, Objectives for their Realization, and Implementation Results

Values	Goals	Objectives	Implementation Results
people sustainability	Academic Distinctiveness and Quality	– Recruit and retain a nationally/ internationally recognized diverse, learning centered faculty and staff. – Enhance the quantity and quality of dialogue with our various communities to ensure our academic relevance and distinctiveness.	– Award-winning Wright State University professor/ filmmaker Julia Reichart and filmmaker Steve Bognar premiered The Last Truck: Closing of a GM Plant on HBO. The documentary was nominated for an Academy Award. – Wright State University conducted the Diversity and Inclusion Project, a cultural assessment survey accompanied by a new website dedicated to the initiative. Following up the survey, several campus Diversity and Inclusion Town Hall Meetings were held to engage students and staff in candid discussions about diversity on campus.
Learning Partnership	Educational Attainment	– Enhance the academic success of students. – Develop effective educational processes to assist students in meeting postgraduate career and educational goals.	– The university developed the Wright State Academy, a five-week intensive course designed to give at-risk students the writing and study skills necessary to succeed in college courses. – Each year, Career Services offers an Etiquette Luncheon, where a certified business etiquette trainer coaches participating students on the finer points of business dining and networking.
Learning	Research and Innovation	– Build a national and international research reputation	– Wright State is now home to seven Centers of Excellence, six of them designated as the state's leading university center for its area of research. These Wright State-based centers partner with businesses and the military, generating new jobs, millions of dollars in economic impact and savings for industry.

	– Foster discovery at all levels in the educational pipeline (K–16+)	– Summer enrichment courses at Wright State for grades K–9 attract children who desire challenge, are interested in learning and personal growth, and have the motivation to succeed. Educators and professionals from the Miami Valley provide a stimulating and challenging learning environment that encourages creativity and critical thinking.
Relationship sustainability	Community Transformation – Increase the opportunities within the curriculum for community engagement. – Offer degree and other education programs consistent with regional and state needs.	– The university developed a class in which students get a hands-on look at how nonprofits manage their resources through fundraising, volunteering and grant writing. Students work with the charity of their choice, and that hard work pays off when they get to give the money they've raised to their chosen organization at the end of the term. – The National Center for Medical Readiness, also known as Calamityville, has been established to better prepare the region, state and nation for emergencies such as weather disasters, terrorist attacks or hazmat situations. http://www.medicalreadiness. org/calamityville/index.html NCMR is developing a state-of-the-art facility to provide a one-of-a-kind training opportunity for the world's medical, public health, public safety, and civilian and military disaster responders.

Source: based on http://www.wright.edu/about/foundational-principles/strategic-plan/implementation-results/ and http://www.wright.edu/foundational-principles/strategic-plan/

Wright State University's mission and core values are reflected not only in fully elaborated strategic plans, but also in a whole array of documents such as policies, procedures, and codes that constitute the ethical infrastructure of its academic community. The university's mission documents have been designed to elaborate on why the university exists, whom it serves, and to what ends. Mission documents include description of the aforementioned Vision 2020, University Aim and Mission Statements (also reflected in College/School and Division Mission Statements), the University Strategic Plans, and the University Ethics Statement, University Diversity Statement, and Faculty Constitution.

The University's Diversity Statement, adopted by the Board of Trustees on March 28, 1991, expresses the university's goal of providing a diverse intellectual, cultural, and social environment on campus that appreciates every individual, without regard to artificial barriers such as "race, gender, age, ethnicity, disability, sexual orientation, socioeconomic status, religious affiliation, or national origin."[59]

Implementing a value of diversity in Wright State University does not end in merely a statement. The school's authorities have taken numerous steps to bring it to life and have it authentically utilized. The strategic plan implemented for 2003–2008 states that the university will actively pursue

- recruitment and retention of a diverse group of students;
- recruitment and retention of a diverse faculty and staff; and
- diversification of and accessibility to curricula.

Since 1996, Wright State student enrollment has increased 8.77%, from 15,697 to 17,074, with most of this increase coming from female students, who accounted for 1,100 of the 1,377 student increase above. Growth in the number of African-American students over the past decade has also been significant; in addition, the university has increased its number of Asian, Hispanic, and Native American students.

Between 1996 and 2005, the faculty increased 16.6%, with a modest increase in gender diversity. Similar to the growth in the number of African-American students, the greatest change in diversity of faculty occurred in the number of African-American faculty whose numbers increased from 31 to 43 between 1996 and 2004. The university will continue to address such disparity in future hires.[60]

Appreciation of the diversity of its learners and constituencies also becomes apparent from the university's mission documents and practices of its colleges, schools, and divisions. It is also apparent from the prominent existence of a number of units specifically created to both enable and exemplify the university's strong commitment to its diverse learners. For example

- in 1970, the university established the Office of Disability Services (ODS) in 1970, 6 years before federal regulations required such action;
- in 2000, the university increased support for the Women's Studies Program and created the African and African-American Studies Program;
- the 2002–2003 publication "Diversity Initiatives: A Directory of Programs at Wright State University" (see Resource Room) offers evidence of its background and development of diversity policies;
- and the university's diversity website presents information about its diversity policies.[61]

The University Ethics Statement supports the mission and core values; it was developed by a broadly representative group of faculty, staff, students, and administrators and was adopted by the Wright State University Board of Trustees on March 28, 1997, to "provide general guidelines for strengthening the integrity of the university."

The Ethics Statement offers guidelines for strengthening the integrity of the university. It sets forth the principles of honesty, respect, justice, and accountability so that the university can better accomplish its mission and serve public interest in an ethical way. Wright State University is committed to the creation of a standing advisory and resource committee to support formal ethics education and to assist the university in developing ethics policies and procedures.

Finally, protecting and upholding the university's integrity is facilitated through formal ethics policies. In addition to the university-wide ethics statement, the university is subject to the Ohio Ethics Policy and the Ohio Ethics Commission. Ethics policies/statements are also adopted and created by various university units, which are systematically updated.

Students at Wright State University are also involved in everyday decisions in the academic community, equipped with a guideline called the Student Policy Guide. Similar to the ethics policy of a university, the policy guide for students is systematically updated and prepared by particular units (colleges, divisions) constituting the university.

For example, Boonshoft School of Medicine in Wright State University begins its student policy guide for 2011–2012 with specification of attributes and core values, such as: Compassion, Commitment to Excellence, Accountability, Integrity, Respect, Humility, Altruism, and Social Responsibility, which creates professionalism in a student's behavior. This should be present in the learning environment and manifested by students. This document also specifies student responsibilities, tasks, the composition of The Honor Code Council, procedures for reporting violations of the Honor Code, and how to appeal decisions by the Council.

Obviously, ethics policies are not the only ones that build ethical infrastructure of the Wright State University. Activities carried out by members of the academic community are realized and supported by Ethical Standards in the Conduct of Research as well as by a policy on Financial Conflict of Interest and Policy and Procedures for Intellectual Property, a revision of which was reviewed and approved by the Board on June 8, 2001.

In summary, we may state that all the documents described earlier that constitute the set for Wright State University's mission, vision, and core values specification are coordinated and elaborated excellently to be used in fulfilling the university's mission and institutionalizing its core values through strategic plan implementation. It is worth emphasizing that the university's website presents vision, aim, mission, ethics, and diversity statements and minutes of all governing bodies; a general announcement listserv is also available to share information and initiate actions that would affect the university community. We should note the widespread use of modern technology for the purposes of communication with academic community; regular meetings arranged with board, administration, faculty, and staff supplement those modern communication tools.

Wright State University's policy transparency is confirmed by the fact that all the annual reports of university's organizational units are widely discussed among the academic members. For this purpose, the university not only uses the mentioned online sources but also two periodicals online: the *Dialogue* newspaper and the student newspaper, *The Guardian,* which are aimed at informing the academic community about the progress of the university's strategic plan implementation and the progress in creating a cultural identity of the school.

Considering institutionalization of core values at Wright State University, it is not possible to ignore two substantial aspects such as the scrupulousness and care of academic authorities for the realization of the written mission, vision, and core values in compliance with the leading values of academic community: integrity. Moreover, the model approach to institutionalization of the university's core value of sustainability should be mentioned. The university's authorities support its integrity through two sets of coordinated activities. In one set, the university presents appropriately informed, disciplined, and ethical daily actions and interactions of individuals from the top to the bottom of the organization; in the other set, the university presents information about elaborated and realized, monitored and regularly redefined policies, procedures, and processes that are conducted in order to institutionalize core axiological assumptions of this university.

Organizational integrity is assessed in many formal ways:

First, in the recent years, Wright State University has taken

- the creation of appropriate policies and procedures that appear in the Wright Way Policies and Procedures Manual, the Faculty Handbook, the AAUP Collective Bargaining Agreement (CBA) with AAUP–WSU, Staff Handbook, and Student Handbook;
- ongoing education and training of employees on university policies and procedures;
- appropriate faculty review and approval processes, including those for the curriculum, through Faculty Senate and Graduate Council;
- ongoing appropriate oversight of University expenditures, processes, etc.[62]

Second, the university symbolizes its irrevocable commitment and sharing of integrity through many community activities.

For example, the Raj Soin College of Business created the Institute for Business Integrity (IBI) in 2003. It was designed to develop future ethical business leaders with the moral competencies to enhance organizational integrity capacity and promote responsible practices in the business community. Its director also serves as the faculty coach for the university student teams, which have earned regional and national recognition by participation in the National Intercollegiate Ethics Bowl Competition. The Wright State University Ethics Bowl Team is the only team in the state of Ohio that has ever won the National Intercollegiate Ethics Bowl Competition after competing against 200 other universities. Third, integrity is reflected in teaching programs by, for instance, implementing the University's Writing across the Curriculum (WAC) Program in 1996. Its goals are such as

- to improve students' writing proficiency—their ability to develop and transmit information for an appropriate audience in an organized, coherent fashion while writing with appropriate style and correct grammar, usage, punctuation, and spelling;
- to encourage students to use writing as a learning tool to explore and structure ideas, to articulate thoughts and questions, and to discover what they know and do not know, thereby empowering students to use writing as a tool of discovery, self-discipline, and thought;
- to demonstrate for students the ways in which writing is integral to all disciplines, essential to the learning and conveying of knowledge in all fields.[63]

The WAC Newsletter offers ongoing training and support workshops for faculty and assistance for students in WI courses. All students can receive free consultations and assistance through the University Writing Center. Ongoing assessments of the WAC program guide its facilitators, showing where goals are being met and where improvement is needed.

Fourth, integrity is reflected in the activity of Business and Fiscal Affairs, which may be proved by the following examples. Internal Controls and Authority Services, founded in 1996, created a "business integrity hotline" and a student audit program. The hotline is a confidential telephone line available 24 hours a day for asking questions or reporting incidents. The student audit program allows senior accounting students to participate in completing and reporting an internal audit. University procurement policies for efficiency, fairness, and auditing controls are regularly reviewed by Business and Fiscal Affairs.

Finally, integrity is reflected in University Advancement. One of the examples is a Communications and Marketing Department as one of the units constituting University Advancement. It is responsible not only for redefining and redesigning the university's image in order to make it compliant with its cultural identity but is also aware that "[o]nline social networks such as Facebook, LinkedIn and Twitter have taken on increasing importance in both personal and professional life" and that those tools "offer unique opportunities for people to interact and build relationships and have great potential to enhance interpersonal and professional communication."[64] This department has elaborated a Social Media Policy to ensure that actions taken on the social Internet by members of the medical school community reflect the school's core values of professionalism, compassion, accountability, integrity, honor, acceptance of diversity, and commitment to ethical behavior.

Despite the fact that Wright State University has achieved much, it is still aware of the necessity for constant improvement in the area of managing values of academic ethos. The university's authorities know that values such as integrity, honesty, and professionalism are, both for people and for organizations, unattainable points of excellence. That is why Wright State University sets new goals and offers opportunities to improve. For instance:

- to give greater visibility in particular to the university's mission statement, including through incorporation into speeches by the President and Provost, and strategic presentations on the university's Web site and publications; in biweekly luncheon meetings with faculty and staff, the president also stresses the university's mission, its strategic plan, etc., and responds to questions about each;
- to continue attempts to develop a university domestic partners policy consistent with the university's diversity statement and with state regulations;

- to continue the university's significant progress in diversifying the faculty and staff, paying particular attention to the under representation of women and people of color in identified colleges.[65]

One of the core values of Wright State University is sustainability as well, which in 2008 was defined in University's Strategic Plan as: "the necessity of preserving our planet [which] compels us to weigh the impact of our decisions, both short term and long term."[66] Is it just a definition, statement, expression of greater intention, or something more? Undoubtedly, this is not just a hollow statement but much more. Many activities that realize the value of sustainability are cultivated among participants of the academic community.

First, in May 2010, President Hopkins signed the Talloires Declaration, committing Wright State to a series of sustainability initiatives, serving as a tangible sign of our continuing dedication to sustainability.

Second, this university not only explains what is sustainability (it gives us many definitions) and why it is so important but also provides the academic community (e.g., at its website) with information regarding, for instance, partners in the local community, who cooperate within sustainability, major summaries of information on ecosystem health and climate change, as well as examples of sustainability presentations. However, explaining and training for academic community on sustainability is not everything.

Third, the university encourages its employees and students to get "to and from the university contributes significantly to our impact on the environment. If feasible, consider walking, riding a bike, taking the bus, or ridesharing"[67] as well as it provides some information about campus shuttle and campus bike rack locations.

Fourth, Wright State currently employs one recycling coordinator, whose responsibilities include baling cardboard, paper shredding, delivery, and pick up of recycling containers servicing the main campus and off-site locations, in addition to transporting cardboard bales to its recycling facility.[68] Moreover, the university not only trains its employees and students on acceptable and unacceptable recycling items, but it also informs about local recycling centers throughout the campus labeled

"Waste" and "Recycling." Wright State has also participated with other national colleges and universities in a 10-week Recyclemania Per Capita Classic competition. The competition measures all cardboard, paper, plastics, and aluminum recycled during the prescribed 10 weeks.

Fifth, Wright State University organizes many actions for promoting sustainability in our everyday life, symbolizing our commitment to build a better world for our descendants. For instance, a Bike to Campus Breakfast is organized annually:

> This event is for Wright State University students and employees. Ride your bike to the front entrance of the Student Union; you will be greeted by bike racks and volunteers. Once you park, you will receive a raffle ticket. Turn in your ticket downstairs in the Atrium for a Free breakfast and a chance to win 15 tickets for the July 7 Dragon's Game.[69]

Other initiatives include Earth Day Photo and Earth Week contests, which is "a reminder that we're not the owners, we just lease some space and that we share Earth with other living things on this wonderful planet."[70] Moreover, in the campus area, students and employees plant vegetable gardens with "potatoes and tomatoes, onions and leeks, kale and pepper plants, and green bean sprouts that are about to pop out of the soil. The list of donations, supporters, helpers and folks who stop by to ask questions is very long and growing."[71]

The list of similar initiatives is very long, and it shows that, for Wright State University, values are not just the statements. They are real lodestars, guidelines in everyday lives of all the members of academic community. Wright State University is an exemplar to follow, which is well prepared for its future as neither changes nor failures disturb what is most significant in here—its cultural identity.

CHAPTER 7

Core Values Management at the University

Insights from International Case Studies

Case Study 1: Reykjavik University

Name: Reykjavik University[1]

Country: Iceland (Reykjavik)

Date of foundation: Founded in January 1988 within The Commercial College of Iceland, School of Computer Science (TVÍ); in September 1998 the School of Computer Science was coupled with a new School of Business and together formed Reykjavik Business University in January 2000 the name was changed into Reykjavik University; in 2005 Reykjavík University was merged with the Technical University of Iceland (THÍ) under the name Reykjavík University

Motto: To increase the competitiveness of business and society

Form: A private university

Rector/President: Ari Kristinn Jónsson

Structure:

Reykjavik University currently includes four schools: School of Business, School of Computer Science, School of Law, and School of Science and Engineering, **University colors:** Red (logo)

Enrollment: More than 3000 students

Employees/Administrates: Over 500 employees from 26 countries

Alumni: *no data*

Notable alumni: *no data*

Brief history:

Reykjavík University has its roots in The Commercial College of Iceland, School of Computer Science (TVÍ), founded in January 1988 and run in The Commercial College of Iceland (VÍ) housing for 10 years.

Reykjavík University started its first semester on September 1, 1998 in a new building under the name Reykjavík School of Business. TVÍ became one of two departments within the school. A name change was inevitable because the school's name was not descriptive for the variety of the school's operations.

In January 2000, the name was changed to Reykjavík University. In the autumn of 2002, the School of Law was established at the University, and in 2005 Reykjavík University merged with the Technical University of Iceland (THÍ) under the name Reykjavík University. Following the merger, the School of Science and Engineering was established, partly built upon the old foundation of THÍ with the addition of new engineering fields.

Reykjavík University sponsors both the Icelandic Center for Research on Software Engineering and the Icelandic Institute of Intelligent Machines. In the autumn 2005, the School of Health and Education was established in Reykjavík University but discontinued in 2010 as a result of strategic focusing.

Throughout the years Reykjavik University has partnered with various companies from industry to form labs and research centers in their three fields of expertise: technology, business, and law.

Vision, Mission, and Core Values of Academic Ethos at Reykjavik University

When studying and characterizing the process of managing core values of academic ethos in Reykjavik University as well as describing its vision, mission, and core values, we should not ignore that it is an organization that needed to build and redefine its cultural identity after a merger in its recent years. Despite the fact that many thought it might not be successful, Reykjavik University managed to work its way into becoming a well-integrated and focused university. In addition, while the two universities could both be considered to be teaching colleges at the time of the merger, Reykjavik University managed at the same time to substantially strengthen its research basis and take the lead in the country in terms of research in the fields of technology, business, and law. It is an exemplar that demonstrates how to manage the cultural identity of a university during and after a merger and how to design the fundamentals for the development of a university of the twenty-first century.

> Reykjavík University (RU) came into being in its present form on 1 June 2005 with the merger of the Technical University of Iceland and the existing Reykjavík University.[2] The merger was motivated by a desire to create a dynamic institute of higher education offering a broad range of program and with the potential to become a leading player in research and international relations.[3]

A merger is always a great challenge and a risk for the organizations that participate in this process. We should not forget the fact that between 30% and 60% of mergers and acquisitions fail to achieve the strategic objectives of the acquirer.[4] The main causes, according to the literature of such a situation, are poor leadership (23%) and cultural differences (unfitness) between the merging organizations (22%).[5] This is the reason why, immediately after announcing the merger, a comparative analysis of organizational cultures of both schools was conducted with the assumption that the result would provide important information that would be helpful for integrating those two entities and, above all, for integrating their organizational cultures (Culture Due Diligence). The research was accepted and consultations began with the authorities of both universities. The research was conducted in the summer of 2005 just after the merger announcement. The objective of the research was a focus on the organizational culture of both the schools, differences and similarities between those schools as well as the individual features of each university. First results were presented in October 2005. The analysis of organizational cultures of Reykjavik University and The Technical University of Iceland was conducted in compliance with Cooper and Cartwright's model of organizational culture. Based on the results, it was possible to conclude that the type of organizational culture in Reykjavik University is a specific mix of task culture and support culture with dominance of the task-oriented culture with features such as

- what you can do matters more than your title;
- service is often customized, depending on who it is;
- organization chart unclear;
- team commitment, zealous belief in organization's mission;
- task requirements determine how work is performed;
- flexibility, high levels of employee autonomy;
- potentially creative environments; maybe exhausting.

The culture of Technical University of Iceland is a specific mix of task culture and support culture with dominance of support orientation that is characterized with

- egalitarianism;
- exists to promote personal growth of individuals;
- typically in cooperatives, and so forth—not profit-seeking organizations;
- success is = realizing your potential;
- very flexible, personal, and informal;
- power comes from charisma, being a good role model;
- common passion unites the group;
- change is welcome, no ownership.

Figure 7.1 illustrates the results of Culture Due Diligence in Departments of Business of Reykjavik University and Technical University of Iceland.

The fundamental conclusion that comes from the "Culture Due Diligence" analysis is that, despite the existence of differences between Reykjavik University and Technical University of Iceland, before the merger there also existed many similarities and many positive common features (such as the pressure for teamwork) and the conviction among employees of those two universities that "what you can do matters more than your title." Thus the organization would benefit from doing every-thing to promote personal growth of individuals.

Culture survey-departments of business, Reykjavik
University and Technical University of Iceland

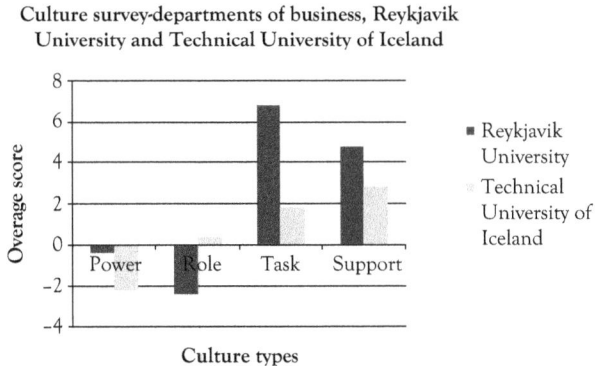

Figure 7.1. Reykjavik University versus Technical University of Iceland—Cooper and Cartwright model.
Source: Based on Bjarnadóttir, A. (2005). Measuring corporate culture. Leadership and change management. October 27, 2005. PowerPoint presentation.

The result of the Culture Due Diligence was taking up joint work on formulating a new vision, mission, and redefining of core values that should be a result of consensus anshould emphasize tradition, values, objectives, and strengths of Reykjavik University and Technical University of Iceland. The new mission of Reykjavik University was expressed as follows:

Reykjavík University (RU) is a university institution dedicated to higher education, research and related activities. The mission of Reykjavík University is to create and disseminate knowledge in order to increase competitiveness and improve quality of life.[6]

Work on the vision statement was carried out incessantly until the publication of Vision 2020 in 2007. In years 2006–2009, Reykjavik University described its vision for the future as follows:

Reykjavík University sets itself the aim of taking its place as a high-powered institute of higher education with an international vision and a strong influence on the development of Icelandic society. It seeks to become the university of choice for ambitious students in Iceland and act as a model for other forward-looking institutes of higher education. Its values are high standards, flexibility, enterprise and integrity.[7]

We should notice that in the vision statement, the core values of Reykjavik University set in 2007 are specified as high standards, flexibility, enterprise, and integrity. In 2007, in a statement called "strategy for Reykjavik University" we may read that

> Our company culture is formed by the values which we uphold in our daily work. Those values describe the behaviour and viewpoints which guide us in our decision making. Furthermore, those values are the foundation for the positions, progress, and success we attain in our work.
>
> We have the ambition to always aim higher, the integrity to be forthright, the agility to seize available opportunities, and the boldness to dare when the right opportunities are in view.
>
> These values set the tone for the expectations we have of ourselves, our co-workers, and our students. At RU, we show ambition and integrity in all our actions and decisions, and we work quickly and assuredly towards constant improvement with an emphasis on agility and boldness.[8]

This set of core values (integrity, ambition, flexibility, and courage) has been presented in those statements of Reykjavik University since then. This example clearly shows that the new Reykjavik University, as a result of consensus and dialogue with academic community, searched for the most appropriate words expressing values constituting its cultural identity after the merger.

The result of the work on its axiological guidelines is the elaboration of Vision 2020 as follows:

> We are building a unique tier. One international university known for its innovative approach to teaching and research collaboration. We operate across borders and beyond boundaries.[9]

Institutionalization of Academic Ethos Core Values at Reykjavik University

Leaders of Reykjavik University, at the time of the merger, focused on building and managing core values of academic ethos. After the merger with the Technical University of Iceland, they not only began working on a redefinition of axiological attitudes of the university but were also aware that it was just an initial step in the long way to enactment and maintenance of academic ethos values at the school. That is why in order to institutionalize Reykjavik University's core values, its leaders reflected those values in particular main objectives, particular measures for evaluation, policies, procedures, codes, and activities aimed at creating a value-driven university.

Figure 7.2 presents the aforementioned activities.

The main purpose of the Reykjavik University was included in the following four statements.

1. We create and disseminate knowledge.
2. We increase competitiveness and quality of life.
3. International and interdisciplinary.
4. The first choice of students and employees.

We create and disseminate knowledge

The role of Reykjavik University is to create and disseminate knowledge. That is what Reykjavik University contributes to the society in which we participate. This university creates new knowledge with research and innovation, which relate to both industry and the scientific community.

In this work, Reykjavik University not only respects creative freedom of the mind but also makes strict demands concerning professional work methods and quality. The University's authorities set ambitious goals and seek cooperation from the best available people. Reykjavík University's academic standing is evaluated internally with regard to three main factors and the aim was to make advances in all three areas over the medium term. These factors are: (a) proportion of teaching staff holding doctoral degrees; (b) number of publications in peer-reviewed journals; and (c) acquiring research grants from competitive funds in Iceland and abroad. Research

Reviewing our strategic jargon

Mission–why we exist
We create and communicate knowledge
to enhance competitiveness and quality

Values–how do we do our job
Integrity & ambition–courage & agility

Vision–what do we want to be
International Interdisciplinary University

Goal–what do we want to achieve next year
Enhance our focus to achieve increased quality. Efficiency
and strategic positioning

Tactical plans–what we need to do
(1) Improve teaching and increase research output in core disciplines
(2) Build a Center on Human behavior and Innovation (CHI)
(3) Consolidate innovation initiatives, and
(4) Organize for interdisciplinary work

Strategic outcome

Satisfied industry and society | Qualified leaders for industry and academia of tomorrow | Innovative teaching & quality research output | Motivated and prepared workforce

As we trusted	How do students do	Are we improving the	Are students and staff
Are we recommended	after graduation	quality of our	eager to come to work
Surveys	Quality of job	teaching and	Job satisfaction
Application	Graduate schools	academic strength	Level of citizenship behavior
Funding	Alumni surveys	Compass measures	

| STAKEHOLDERS | CUSTOMERS | PROCESSES | LEARNING |

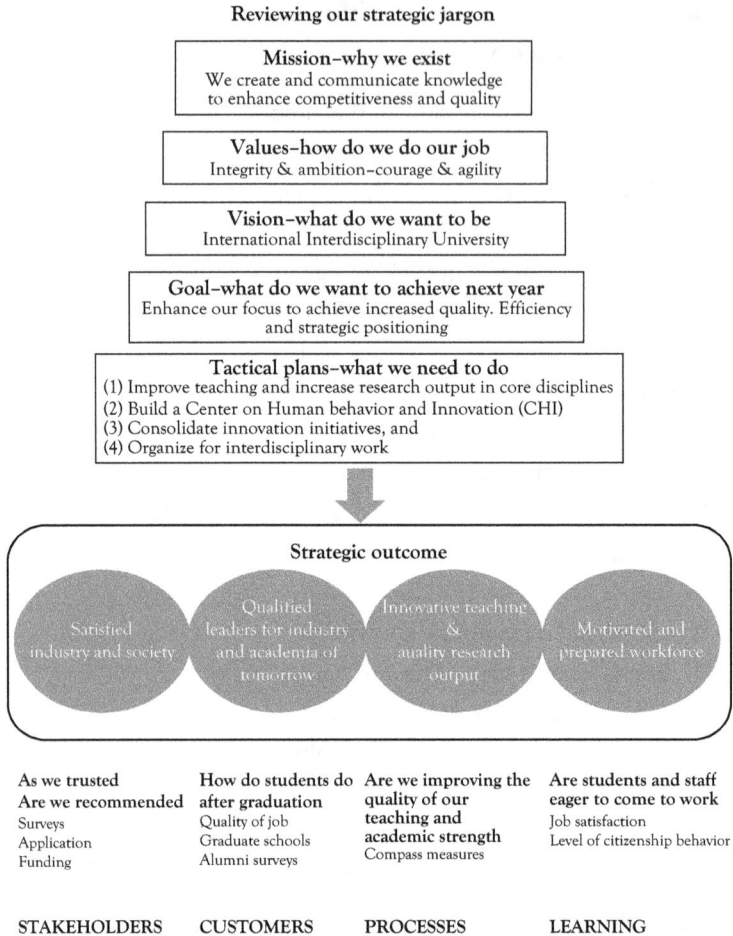

Figure 7.2. Reviewing Reykjavik University's strategic Jargon.
Source: Based on *Strategic Arguments. RU strategy and focus 2009–2010*.

and innovation are the basis for powerful knowledge creation on the part
of Reykjavik University. Its "uniqueness" as a school is determined by

- lively teaching methods and active participation from
  students;
- strong ties with industry;
- cooperation with foreign academics and guest lecturers;
- possibilities to adapt teaching methods and access to our
  services according to the needs of a modern community.

We increase competitiveness and quality of life

Reykjavík University places great importance on quality of teaching and personal contact between students and staff.

This may also be proven by various initiatives taken by the University. Because of limited class sizes, a dean is able to meet with every student at the beginning of the academic year. Teachers regularly meet to discuss new teaching methods, and students are encouraged to seek out mentors for guidance.[10] The net result is quality assurance on a high level.

> The quality assurance system of Reykjavík University comprises four parts: study and teaching, research, academic staff, and support services. The system was reviewed and documented in its current form in 2009.
>
> Emphasis is placed on innovation in teaching, diversity of teaching methods, and assessment of teacher and student performance (Teaching Quality Handbook). Key processes in the quality assurance system for teaching are the systems for the approval of new study programmes, teacher training and courses for teaching staff, and the compilation of various statistics and metrics relating to studies and teaching.
>
> Quality assurance in research: The quality assurance system for research builds on the University's annual research evaluation of academic staff. (…)Quality assurance in research covers two key processes. Firstly, all academic staff undergo an annual individual research evaluation. This evaluation has been conducted in the University every year, starting in 2007. Secondly, it is planned to carry out regular audits of the research and research policies of the different Schools of the University (School evaluation) to be used in policy-making within the Schools and in the implementation of research plans. (…)
>
> Quality assurance for academic staff: The quality assurance system for academic staff covers the processes that relate to staff recruitment and selection, career development, and promotion within the University's academic career structure. (…)Among the key

processes in the quality assurance system for academic staff are the rules on recruitment for academic posts, the processes for evaluation for promotion and the granting of academic titles, and the rules on continuing education and surveys of staff opinion.

Quality assurance in support services: The quality assurance system for support services covers the processes and evaluative procedures that relate to support services for staff and students, including annual opinion surveys on services conducted among staff and students.[11]

An integral part of a document that supports this system performance is "Teaching Quality Handbook," which is aimed at providing instructors at RU with step-by-step guidelines on various aspects of the teaching process, in order to ensure consistency and quality:[12]

This handbook is applicable to all credit-bearing courses taught at RU, both undergraduate and graduate. The first four sections deal with various practical issues involved in the teaching process (…). The final section describes the Teaching Quality Assurance System at RU.[13]

In order to assure the quality of all teaching at RU and to fulfill contracts made with the government, the University and/or individual schools regularly provide teaching quality seminars and/or teaching days for its staff. All permanent and part-time teachers are required to attend these seminars unless special circumstances preclude it.[14]

The second element of the Teaching Quality Handbook was called "The Teaching Itself and Interactions with Students." It begins with a definition of an excellent teacher:

First and foremost an excellent teacher must command expertise in their field. An expert can focus on the essentials in a subject, explain the material at the appropriate level of abstraction, and has the self-confidence and motivation necessary to teach well.

An excellent teacher should also possess

a. enthusiasm for the subject matter;
b. enthusiasm for the development of students as individuals;
c. enthusiasm for the teaching methods that he or she uses.[15]

In the next part, some examples are given of particular behaviors that should be implemented by teachers in order to ensure the quality of teaching and developing ambition to be excellent among students. For example, the following guidelines should be applied by a teacher to encourage individual growth.

- Active participation by students in class: class discussions, role plays and cases, peer assessment and self assessment.
- Variety in projects and experiences: individual projects, practical assignments, academic projects and participation in research.
- Discussion boards on-line, blogs, web-chat and on-line office hours.
- Clear and timely feedback on students' work.[16]

This section also includes examples of teachers' behaviors in class and outside it that reflect the core values of integrity. For instance

- Teachers must show integrity at all times and ensure professionalism in their appearance and interactions.
- Teachers must treat students with respect and integrity and should provide support as much as possible through their studies.
- Teachers should strive to respond to e-mails sent by students within two working days. Teachers can ask students to use the course website (discussion forum) for questions and debate, so that the answers can benefit all students.
- Teachers shall announce their absence in a timely manner both on the course website and to the school office.
- Teachers shall, if possible, stay for a few minutes after each class to allow students the opportunity to approach them.

- Teachers must advertise office hours outside teaching hours for students, or be willing to schedule them when the need arises.
- Teachers shall arrive punctually for all lectures (preferably 5 minutes early), and be ready to start teaching at the given time.[17]

The third element of the "Teaching Quality Handbook" is called "Evaluating Student Performance" and it is also an evidence that Reykjavik University makes a vigorous effort to have a core value such as integrity not only to serve as a slogan but also to be a guide to particular behaviors for members of academic community:

Reykjavik University places great emphasis on academic integrity and the high quality of scholarly work. RU emphasizes academic integrity and ethical behavior by its staff and students. An important part of academic integrity is the respect for copyright and the full participation of all members in all work groups. In order to clarify our expectations in this area, we have created the following project work code of conduct. The following rules apply to all aspects of project work:

Your original work: Reykjavik University requires that your projects be your original work. (…)Plagiarism is unacceptable at all times, and all sources of information must be acknowledged in a scholarly fashion.

Your contribution: Reykjavik University requires that you always put forth your best effort in group work and make sure that your contribution is equivalent to that of others.

Individual and group projects: In individual projects the student must work on all parts of the project alone.

The penalty for violation of these rules ranges from the grade of 0 for the project, to 0 in the course and even to suspension from further studies. Teachers are encouraged to introduce the above code of conduct and its meaning for the particular course assignments at the beginning of the course.[18]

At Reykjavik University, everything that concerns core values and objectives for their institutionalization does not happen by accident. Reykjavik

University gives evidence for this by clearly showing that academic ethos management is a planned, conscious process with consequences.

The last two modules of Teaching Quality Handbook, "Teaching Evaluations by Students" and "Teaching Quality Assurance System at RU," are elaborated to "ensure quality in teaching, Reykjavík University has put in place a quality assurance system for teaching. This system is part of the overall university Quality Assurance System that deals with teaching, research, academic staff and support services."[19]

It is also commendable to mention another document elaborated on in Reykjavik University's "General Rules of study and Examinations" that specifies student responsibilities and rights during studying and examination.

International and interdisciplinary

The officers of Reykjavík University believe that personal, corporate and national competitiveness in the twenty-first century century will to a large extent be determined by the ability to utilize knowledge in the interests of progress and participation in the international community. (…)The boundaries between academic disciplines are becoming ever more blurred, creating an increasing need for syncretic approaches to learning.[20]

The above statements are not just declarations of beliefs or willingness as much as they are truly reflected in the university's reality. To fulfill those declarations and to secure RU a place as an international university:

Reykjavik University will stop doing noncore programs (Med, BS Sport Science, MPH, BS Math) and unstructured centers, fields, etc.

Reykjavik University will do more enhance the quality of our programs and research in the areas of Technology, Business and Law, promote and facilitate innovation and entrepreneurship, structure for interdisciplinary work—not just talk about it, explore possibilities for participating in the strategic networks of universities, increase number of international students (exchange and degree seeking) and increase number of international teachers.[21]

The First Choice of Students and Employees

"RU always aims for excellent results. Reykjavík University sets itself the goal of becoming the university of first choice for students in Iceland wishing to undertake higher studies in the disciplines offered by the University."[22] To achieve this, it is not enough to attract promising students and offer them exceptional teaching along with training in the utilization of the knowledge they acquire. Each organization is, above all, a group of people with their knowledge, character value opinions, and attitudes. "For this reason, the University seeks to become the institution of choice for those wishing to work in a university environment in Iceland. This aim is fostered by a strong human resources policy. The University wishes its staff and students to view their time there as a rewarding and fulfilling experience."[23] Because of this, RU needs to offer

- a demanding but encouraging work environment which attracts the most qualified individuals in each field;
- purposeful continuing education for staff members and an environment where ability, freedom, and diversity are applauded;
- a reward and advancement system which encourages research activity, progressive teaching methods, and active collaboration with industry;
- an international work environment which creates fertile ground for knowledge creation and dissemination, and which cultivates strong ties with the economy;
- a work environment where equality is always maintained and where individuals are not discriminated against based on gender, age, religion, nationality, race, disability, sexual orientation, or political view.[24]

Some would say this is a model objective for any university. Yes, but at Reykjavik University it is not only a statement. It is a reality built by its leaders and the whole academic community. Reykjavik University "in the summer of 2007 signed two documents developed by the European Commission (Directorate-General for Research) aimed at improving the career development prospects of individuals wishing to build a career in research in Europe." These documents are the European Charter for Researchers and the Code of Conduct for the Recruitment of Researchers.

The main principles of the Charter and the Code are as follows:

- Open recruitment, clear selection criteria, career development, international and intersectoral mobility, professional recognition.
- Special emphasis on postdoctoral appointments and the development of junior researchers.[25]

All Icelandic universities signed these documents in 2007, but Reykjavik University is the first Icelandic university to participate in a formal implementation program.[26]

> In June 2009 Reykjavik University accepted an invitation by the European Commission to join the Institutional Human Resources Strategy group, which is a group of about 40 institutions committed to incorporate the Charter and the Code into their human resources strategy. (…) A working group was established in September 2009, to conduct an internal analysis of Reykjavik University vis a vis the principles underlying the Charter and the Code.[27]

A thorough analysis of the working situation of young researchers, conducted by a task force in 2010, indicated that there still were some things to improve, but human resources management in Reykjavik University is considered a significant strength of this higher school and a very important pillar for enacting and maintaining its core values.

Has Reykjavik University managed after 7 years since its merger to build a strong cultural identity of academic community based on four main pillars—core values of Reykjavik University? Staff surveys and conversation with former leaders give a positive indication! There is detailed, internal documentation of the school in the form of numerous procedures, policies, codes, and strategies that show the University's strengths; there is information gleaned in direct conversations with leaders (former rector/president of Reykjavik University or the former executive director of Human Resources and Quality and a few other

Reykjavik University's employees). Another indicator of success is the results of the research conducted among Reykjavik University employees in 2007 aimed at measuring how well is one's focus on his or her top goals and leading indicator of how well one will execute current and future goals.

When answering a survey point in 2007, "If you know any of the top four goals (Markmið) of Reykjavik University, please list them," more than 71% respondents indicated "increase research activity and output," and more than 77% of them know the main objectives of Reykjavik University, such as "becoming an international university" and "increase quality of teaching and the use of innovative teaching methods."

When responding to the following point on the survey; "If you know any of the top four measures that indicate whether Reykjavik University is achieving its most important goals, please list them," 34% indicated "number of international students, number of international faculty members, number of courses taught in English" and more than 30% "number of publications, research grants, number of citations."

However, what is much more important is the fact that on the question of whether organizational values and commitments are honored, 62% of respondents answered positively.

The same survey reaffirmed that the strategy is clear and is linked to organizational goals (77%), workers are focused on top organizational goals (68%), individual workers are valued and motivated (80%), and workers have the resources and freedom to do their job (59%). In addition, 65% of the respondents confirmed that at Reykjavik University there is a climate of mutual understanding and creative dialogue. The same research also confirmed that there are areas that require additional work such as smooth teamwork across functions and systemic approach to scheduling priorities. Employees of Reykjavik University also indicated most significant barriers that make it difficult for one to achieve his or her most important work goals including, for example

- lack of resources (46%);
- poor information systems (20%);
- lack of recognition or reward (11%);
- information overload (14%).

This research was conducted 2 years after the merger and the results confirm that in 2007 Reykjavik University was on its way to success in the process of creating a value-driven university.

Although Reykjavik University has experienced several difficult challenges following the Icelandic economic meltdown in the fall of 2008, the activities, initiatives, and attitudes described earlier taken since 2007 until the present day continue to enhance the cultural identity of Reykjavik University based on a clear focus (technology, business, and law), a clear strategy; aiming at teaching excellence, outstanding research, and effective industry collaboration, emphasizing internationalization, cross-disciplinary work and innovation; and last but not least, a personal and collaborative spirit among faculty and staff.

Case Study 2: IAE Business School (at Austral University)

Name: IAE Business School (Austral University)[28]
Country: Argentina (Pilar, province of Buenos Aires)
Date of foundation: Founded in 1978
Motto: *no data*
Form: Business School being a part of a private Catholic university
Dean: Marcelo Paladino
Structure:

IAE is one of six academic units, including the Schools of Communications, Law, Engineering, Biomedical Sciences and Business Sciences, besides the Austral Hospital and Austral Park, as encompassed within Austral University.

IAE Business School includes nine departments: Organizational Behavior; Marketing; Business Policy; Finance; Economy; Business, Society, and Economy; Operations and Technology Management; Management and Control Systems.

University colors: *no data*
Enrollment: 6500
Employees/Administrates: 84 faculties, including 49 full-time professors, 28 PhD professors, 7 PhD candidates
Alumni: 12,000 from 50 different countries

Notable alumni: *no data*

Brief history:

IAE Business School was founded in 1978 and is now part of Austral University, which was founded in 1991.

IAE received three leading international accreditations for Management Education outstanding quality: EQUIS (European Quality Improvement System, Europe), AACSB (The Association to Advance Collegiate Schools of Business, United States), and AMBA (Association of MBA, UK). It has been the first Argentine Business School and the fourth in Latin America to receive these three accreditations.

It has been placed among world's top business schools in many prestigious rankings:

- as Argentina's leading business school, according to Apertura's MBA rankings since 2007;
- first in continuing education for executives, according to América Economía magazine in 2008 and third in 2011;
- twenty-fifth overall, eleventh in customized executive education and first in the International Clients category on a worldwide basis (FT Executive Education Ranking 2008);
- in 2009, its 1-year full time MBA was placed eighth globally and was the only in Latin America among the most prestigious short-term master programs as set forth by the *Wall Street Journal.*

IAE has visiting foreign professors from world's leading business schools such as Harvard, IPADE, Darden, IESE, MIT, Michigan University, and London Business School. Its full-time professors also teach at top-tier business schools in the United States, Spain, Mexico, China, Slovenia, Venezuela, Brazil, to name a few.

Vision, Mission, and Core Values of Academic Ethos at IAE Business School

According to the Executive Education ranking of the *Financial Times*, IAE is among the top 26 schools of the world. *América*

Economía magazine places it at the third position in executive education in Latin America and Apertura considers it to be the best business school of Argentina.[29]

The above information is fully compliant with and fully confirms the vision and mission statement of this higher school. It also proves that IAE moves forward in the direction determined by its axiological imperatives and does it in an involved and well-considered way.

At the website of this school as well as in IAE Business School Annual Report from 2011, we find the following statement of vision for 2015 and the mission of this school. The Vision for 2015 for IAE Business School is "to become a top management and business school recognized around the world for its leadership in: Knowledge of Emerging Economies." It also aspires to be a business school in Latin America known for its leadership in

- the fostering of development and integration, on a local and regional basis in a global context;
- the knowledge and expertise in emerging economies, focused on Latin America;
- the responsibility to offer service to all global and regional companies;
- the flexibility to develop cooperation projects with companies and other institutions;
- the rigor and relevance of its research and the quality of its teaching, both with a humanist focus;
- the intensity of its bond with companies and alumni;
- the service, warmth, and special dedication offered by the entire institution.[30]

IAE's mission statement "to contribute to knowledge development and personal growth of business men and women, strengthening their managerial skills as well as the human virtues required for management"[31] was developed through the interaction of the school's founders with a group of managers in the late 1970s. Because it is foundational, it describes the essence of the School's spirit and has not changed since then.

The School's mission includes an explicit commitment to an ethically and a socially responsible behavior in the management profession. All activities at the IAE are conducted with the human being at the core of the business community and economic activity. The core values shared at the School are

- promotion of the human being from his or her dignity and transcendent destiny;
- work as a necessary activity for personal development and as means for serving others;
- common good perspective, which implies going beyond what is individual and immediate to consider the whole;
- search for truth.

The virtues derived from the conduct expected at IAE are

- friendship: generosity, transparency, loyalty;
- professionalism: spirit of self-improvement, order, and responsibility;
- humility: openness to learning.

Institutionalization of Academic Ethos Core Values at IAE Business School

From the analysis of internal documentation of the IAE Business School, conversations with its representatives, and several on-campus visits during conferences and scientific meetings, there emerges an impression that all activities, formulated strategies, and realized programs at IAE are conducted with the human being at the core of the business community and economic activity. Human promotion, based on human beings' individual dignity, and transcendent destiny and work as a necessary activity to grow personally and to serve others[32] are the core of cultural identity of IAE Business School.

So it is not surprising that through the creation of the Business, Society, and Economics Area in 1999, this school of higher education has been at the forefront of corporate responsibility. In fact, the area's research production[33] in the first decade was dedicated to the critical issues of Corporate Social Responsibility.[34]

For a long time, IAE's authorities have been aware that there is an important need for business leaders of the future to constantly adapt to new and demanding global situations, which requires skill sets beyond academic knowledge and the development of personal and social capabilities.[35] Therefore, IAE strives to educate students who are not only able to perform well on the subjects of strategy and finance but are also capable of gauging the proper course of business ethics, knowing what is right and what is wrong, then making sound decisions, including ethical, environmental, social, and human rights decisions, thus elevating managerial practice into opportunities for personal growth. IAE offers a vision for the proper course of business, enriching the path to efficiency with a firm commitment to social development.[36]

The aforementioned statements are not just empty words at IAE. They have become a practice in various actions that are taken by the academic community in order to enact their core values. This enactment and maintenance of academic ethos values is best illustrated and practiced during implementation of the principles for responsible management education.

As an institution of higher learning involved in the education of current and future managers, IAE Business School is committed to engaging in a continuous process of improvement of the following principles and their application, reporting on progress to all its stakeholders, and exchanging effective practices with other academic institutions:

- Principle 1—Purpose:
  We will develop the capabilities of students to be future
  generators of sustainable value for business and society at large
  and to work for an inclusive and sustainable global economy.
- Principle 2—Values:
  We will incorporate into our academic activities and curricula
  the values of global social responsibility as portrayed in
  international initiatives such as the United Nations Global
  Compact.

- Principle 3—Method:
  We will create educational frameworks, materials, processes,
  and environments that enable effective learning experiences
  for responsible leadership.
- Principle 4—Research:
  We will engage in conceptual and empirical research that
  advances our understanding about the role, dynamics, and
  impact of corporations in the creation of sustainable social,
  environmental, and economic value.
- Principle 5—Partnership:
  We will interact with managers of business corporations to
  extend our knowledge of their challenges in meeting social
  and environmental responsibilities and to explore jointly
  effective approaches to meeting these challenges.
- Principle 6—Dialogue:
  We will facilitate and support dialogue and debate among
  educators, business, government, consumers, media,
  civil society organizations, and other interested groups
  and stakeholders on critical issues related to global social
  responsibility and sustainability. We understand that our own
  organizational practices should serve as example of the values
  and attitudes we convey to our students.[37]

IAE's mission includes commitment to an ethically and a socially responsible behavior in the management profession. IAE activities are conducted with *people* at the core of the business community and economic activity, placing implementation of the PRME principles in the IAE Business School on solid ground.[38]

Having analyzed the achievements of IAE's academic community in implementing the above principles, it is impossible to overlook that this school is on its way to its mission's fulfillment, and its authorities do manage IAE's cultural identity in a well-considered and deliberate manner.

The following examples will be the best evidence confirming the thesis formulated earlier:

As part of the School's mission of values and ethics, the MBA program promotes personal and professional development. The

Anthropologic Education Department offers IAE professors sound ethics training, resulting in a systemwide preparedness to teach the ethics of business and the business of ethics – the moral imperatives on a global scale and the moral right-and-wrong on a deeper, more personal level.

IAE offers a series of courses on Corporate Social Responsibility and on companies' senior management responsibilities as presented through the Business, Society and Economics Area and the Business Policy Academic Area.[39]

IAE also offers panel discussion programs outside of school that look at Social Responsibility in the Media. The panel is composed of a faculty member, leading politicians, and representatives from top national newspapers.[40]

In an effort to enact the values of academic ethos, the IAE Business School does not forget about projects and programs that are strictly directed to its students. These initiatives include (among others)

- The Social Field Work is a project where students work with an NGO (Non-Governmental Organization), or a Community Service organization by which they have a hands-on experience and apply business management skills to the distinctive setting of these institutions.
- Regional Leadership Training, which gives MBA students another opportunity to develop transformational leadership. Set as a simple corporate responsibility practice, they make contact with local leaders working in sustainable economies. This leads them to discover the cultural mind-set of the Latin American native, making them aware of the need for integration in the region, and of the importance of a greater participation in relations with the government.
- IAE Business School's training programs for current and future leaders have been very much geared to the private sector. IAE has taken the challenge of contributing to build cooperative ties between the public and the private sectors. In 2001, the GESE Centre—the Government, Business, Society Centre

was founded with the aim of contributing to social capital development, improving public policies and government practices, strengthening business and, thus, fostering economic growth and greater social equity, not only nationally but also in different regions, provinces and cities nationwide.

- The "Government Program for Local Community Leadership Development" designed by GESE was launched for the first time in 2003. This program hinges on two theoretical pillars: government management efficiency and political leaders' social responsibility. Knowledge of key importance for management is presented to public administration in the areas of general managerial issues, soft skills, and specific knowledge in the field of public administration.

The emphasis at the IAE Business School is on personal development as a hallmark of effective leadership—both for current students and for alumni. The positive track record of the alumni in the business world serves as testament to the commitment of these alumni and the School's success in achieving its objectives.[41]

For realization of the above objectives at the IAE, a special Alumni Department was established that formulated the following goals to achieve in the years 2009–2015:

- to encourage all 11,000 alumni to contribute to IAE's institutional development before the end of 2011;
- to create 15 regional Alumni clubs;[42]
- to help clubs to become more autonomous, so that they can enhance their networking, research, activity building, and fundraising capabilities until the end of 2015;
- to publish at least four issues a year of magazine for alumni;
- to address the magazine for alumni not only to IAE's graduates but also to opinion leaders and leverage it to disseminate IAE operations among alumni, local and foreign business, political, economic, and third-sector communities (the goal formulated to achieve until the end of 2015);
- to communicate with alumni with weekly newsletter and social networks;

- to provide more fluent communication with alumni by building a community in social networks (where alumni are constantly connected) and creating new academic, relevant contents for alumni.

To underscore its mission statement, the IAE Business School analyzes the methodologies of conducting business in emerging markets, with an initial focus on specific regions. The research aids members in a better understanding of the role of corporations in the creation of sustainable social, environmental, and economic values in Latin America. This is enacted individually by each scholar and cooperatively through its Academic Areas and Research Centers.[43]

Research Centers at IAE (for example, Entrepreneurship, Negotiation, Governance and Transparency, and ENOVA-Thinking) are integrated by a group of professors and research assistants. This multidisciplinary team is united by a research interest, usually within a specific sector or area, and supported by a long-term research and development plan.[44]

When discussing the Research Centers at the IAE Business School, it is necessary to mention the one activity that is crucial for implementing PRME and enacting the mission and values of academic ethos at this school, namely the Governance and Transparency Center. Its mission is expressed in as follows:

The Center pursues the education and training of business leaders and senior management through the development of academic and practical material, creating awareness and fostering discussion about organizational dilemmas concerning good business practices and corruption. It also seeks to establish itself as a referent in the study of the challenges that business firms face on a daily basis when dealing with transparency and integrity issues in their own environments.[45]

And its main goals are

- To promote and disseminate research in business ethics, compliance, corporate governance, and transparency.

- To provide practical research results to leaders in business, public policy, and education, and to help them understand and face the complex compliance and integrity problems that present themselves in business practices at local, regional, and global levels.
- To examine the presence of organizational incentives that promote ethical practices, along with processes and decision-taking features associated with governance and integrity failures.

The Center for Governance and Transparency coordinates the Principles for Responsible Management Education (PRME) Anticorruption in Curriculum Change Working Group. The PRME are inspired by internationally accepted values such as the principles of the United Nations Global Compact. They seek to establish a process of continuous improvement process among management education institutions in order to develop a new generation of business leaders capable of managing the complex challenges faced by business and society in the twenty-first century.

Despite of so many achievements in the process of its mission and core values enactment, IAE's authorities are fully aware of the fact that whoever does not develop, moves back. That is why they take new initiatives for improving their cultural identity management, and they constantly set new and ambitious goals.

Examples for such objectives that academic community of IAE Business School wants to realize in the near future are

- To continue integrating more ethical dilemmas and challenges in all specific courses, giving the whole program a strong ethical character; expanding Social Field Work to other realities during its different stages in order to integrate the social complexity to the FT MBA program and to its learning experience.
- To develop different activities to attract alumni in order to keep working in the human formation of those students who finish their programs but are still part of IAE Business School.
- To make IAE's various programs (EMBA, MBA, etc.) further advance their commitment of embedding social responsibility

issues within their academic activities, in particular in relation with civil society organizations that tackle poverty, inequality, and public policy issues.

- To implement the pilot version of PRME' Anticorruption Working Group toolkit in conjunction with the previous introduction of anticorruption topics and problems in compliance and business ethics modules. This will allow IAE to be one of the first institutions that will be able to test the toolkit.
- To continue the Governance and Transparency Centre's collaboration with the PRME Inspirational Guide and to produce short videos with anticorruption cases for teaching and training purposes.
- To complete by Center for Governance and Transparency the edition of a book on compliance in Argentina and the writing of technical notes (e.g., compliance training), papers, and articles in the press.

The initiatives described earlier that are taken by the academic society at IAE Business School clearly show that, at this school, the authorities, scientific employees, administrators, and students are "walking the talk."

This school may also be a model for the other higher schools as it shows how to manage cultural identity in order to follow the changes in the surrounding world on the one hand and how to keep its organizational DNA—its core values—on the other hand.

CHAPTER 8

Core Values Management at the World's Oldest Universities

Case Study 1: Jagiellonian University

Name: Jagiellonian University in Kraków.[1]

Country: Poland (Krakow).

Date of foundation: Founded in 1364 (as the second university in Central Europe) by King Casimir III the Great, who received permission from the Pope to establish a university in Krakow, the capital of the Kingdom of Poland.

Motto: PLUS RATIO QUAM VIS ("let reason prevail over force").

Form: A public university.

Rector/President: Professor Karol Musioł, PhD (from September 1, 2012, Prof Wojciech Nowak, PhD).

Structure: Jagiellonian University is composed of 17 faculties (which have different organizational sub-structures): Law and Administration, Medicine, Pharmacy and Medical Analysis, Health Care, Philosophy, History, Philology, Polish Language and Literature, Physics, Astronomy and Applied Computer Science, Mathematics and Computer Science, Chemistry, Biology and Earth Sciences, Management and Social Communication, International and Political Studies, Biochemistry, and Biophysics and Biotechnology.

University colors: Blue and yellow.

Enrollment: Total 51,601 students, including 2,941 PhD students and 2,648 postdiploma students.

Employees/Administrates: Total 7,083, including 6,499 faculty and 584 staff.

Alumni: *no data.*

Notable alumni: Marcin Bylica of Olkusz (chief astrologer to King Matthias Corvinus in Buda), Marcin Biem (astrologer who devised a reform of the Julian calendar), Jan of Glogow (the author of numerous mathematical and astronomical tracts, known all over Europe), Nicolaus Copernicus (astronomer), Jan Virdung of Hassfurt (a professor at Heidelberg University), Johann Vollmar (a professor at Wittenberg), Konrad Celtis (astronomer), Saint John Cantius (philosopher, physicist, theologian), Erasmus Horitz (astronomer), Stefan Roslein (astronomer), Maciej Miechowita (professor of medicine, prominent physician, historian, author), Adam of Bochen (professor of medicine), Jan Dlugosz (historian), Jan Kochanowski (author), Andrzej Frycz Modrzewski (author), Marcin Kromer (author), Mikolaj Rej (author), John III Sobieski (King of Poland), Karol Olszewski (chemist), Zygmunt Wroblewski (physicist, who were the first to liquefy oxygen and nitrogen from the air in 1883, and later also other gases), Napoleon Cybulski (physiologist, who explained the functioning of adrenaline), Tadeusz Browicz (anatomopathologist, who identified the typhoid microbe), Marian Smoluchowski (physicist, the author of major works on the kinetic theory of matter); Leon Marchlewski (chemist, who conducted research on chlorophyll), Paulin Kazimierz Zurawski and Stanislaw Zaremba (whose outstanding research gave origin to a new school of mathematics), Edmund Krzymuski (professor of penal law), Fryderyk Zoll Jr (professor of civil law), Stanislaw Wroblewski (professor of Roman and civil law), Wojciech Boguslawski (actor, theater director, founder of the national opera), Karol Wojtyla (Pope John Paul II).

Brief History

In 1364, after many years of endeavor, King Casimir the Great received permission from the Pope to establish a university in Krakow, the capital of the Kingdom of Poland. It was the second university to be founded in Central Europe, after Prague in 1348. Soon afterwards, other universities were established in the area: in Vienna (1365), Pécs (1367), Erfurt (1379), and Heidelberg (1386). However, the Studium Generale in Krakow, as the school was then called, started functioning practically only in 1367. It consisted of three faculties: liberal arts, medicine, and law. King Casimir's premature death in 1370 and the total lack of interest in the University demonstrated by his successor, King Louis of Anjou (King of Poland and Hungary), led to its gradual collapse.

The University (or the Academy, as it was called then) was restored, due to the endeavors of Queen Jadwiga, who pleaded its case with the Pope in Avignon and later bequeathed her personal effects to the University, which was re-established in 1400, after its benefactress's death. Henceforth it was a full medieval university, consisting of four faculties (including theology). As it followed the pattern of the University of Paris, its Rector was elected by the professors. Colleges with accommodation for the professors and dormitories for students were founded. The restored Krakow University soon established itself in the world of learning.

In the seventh century, the Academy—involved in a violent conflict with the Jesuits who, supported by King Sigismund III, attempted to control it—increasingly conservative and scholastic, lost international academic status. It shared the nation's declining position on the European stage. However, in spite of adversity, the Academy managed to establish a wide network of associated schools, known as "Academic Colonies." The first of them was its own secondary school, Nowodworski College, founded after the reform of the teaching system in 1586. But the Academy also experienced the siege of Krakow by the Swedes in 1655 and was plundered after the surrender of the city.

In the eighteenth century, the University continued to decline, yet some signs of change became gradually apparent. The systematic teaching of German and French was introduced, as well as lectures in Polish law, geography, and military engineering. Fundamental reform at the University, such as new organizational structure, was introduced and a number of academic facilities were founded, such as the astronomical observatory, the botanical gardens, clinics, and laboratories. All lectures were in Polish, and scholars educated at foreign universities in the spirit of the Enlightenment were appointed professors, to disseminate Enlightenment ideas among students.

The third and final Partition of Poland posed a serious threat to the very existence of the University, but fortunately it was saved by the intervention of Professors Jan Sniadecki and Jozef Bogucki in Vienna. However, the University was subjected to the process of obliterating its Polish character and to its gradual reduction to the secondary school status. This threat disappeared after Austria's defeat in the war with France in 1809, when Krakow was incorporated into the Duchy of Warsaw, but then, when it gained the status of the Free City of Krakow (1825–1846), it was subjected to a number of restrictive and harassing acts from the "protector" powers. In 1848, Krakow was again incorporated into the Austrian Empire, but after many years it gradually became a self-governing body. It was the beginning of another golden age for the University, which had been renamed the Jagiellonian University in 1817.

The number of chairs increased threefold, so that by the last academic year before the First World War there were 97 of them, while the number of students in the same year was over 3,000. They were mostly male, but in 1897 the first female students were admitted to study pharmacy. They were gradually accepted by other faculties; the last of them to admit women was the Law Faculty in 1918.

After Poland achieved independence in 1918, the number of Polish universities increased from two (Krakow and Lvov) to five, as the universities in Warsaw and Vilnius were restored and the university in Poznan was founded. The academic staff of those schools was largely drawn from the resources of the Jagiellonian University. In the interwar years, Krakow University was considerably expanded. New departments were established, such as the Department of Pedagogy and the Slavic Department in the Philosophy Faculty, and the Physical Education Department in the Faculty of Medicine. However, many political conflicts between students of widely different political views often resulted in violence. The Senate of the Jagiellonian University repeatedly protested against the authoritarian rule of the government, particularly against the trial of opposition politicians at Brest in 1931, as well as against limiting the Universities' autonomy. The Great Depression in the years 1930–1934 severely affected the finances of the young Polish state, which resulted in drastic cuts in expenditure on education.

The Jagiellonian University was dramatically affected by the German occupation of Poland: 144 University staff were arrested by the Gestapo, together with some students, 21 professors of the Academy of Mining and others, and sent to a concentration camp. In total 183 persons were imprisoned. The University was closed, its property dismantled, destroyed, looted, or sent to Germany. The University suffered losses also from the Soviets. Among the Polish prisoners of wars (POWs) murdered at Katyn and Kharkov were 14 Reserve Officers, University teachers, and graduates. Yet the other university staff resolved to persevere in the face of adversity. University courses were taught in a clandestine way, flaunting the strict Nazi ban on all but the most basic education. During the war period this underground university had about 800 students.

At the end of the Second World War, lectures began in February 1945, with more than 5,000 students registering. It appeared that this was the period of both reconstruction and rapid expansion. The first three post-war years were promising. Many academicians who had been forced to leave Lvov and Vilnius or those who could not return to Warsaw, virtually flattened by the war, found employment at the Jagiellonian University.

However, the year 1948 marked the beginning of the worst period in the University's postwar history. Stalinism cast its ominous shadow on higher education. The Polish United Workers' Party was in full control of every aspect of university life. Some professors were dismissed. The great change that came with the end of Stalinism in 1956 affected the University, as it did the whole country. The professors who had been dismissed were allowed to resume their jobs, and the University self-government was restored, the government, however, reserving the right to extensive control, particularly concerning academic promotion.

In 1968, students at the University were actively involved in political protests against the regime, which was followed by repressive measures against the most active protesters and some of the staff, particularly those of Jewish origin. Some academicians decided to emigrate from Poland. Still, when compared with the situation at other universities, repressive measures at the Jagiellonian University were considerably limited. This was certainly due both to the University authorities, who firmly defended the fundamental principles of academic ethics and cooperation, and to virtually all the staff.

The ancient Jagiellonian University, covered with the moss of centuries, today is a young, innovative place. In 1999, the Research Centre for the Life Sciences was opened, and in 2002 this was followed by the opening of the Institute of Molecular Biology and Biotechnology building, with the most up-to-date scientific and technological infrastructure in Poland, and the Institute of Environmental Protection. In 2005, the new site for the Institute of Geography and Spatial Management was opened. The infrastructure at the very center of Cracow is also being transformed and modernized—in 2005 the Auditorium Maximum was opened. Technological and Academic Incubator of Technology Park specializing in the Life Sciences was switched on in May 2006. In October 2006, the Jagiellonian University CMs Faculty of Medicine opened its Lecture–Conference Centre.

Vision, Mission, and Core Values of Academic Ethos at Jagiellonian University

On the first page of the Statute of Jagiellonian University enacted on June 7, 2006, there is a statement that clearly emphasizes its aged cultural heritage as follows:

> The Jagiellonian University—Alma Mater Jagellonica—was established by King Kazimierz the Great, renovated by King Wladyslaw Jagiello. University continues its ancient heritage of service for science and education through carrying out scientific research, constant quest for the truth and promoting it with sense of moral responsibility for the Nation and the Republic of Poland.
>
> In its activity the University lives up to a principle of *PLUS RATIO QUAM VIS*.[2]

In the same document within a section named General Terms there occurs also a mission statement of Jagiellonian University:

> The mission of the University is to educate foster culture in society and carry out scientific research. Due to its own activity and personal example of academic society members, the University prepares mature, self-reliant people for the home country, who are ready to solve everyday problems, which the modern life brings

up. The University not only takes part in development of science, health protection, art and other fields of culture but also educates and up-brings students and academic personnel according to ideas of humanism and tolerance, spirit of respect for truth and hard work, the law and justice, human dignity, patriotism, democracy, honour and responsibility for Society and Homeland.[3]

The core principles statement for performance of this organization include freedom of scientific research and promoting creative scientific; this is expressed in the unity of science and education, or operating by keeping constant contact with local and foreign research institutes, community centers, education and didactic institutions, cultural and economical units, and health care centers.

The Jagiellonian University Senate adopted the University Code of Ethics on June 25, 2003 to set forth the principles and values necessary to guide and govern the academic community.[4] Science and higher education are being deeply restructured in Poland. There are still some crisis phenomena typical for the economic structural change of a state. Structure and conditions for a university's performance are changing. Private higher education has developed to the great extent, and next-to-free graduate and undergraduate studies there extended various forms of highly charged educational services.[5] Scientists, especially professors, take jobs at many schools, which influences their relations with their alma maters and the level of their dedication to scientific research. Not all resist the temptation to act in an unscientific way (participating in politics, elaborating expert's reports ordered by private companies, diffusing views in mass media that hardly qualify as "scientific").

Detrimental phenomena accumulate in scientists' awareness, motivation, activity, and ethical attitudes, leading to an overall decline in standards and morale. Such a decline in ethics has a direct impact on the health of academic research and the well-being of the entire nation. The University Code of Ethics stands through time as the light of reason over force, guiding the conduct (and censuring the misconduct) of academicians in all fields of study. Their reflection in the attitudes and activities of the members of the university community support the sustainability of key moral values shaped by a long-standing university tradition.[6]

The core values of Jagiellonian University are[7]

- Truth, which is the fundamental of a scientist. It includes discovering the truth and formulating views and theories that are true as well as announcing and bringing up academic students.
- Responsibility for scientific technique, the whole discipline as well as institution and environment and for the way of exploiting scientist's authority beyond the university and science, including application of research results in practice.
- Good will—the duty of every master is to inspire other masters and to transfer the widest, most reliable, and clearest message of the whole body of knowledge to lecture listeners and publication readers. It is also the creation of a "good job" atmosphere that encourages energy and enthusiasm of all participants of academic life, the atmosphere that would be free from small-mindedness, discouraging criticism, competitive hurry, and false simulation of scientific activity.
- Justice—the higher school is a school of justice, practical learning of its recognition, defining, application, and respect for its principles.
- Reliability—science is a domain of extraordinary solidity, precision, reliable attitude to facts, achievements of predecessors, and precise language used for creating theories and knowledge diffusion.
- Tolerance—no period, school, method, or even the brightest mind should hinder the course of true science. Cognitive wisdom requires caution and the recognition of the importance of diversity, its understanding, and estimated acceptance or tolerance. Tolerance is understood as the cautious listening to the opinions of others, even to those that are contrary to the binding ones and especially contrary to our personal ones.
- Loyalty—Loyalty to the mother academic community may be expressed in everyday conduct as well as in special moments that require courage, commitment, and persistence and an abdication of private interest and opportunism. Loyalty may be expressed by the labor discipline and support for the democratically chosen authority as well as by the reliability toward colleagues, students, and all members of the academic

community by helping with joint initiatives, especially those supporting the university's and its members' prestige.

- Independence—Scientific creativity is a process of two actions: of transforming the achievements of predecessors and present authors and of contributing the effects of research results that were independently prepared, conducted, and elaborated. Any violation of the principle of independence such as plagiarism, cryptoplagiarism, or autoplagiarism is the violation of the fundamental rules and the idea of the science mission.

- Honesty—It is connected with the attitude to other people, public issues of any public range, and the level of personal responsibility, and within the scientific and didactic activity—the application of clear and unambiguous criteria of conduct and evaluation.

- Dignity—It provokes the internal strength that does not allow withdrawal from personal beliefs or ethical principles or let the person give in to pressure, comfort temptations, and false aspirations for honors and awards. Dignity is not the privilege of any chosen social group, environment, or position. The equal right to dignity is possessed not only by the respected professor, but also by the scientific worker, or by a secretary, librarian, storekeeper, or by the worker of cleaning services.

- Freedom of science, freedom of scientists—ethical values arise, are in force, and express themselves openly within the communities of free people. Freedom is the precondition for the choice of values, searching for them, and their subsequent creation. The subjective freedom of scientists is necessary here. Those scientists conducting in accordance with their mind, experience, and individual conscience are able to develop fully their talents to discover and ability to defend the pressure of negative external factors or internal enslavement.

The Code of Good University Practices supplements the Jagiellonian University Code of Ethics; it was compiled by the Polish Rectors Foundation and passed by the Plenary Assembly of the Polish Rectors Conference on April 26, 2007.[8] In this document are formulated fundamental principles and good manners in leading a university that go beyond the rules of common law and other legal regulations referring to higher schools' performance.[9] These principles include: public service; impartiality within public affairs; autonomy and responsibility; power sharing and balance in the higher school; transparency; dignity, respect, and tolerance; and the principle of universalism of research and education.

The document also includes sections referring to good practices of a rector's conduct, such as: responsibility for university's development; the culture of senate sessions; avoidance of decisions concerning the Rector's own issues; education quality concerns; respect for the university's tradition; and the Rector's cooperation with his or her predecessors. Moreover, some sections referring to good practices of senate conduct are present in this document. They take into considerations issues such as cooperation between senate and faculty councils, student participation in senate sessions, responsibility for programs of education, ways of voting, and evaluation of a Rector's activity.

Institutionalization of Academic Ethos Core Values at Jagiellonian University

Jagiellonian University is immersed in tradition. This tradition and its results, such as various rituals, ceremonies, and architecture symbols, express core values of this higher school. Academic customs embedded in the 600-year history of Jagiellonian University make its values as vibrant as today; they are bequeathed to subsequent generations of people managing Jagiellonian University.

In the process of maintaining, enacting, and directing Jagiellonian University's core values, there is a wide range of ceremonies, rituals, architecture symbols such as the external architecture of campus buildings, monuments, logos, seals or colors, or the physical symbols as a dress code (ceremonial gowns), rings, symbols of prestige, symbols of hierarchy or social position as, for instance, presidential costume, chain, mace. Below, I will characterize briefly some of them.

Jagiellonian University preserves and promulgates its many rich customs and traditions. Regular and special academic celebrations are the proof for what are these great academic traditions and customs.[10]

According to the custom Rector, Deans, professors, and people with a degree of doctor habilitated have the privilege to wear traditional gowns and to carry an insignia of their authority. The style and colors of the gowns and the type of insignia correspond to the customs formed at the University. The Rector insignias are: a scepter, a chain, and a ring.[11]

The colors of particular faculties are

- black for Law and Administration;
- claret (deep red) for Medicine;
- claret with blue rim for Pharmacy and Medical Analysis;
- claret for Health Care;
- silver for Philosophy;
- blue for History;
- navy blue for Philology;
- navy blue with blue rim for Polish Language and Literature;
- purple for Physics and Astronomy;
- purple with blue rim for Applied Computer Science, Mathematics and Computer Science;
- yellow for Chemistry;
- green for Biology and Earth Sciences;
- brown for Management and Social Communication;
- carmine for International and Political Studies;
- ecru for Biochemistry, Biophysics and Biotechnology.

Life of the academic community is enhanced by specified rituals and ceremonies that come from the fifteenth century and are cultivated in modern times. They not only create a sense of community among participants of Jagiellonian University's academic society but are also the basis for the cultivated cultural identity of the entire university.

The most significant ceremonies and rituals of academic tradition that are currently practiced at Jagiellonian University include: May 12 is when the school commemorates the founding of the Jagiellonian University and is a holiday for the whole academic community; November 6 is when the school commemorates the day when the professors and other members of the university community were imprisoned by Nazis in 1939 (it is the Commemoration Day about Them; and it is also the

Commemoration Day about All Deceased Workers of the University); new PhDs promoting, or awarding honorary doctorates (doctorates *honoris causa*); and finally, the day of inauguration of the new academic year (usually October 1). On this day, Krakow inhabitants and tourists may see the ceremonial parade of professors from the oldest Polish university marching from the academic St. Anna Collegiate Church and Collegium Maius edifice to the Auditorium Maximum (before the year 2005 the march used to end in the Collegium Novum).

Although during the past 640 years the Almae Matris inauguration ceremonies of this kind did not always take place, they date back to the very beginning of the Jagiellonian University. The first ceremony of this kind, information about which has been preserved in documents, is connected with the University's renewal. It took place on Monday, July 26, 1400 at the place of today's Collegium Maius. Maciej Radzyminski—a historiographer of Krakow University from seventeenth century—created an imaginary description of this first inauguration. He was inspired by the ceremonies typical for his times (over 200 years later). The description illustrates the ceremonial parade of eminent hosts and professors in their gowns marching from the Wawel Castle, along the Royal Way to the Market Square, and then to Collegium Maius. There is no mention of this march in sources dated for 1400, but in the mid-seventeenth century, such parades were the element of the old academic tradition. They obviously result from the religious processions, which is why its participants were arranged according to their status—from students to the Rector holding the highest office (so-called *ordo canonicus*), who was preceded with people carrying the Rector's mace (named *pedli*).

Other parts of the religious processions included professors wearing garments derived from the higher clergy. When the Collegium Novum was erected in Krakow in 1887, it became the place of ceremonial inaugurations of the successive academic years, but the march still started from Collegium Maius, and it has not changed over time. The constant element of the inauguration (apart from the Rector's report of Almae Matris activity of the precedent year) is a lecture by a professor from the university who is widely respected in the scientific community for his or her achievements, as well as the ritual of matriculation of chosen representatives of new students. Moreover, this ceremony always ends with singing a song, *Gaudeamus Igitur* (in Anglo-Saxon countries known as *De brevitate vitae*), what, for over the past 100 years, has been realized by the academic choir of the Jagiellonian University.[12] During the ritual of matriculation, new students and doctors are included into the academic community, and they take the following oath:

> Aware of the great tradition and accomplishments of the Jagiellonian University as well as the responsibilities of a member of the academic community, I hereby solemnly swear:
>
> - I will seek the truth, the fundament of all science;
> - I will gain lasting knowledge and abilities for the good of my Homeland;
> - I will uphold the norms, social standards and traditions of the University;
> - I will cultivate the good name of our University and the honor of its students.[13]

The oath indicates that the civil duty of a student is to respect tradition and customs of the University and take care of its image.

A statute of the Jagiellonian University specifies the rights and duties of its employees. The basic duties of research and didactic employees include educating and up-bringing students, supervising students' work (taking into account merit and methods), conducting scientific research and developmental works, developing scientific or artistic creativity, and participating in organizational work at the University. Moreover, employees of the professor or doctor habilitated degree have a duty to educate the scientific staff. All the academic teachers are obliged to comply with the University's System for Education Quality Improvement and adopted education courses.

Core values of Jagiellonian University's academic ethos are expressed within its ceremonies, rituals, and documents of the school such as statutes, codes of academic values, or codes of good manner in higher schools; symbols also illustrate what the core of Jagiellonian University's cultural identity is, namely its values constituting academic ethos.

When describing Jagiellonian University's tradition, it is necessary to mention the edifice of Collegium Maius:

> Collegium Maius, situated at the corner of St. Anna and Jagiellonska Streets, is the oldest university edifice in Poland. Its history goes back to the year 1,400, when King Wladyslaw Jagiello purchased the Pecherz family's corner house and donated it to the University. The actual walls of the Pecherz house have been preserved in their foundations and on the side overlooking Jagiellonska Street. This is easily traceable by observing the wild-stone composition, so typical of the fourteenth century. The house was not large and hardly could hold the University activities. During the fifteenth century Collegium Maius was extended. The University was able to purchase the houses contiguous to the College and to combine them into a harmonious whole, complete with a courtyard enclosed with a ring of arcades, interrupted with the professor's staircase, leading up to the first-floor balconies.
>
> On the ground floor there were lectoria, i.e. lecture rooms, low-vaulted, dark and often wet rooms. On the first floor were the Library (added c.1515–1519), the Stuba Communis (refectory for Professors), the Treasury rooms and the Assembly Hall. The Professor chambers were located all over the building.
>
> Up to the second half of nineteenth century the appearance and interior arrangements of the Collegium Maius didn't change much. The neogothic reconstruction in the years 1840–1870, changed the original face of the Collegium and transformed it into the University Library, which used the building up to 1940. Between 1949 and 1964, on the personal initiative of Prof. Karol Estreicher Jr., the whole building underwent a major refurbishment and conservation, shedding all superfluous neogothic additions, that effectively blurred the austere elegance of its original structure. It this time the Collegium Maius was also designated as the seat of the Jagellonian University Museum, home to ancient university collections, including the collection of the old scientific instruments.[14]

After its thorough renovation, the lower levels of the Collegium Maius became a place for conferences in the so-called "Casimir the Great Hall," and for meetings "At Pecherz" café; additionally, all the rooms may be used as exhibition halls. It also has a representative function as the museum hosts the most important academic conferences and Jagiellonian University Senate sessions. It has been visited by the most eminent university guests including John Paul II, Queen Elisabeth II, and the emperor and empress of Japan.

Collegium Maius is not the only museum located in the Jagiellonian University's buildings as evidence of its long tradition and history. The Zoological Museum was established in 1782 as the Studio of Natural History, and the Jagiellonian University Museum of Pharmacy founded in Krakow in 1946 is the largest institution of its kind in Poland and one of the few such museums in the world. Jagiellonian University possesses one of the oldest collections gathered since 1782, and in 1900, as an initiative of Professor Walery Jaworski, the Museum of Faculty of Medicine was founded at the Jagiellonian University.[15]

Jagiellonian University has its emblems, seal, flags, and songs. Two crossed maces emblazoned on a blue shield topped with a crown adorn the University coat of arms. A separate coat of arms with a picture of Saint Stanislaw over a shield and a crowned white eagle on a red background is used for special celebrations and also serves as the primary seal of the Jagiellonian University. The University flag has crossed gold maces topped with a crown placed in the background. During academic celebrations, *Gaude Mater Polonia* is traditionally performed.[16]

Conduct compliant with the values of academic ethos are appreciated and rewarded at the Jagiellonian University. The most prestigious honor at the Jagiellonian University is the award of honorary doctorate (doctorate *honoris causa*). Awarding honorary doctorates (doctorates *honoris causa*) dates back to the 1810s and is modeled after the practices of German and Austrian universities. In April 1815, the Jagiellonian University referred to those universities when it requested from the educational authorities in Warsaw the right to "award doctorates to the men of letters distinguished for their wise and valuable writings." The doctorates were called *honorifica* (not to be mistaken for those awarded under the ordinary procedures).[17] The first honor of this kind was awarded in 1816 to Feliks Bentkowski and Paweł Czajkowski; in 2011, eminent persons such as Gaetano Platania (the historian with great achievements for the research on history of Poland), Peter-Christian Müller-Graf (one of the most eminent German lawyers of these days), Thomas L. Saaty (one of the most eminent American mathematicians), and Hans Joachim Meyer (a widely respected authority in general surgery) were honored.[18]

Other honors at Jagiellonian University include the Pro Arte Docendi Award, given to eminent University teachers for the high quality of their teaching, their mastery of imparting knowledge to their students, use of innovative methodologies of teaching, outstanding educational achievements, individual work with top students, and cooperation with student societies. The award, presented at the convocation of the new school year, may be given to individuals or groups.[19] Moreover, the Merentibus Medal may also be awarded for services rendered at the University. It can be given either to a person or to an institution, from both Poland and abroad. In certain instances, the medal can be awarded to University staff members. Following a proposal from the Rector, the decision to present someone with the medal is undertaken by the Jagiellonian University Senate. An entry into the Book of the Awarded justifying the decision is made each time the medal is awarded. The Rector presents the medal during University ceremonies. At the ceremony, the medal winner also receives a special certificate, and the entry from the Book of the Awarded is read aloud.[20]

However, it is not only the past and tradition that live on at the Jagiellonian University as authorities of this higher school care for cultivating fresh values of academic ethos and creating a robust academic community through various initiatives. One example of such activity taken by the Rector for creating the sense of membership of this outstanding, aged university is a picnic day for Jagiellonian University's employees. It is part of tradition at the Jagiellonian University that every May the Jagiellonian University Rector invites his employees for an annual picnic and provides attractions such as games, snacks, gifts, and dance classes.[21]

Fulfilling its mission, the Jagiellonian University does not forget its role in natural resources preservation for the future generations. Evidence for such conduct may be the initiative named "eco style student," which is aimed at promoting and teaching water and energy conservation. Similar instances for actions taken by the Jagiellonian University's authorities and academic community that fulfill university's mission and enact values of academic ethos are numerous and would provide enough material for more than a single book.

Having studied and analyzed the above examples, it may be categorically stated that the Jagiellonian University is an excellent model of the ideal balance between modernity and tradition, today's customs and those from the fifteenth century. Moreover, the university may be a kind of guidebook describing the way for cultivating values of academic ethos for centuries without the loss of the most important element of its identity and culture—its core values, and at the same time for changing everything else at the university. It is an exemplar that should be followed as it proves that the source for persistence and development of higher schools is their loyalty to academic values and incessant process of their enacting and protection for and on behalf of the successive generations.

Case Study 2: Hamline University

Name: Hamline University.[22]

Country: United States of America (Saint Paul, Minneapolis, MN).

Date of foundation: In the year 1854, named after Bishop Leonidas Lent Hamline of the United Methodist Church.

Motto: Looking back, Thinking forward.

Form: A private liberal arts college.

Rector/President: Linda N. Hanson.

Structure: Hamline University includes the following five schools and colleges: College of Liberal Arts, School of Education, Graduate School of Liberal Studies, Hamline University School of Law, and Hamline University School of Business.

University colors: Burgundy and gray.

Enrollment: Nearly 5,000 students, including 1,866 undergraduate students.

Employees/Administrates: *No data.*

Alumni: *No data.*

Notable alumni: Barb Goodwin (member of Minnesota State Senate), Martin Maginnis (member of US House of Representatives), Van Tran (current member of California State Assembly), Kerry Trask (candidate for Wisconsin State Assembly), Tom Dooher (president of Education Minnesota, AFT, NEA, AFL-CIO), Anna Arnold Hedgeman (civil rights leader and Hamline's first African-American graduate), Gordon Hintz (member of Wisconsin State Assembly), Yi Gang (deputy governor of the People's Bank of China), Duane Benson (American football linebacker), Carl Cramer (professional football player), Lew Drill (former professional baseball player), William Fawcett (actor), Coleen Gray (actress), Paul Magers (television news anchor), John Bessler (professor of law), Arthur Gillette (surgeon), John Kenneth Hilliard (academic and Academy Award recipient), Robert LeFevre (libertarian theorist), Deane Montgomery (prominent mathematician and recipient of the Leroy P. Steele Prize), Dwight D. Opperman (chairmen of Key investments and one of Forbes 400 richest Americans), Max Winter (former part owner of Minneapolis Lakers and Minnesota Vikings).

Brief History:

Hamline University is Minnesota's oldest university. Named in the honor of Leonidas Lent Hamline, a Methodist bishop who donated the funds, Hamline's first home was in the town of Red Wing in what was then the Territory of Minnesota.

The first classes were held on the second floor of the village general store. Classes were in the second term when students moved into the Red Wing building in January 1856. Seventy-three students enrolled at Hamline in the opening year.

Hamline graduated its first class in 1859: two sisters, Elizabeth A. Sorin and Emily R. Sorin, who were not only Hamline's first graduates, but also the first graduates of any college or university in Minnesota.

Three courses of study were open to candidates for a degree:

- The "Classical Program": Greek, Latin, English language and literature, and mathematics;
- The "Scientific Course": included the studies of the classical program but substituted German for Greek and Latin;

- The "Lady Baccalaureate of Arts": a separate course for women, omitting Greek and abridging Latin and mathematics while introducing French and German and the fine arts.

On July 6, 1869, the Red Wing location was closed. It is believed that the building was torn down around 1872.

Building operations for the new University Hall began in 1873, but the Depression had overtaken the planners and there were repeated postponements and delays. The doors finally opened on September 22, 1880, and Hamline's history in Saint Paul began. The catalog for that year lists 113 students, with all but five of them preparatory students.

Tragedy shocked the campus on February 7, 1883 when the new building, barely 2.5 years old, burned to the ground. With frontier fortitude, the plans for a new University Hall were prepared. Eleven months later, the new structure, the present Old Main, was dedicated in the presence of a throng whose carriages were parked all over the campus.

During the First World War in April 1917, the students responded to the call to duty in a variety of ways, seeming to grasp the issues at stake and the parts that would be required of them in the war. In the fall of 1918, a unit of the Students' Army Training Corps was established at Hamline and almost every male student became an enlisted member. The Science Hall was used for military purposes, with the basement becoming the mess hall, and the museum and several classrooms being marked for squad rooms and sleeping quarters.

A new venture was launched in 1940 when Hamline University and Asbury Methodist Hospital of Minneapolis established the Hamline-Asbury School of Nursing, offering a 5-year program (later a 4-year program) leading to the degree of bachelor of science in nursing.

A flood of veterans entered or returned to college after the Second World War under the G.I. Bill of Rights. The first reached the campus in the fall of 1946, when registrations passed 1000 for the first time.

The School of Nursing was discontinued in 1962 following the decision to concentrate resources and staff on the liberal arts program.

During the 1960s, Hamline began to address matters such as the racial diversity of its students and faculty, institutional racism, and the education of culturally disadvantaged students. Hamline felt the impact of deepening racial turmoil during this decade. In 1968, black students on campus founded PRIDE—Promoting Racial Identity, Dignity, and Equality.

The university launched an innovative MBA program in 2008, aligned undergraduate and graduate programs in School of Business (including business, management, public administration, and nonprofit management) and School of Education, created centers for Business Law and Health Law, and created an in-residence MFA in Young Adult and Children's Literature.

In 2008, Hamline University expanded to a 33,000-square-foot location in Minneapolis and now offers master's level programs in business and education. Hamline has established a relationship with the United International College, the first liberal arts college in mainland China, and the Shanghai Institute for Foreign Trade.

Vision, Mission, and Core Values of Academic Ethos at Hamline University

In 2006, Dr. Linda N. Hanson, Hamline University's 19th president, decided to lead "the university through the development of a comprehensive, university-wide strategic plan, Creating Pathways to Distinction, which describes Hamline's academic vision and strategies to innovate in the tradition of liberal arts and professional education; to be dynamic and actively inclusive; to be locally engaged and globally connected; and to invest in the growth of persons."[23] Hamline built on this in 2006–2007 with a plan that fully focused on its mission, values, and goals for the future. This innovative program, Creating Pathways to Distinction, involved more than 200 trustees, faculty and staff members, and students. The Hamline University community looked at its existing system of education and determined how to create a stronger, more dynamic system that would be more timely, more sensitive to needs, and ultimately would benefit all in the Hamline community[24]. In the Hamline University Strategic plan for 2007–2012, as well as in the updated version of this document from 2011, we may find the following statements of vision, mission, and core values of Hamline University.

Vision of Hamline University:

To become a dynamic, learning-centered university rooted in the tradition of liberal education, locally engaged and globally connected, and dedicated to the personal and professional growth of every member of our diverse community.[25]

Mission of Hamline University

To create a diverse and collaborative community of learners dedicated to the development of students' knowledge, values and skills for successful lives of leadership, scholarship, and service.[26]

Core values of Hamline University

Hamline University recognizes its roots in the traditions and values of the United Methodist Church, and aspires to the highest standards for
1. Creation, dissemination, and practical application of knowledge.
2. Rigor, creativity, and innovation in teaching, learning, and research.
3. Multicultural competencies in local and global contexts.
4. The development and education of the whole person.
5. An individual and community ethic of social justice, civic responsibility, and inclusive leadership and service.[27]

Institutionalization of Academic Ethos Core Values at Hamline University

The identity of the Hamline University is deeply rooted in tradition and values of United Methodist Church. The church and army are the oldest organizations that are managed with the use of core values. So it is not surprising that Hamline University has taken the best practices of implementing values for organization's identity creating through its tradition and identity. Immersion of University's identity within the values of United Methodist Church as well as its history full of military service made an institutional pattern of core values for this university.

Academic community members in Hamline University participate actively in the process of core values redefinition, formulating declarations of the university's vision. University leaders are also aware of the fact that in order to make those written vision and mission statements feasible, core values as the core of university's identity need to reflect strategic directions and objectives.

At Hamline University, its identity, initiatives, and inspiration are built upon a solid foundation of a clearly defined mission, sharply rendered values, and mature vision.[28]

Table 8.1 presents the way in which core values of the Hamline University are reflected in strategic directions and initiatives for their realization in this university. It also indicates the achievements in core value enactment at Hamline University in the past 4 years. Moreover, Table 8.1 is evidence that through personal and collective efforts, Hamline University was able to achieve its objectives of enacting core values.

Hamline University has also elaborated on an array of tools in the form of policies and procedures that enable the school to fulfill objectives and tasks for its core values enactment. Those documents are accessible at the university's website as faculty/staff/student policies and handbooks. Particular attention should be paid to the legibility of its location in particular webmarks "resources for": faculty and staff, current/admitted students as well as families/parents, and veterans.

Among the various policies for faculty and staff, the Diversity Policy stands out, where we can read:

Hamline University commits itself to inviting, supporting and affirming cultural diversity on the campus. All university programs and practices, academic and co-curricular, shall be designed to create a learning environment in which cultural differences are valued.

To ensure the achievement of these policy goals, Hamline University is committed to:

Encouraging all organizations to have as part of their constitution and by-laws, a cultural diversity policy that states explicitly the organization's commitment to fostering cultural diversity on campus;

Table 8.1. Reflecting core Values of the Hamline University in Strategic Directions and Initiatives for Their Realization

Core Values	Strategic Direction	2007–2012		2012–2017	
		Objective	Initiative	Achievement	Objective	Initiative
Regarding ALL the Hamline University core values	Create a cohesive identity as a mission-driven university	Hamline University's mission, values, and vision will be better understood and acknowledged as the foundation and inspiration for our institutional identity.	– Review and align all other published missions, visions, and statements of purpose in schools, programs, and departments with the university mission.	– Integrated all five schools under the common vision through marketing plans, publications, and programming – Launched a new university website that conveys the university's mission, values, and vision – Developed a strategic social media plan, including the use of Facebook, Twitter, and YouTube to disseminate the mission to a wider audience		

(Continued)

Table 8.1. (Continued)

Core Values	Strategic Direction	2007–2012			2012–2017	
		Objective	Initiative	Achievement	Objective	Initiative
Regarding ALL the Hamline University core values	Connect teaching, scholarship, and university-wide learning outcomes with the mission and core values to advance a distinctively Hamline experience that is valued and realized by all learners.	Hamline University will support faculty, staff, and students in their teaching, learning, and research to continually improve as a learning-centered university.	– Create a Center for Teaching and Scholarship – Establish clear and reasonable expectations for teaching, scholarship, and service to optimize potential of faculty members for scholarly and artistic production	– Created the Center for Teaching and Learning, which supports the collaboration, research, teaching, and continuing education of Hamline faculty members – Developed an academic program review process to ensure that programs are of high quality and are responsive to the needs of students in the twenty-first century – Established university-wide policies for faculty rank, tenure, and evaluation to attract quality, reputation, and diversity in candidates	– Hamline University will retain and strengthen its commitment to a liberal education while infusing all aspects of the curriculum with an intensified emphasis on high-impact learning, allowing students to gain the knowledge, cultural awareness, skills, and professionalism needed to lead successful and ethical lives of leadership, scholarship and service.	– Coordinate educational opportunities with mentoring, internship opportunities, and career preparation. – Obtain individual, corporate, and foundation donors to support the intensified emphasis on high-impact learning.

(Continued)

Core Values	Strategic Direction	2007–2012			2012–2017	
		Objective	Initiative	Achievement	Objective	Initiative
Regarding values of: – Multicultural competencies in local and global contexts – The development and education of the whole person – An individual and community ethic of social justice, civic responsibility, and inclusive leadership and service	– Serve the changing needs of society, locally and globally, by investing in the personal and professional growth of our students	– Hamline's educational opportunities will align with student and market needs to increase the success of Hamline students in the workplace and enhance their preparation to be contributing members of society.	– Provide enhanced language learning opportunities.	– Implemented new study abroad programs at the undergraduate and graduate levels, including: School of Business programs in: China, Dubai, Finland, Germany, Italy, Japan, and Spain.		

(Continued)

Table 8.1. (*Continued*)

Core Values	Strategic Direction	2007–2012			2012–2017	
		Objective	Initiative	Achievement	Objective	Initiative
Regarding values of: – The development and education of the whole person – An individual and community ethic of social justice, civic responsibility, and inclusive leadership and service	Become an exemplar in the integration of diversity to achieve and sustain an inclusive community	Hamline University will integrate and operationalize diversity in the service of social justice and equality through inclusive excellence in: the university's structural and functional organization and academic life and everyday culture	– Develop and implement diversity standards for business practices and vendor relationships that align with the university's diversity agenda. – Utilize best practices and require accountability in recruiting, hiring, retaining, and developing a diverse community of trustees, faculty, staff, and students.	– Established the Diversity Integration Standing Committee (DISC) and the Office of Diversity Integration – Established the Wesley Center for Spirituality, Social Justice, and Service Learning, which develops programs that promote compassion, service, inclusiveness, civic involvement, personal and spiritual wholeness, and social justice on campus and in the wider community – Sponsored an undergraduate faculty conference on teaching and diversity – Successfully recruited diverse students, faculty and staff members, and members of the Board of Trustees	– Hamline University will integrate and put into action diversity principles and policies, consistent with our commitment to equity, access and social justice.	– Increase the numerical representation of various racial, ethnic, gender, class or national groups among students, faculty, staff and trustees.

Source: Author's own study based on: *Creating Pathways to distinction. Hamline University Strategic Plan 2011. Update* and *Hamline's Strategic Plan. Pathways 20 2013–2017*.

- Encouraging inclusiveness in all organizations while respecting the different needs of organizations composed of groups that have been or currently are denied equal opportunity.
- Developing and maintaining academic/co-curricular programs and university climate that promises a responsible, civil and open exchange of ideas.
- Educating all members of the campus community about diversity and forms of discrimination, such as racism, sexism, and homophobia.
- Maintaining a respectful environment free from all forms of harassment, hostility and violence.
- Recruiting and working to retain students, staff and faculty who are members of historically or otherwise under-represented groups.
- Providing the necessary financial and academic support to recruit and retain diverse students, faculty and staff.
- The University's Cultural Diversity Committee shall act as a resource for the implementation of this policy and shall report annually to the President and the University Council. The President shall ensure that procedures are developed to implement this policy. The procedures shall include defined terms and ideas to assist organizations in implementing this policy.[29]

Its specific supplement addresses discrimination of any sort. The Harassment Policy encompasses all groups (faculty, staff, and students) in the Hamline University community. It starts with a declaration that:

Hamline University will not tolerate harassment, discrimination, or retaliation based on race; color; gender/sex; ethnic background; national origin; sexual orientation; gender presentation; marital, domestic partner or parental status; status with regard to public assistance; disability; religion; age; or veteran status in its employment or educational opportunities.[30]

There is also a clearly defined policy of strategic objectives and methods for their realization that is a consequence of the vision, mission, and core values.

> Hamline's mission is "to create a diverse and collaborative community of learners dedicated to the development of students' knowledge, values, and skills for successful lives of leadership, scholarship, and service." The strategic plan identifies as one of its goals that of becoming "an exemplar in the integration of diversity to achieve and sustain an inclusive community." Strategic Direction, 4. Discrimination, harassment, or retaliation designed to silence, stigmatize, marginalize, or exclude any individual based on his or her inclusion in a protected class as identified below is incompatible with the University mission and vision to educate, to seek truth, and to sustain an inclusive community.

Students of Hamline University are also supported by the university's authorities and administrators with valuable documents that serve as independent guidelines for their ethical decisions and actions aimed at studying the unique identity of Hamline University that is based on its core values.[31]

Undergraduate and graduate students have a number of relevant policies and procedures that should be obeyed if the students want to be successful participants of academic community at Hamline University. The basic document for each student is the Student Handbook 2011–2012, which addresses key topics, such as Hamline's mission, governance and laws, principles of community, full services, graduate student policies, undergraduate student policies, policies for resident students, student organization information, and other questions and concerns.[32]

Hamilton University elaborated on a wide orientation program for admitted students that includes:

> Piper Preview is the first of two required orientation programs for all incoming first-year students. During this 2-day/overnight program, you and your parents/family members will get the opportunity to
> - Meet your New Student Mentor (orientation leader) and other incoming Pipers.
> - Learn from faculty and staff what it takes to be academically successful.

- Choose your classes and register online.
- Speak with offices and departments to get all your questions answered.
- Get a sneak peek into life on campus with entertainment and a night in the residence halls.
- Leave with a feeling of pride and confidence knowing that Hamline was the right choice for you.[33]
- Piper Passages is the second required orientation program for all first-year students. A few days before classes start, students who plan on living in the residence halls will move in, commuter students will have a Commuter Student Pre-Orientation Program, and parents and family members will also participate in a variety of orientation sessions.[34]

Parents and guardians of students are also treated at the Hamilton University as integrated and important parts of the academic community. Interesting and recommendable initiatives include the Parent Network and Parent E-Newsletter.

> The Parent Network is a representative group of the Parents Association and acts as a liaison between the University and the parents. And as a parent, you are already a member!

> The Parent E-Newsletter is an excellent resource, providing updates and stories about life on campus, Hamline students, faculty, and other events and useful information about Hamline.[35]

Hamline University is proud of its long history of military service that started during the Civil War. In honor of the women and men of the military, the university is fully dedicated to offering veterans a superior academic experience.[36] Hamline exhibits its pride in its veterans by helping them make the transition from military to school smooth, accessible, and richly rewarding.[37]

Hamline University includes its graduates as the custodians of Hamline University's values:

> Hamline owes its strong reputation for academic excellence and moral values to the leadership, generosity, and success of its alumni.

It is thanks to alumni and their belief in John Wesley's quote, "Do all the good you can, in all the ways that you can . . ." that Hamline has such beautiful and technologically advanced facilities, scholarships that allow students to reach their academic potential, and inspiration on how to live a life of leadership, service, and scholarship.[38]

All the mentioned policies, procedures, and initiatives for enacting core values at the Hamline University are supported by the Office of the Ombudsman. This office has existed at the Hamline University since 1998 as Ombuds services on a part-time basis, and since 2005 as Hamline University's Ombudsman Office.

> The Ombudsman is a confidential, neutral and informal resource to whom students, faculty and staff can bring any university-related question, concern, or conflict. The Ombuds is an alternative to existing university problem-solving services and can help to surface concerns, resolve disputes, manage conflict, explain of University's policies and procedures, and educate individuals in more productive ways of communicating. The Ombudsman can function in a number of ways: as an impartial listener, as a resource for assistance, as a confidential advisor, as a facilitator of discussions or meetings and as an informal mediator or negotiator. Communications with the Ombudsman are entirely confidential, except in the case of imminent risk of serious harm. This confidentiality allows visitors to explore options and generate possible avenues for resolution without involving formal channels.

> The Ombudsman Office is not an office of notice for the university.[39]

> Hamline's Ombudsman adheres to the Standards of Practice and Code of Ethics of the International Ombudsman Association. The Ombuds Office is confidential, neutral, informal and independent.[40]

Having analyzed the values of academic ethos of Hamline University, there emerges an impression that the value that best describes the spirit of the university and that interprets its vision and mission of the United Methodist Church is the diversity:

> This diversity is not merely a characteristic of Hamline, but an integral part of its identity and values. It's who we are, what we do, and how we see the world. Hamline isn't a place where you "fit in," conforming to the Hamline mold. Rather, Hamline "fits in" you, welcoming your unique contributions and valuing who you are.[41]

Diversity at the Hamline University is not just a beautiful decoration, a proper declaration. It is a deeply rooted value in the academic community supported with tools for particular policies, procedures, and initiatives for its institutionalization. It is a carefully cultivated and deeply shared core value.

It is worth noting that in 2002 Hamline University formulated a definition for the term "diversity" that not only draws on its own policies and definitions but also turns a keen eye toward the concerns of those outside the community; case in point, by examining definitions from the University of Central Florida:

> Diversity refers to the variety of backgrounds and characteristics found among humankind; thus, it encompasses all aspects of human similarities and differences.[42]

Authorities at the Hamline University are fully aware that for fulfilling its mission as "a diverse community of learners with students at the center that transforms lives,"[43] it is not enough just to elaborate a diversity policy. Policies must be a complete, active, vital collaboration among administrations, schools, and programs.[44] That is why at the Hamline University, the value "diversity" is integrated "across five major focus areas":

> Student learning inside the classroom (faculty development and academic affairs);
> Students outside the classroom (student affairs);
> Faculty recruitment and retention;

Staff recruitment, development, and retention;
External relations and partnerships.[45]

The Office of Diversity Integration is responsible for all activities within these areas; it supports university programs with a keen eye toward ensuring comprehensive advocacy on behalf of all diversity and equality practices.[46] Exemplar activity by this unit includes:

- developing and coordinating diversity-centered events with faculty, staff, and students;
- initiating development and training opportunities;
- supporting innovative scholarly and curricular techniques;
- creating a welcoming campus environment for all students, regardless his or her background;
- maintaining an archive of diversity-related documents and resources;
- developing relationships with organizations beyond the walls of academia in the community at large.[47]

The University's authorities do know that communicating a particular value, explaining its meaning, and even creating appropriate infrastructure in a form of policies and procedures is not enough. Implementation of particular value depends not only on the awareness of the value's essence among members of academic community, but also on their knowledge and capabilities to take particular actions for its implementation.

That is why the Hamline University elaborated and implemented "The Staff Diversity Development Initiative, [which] is a framework for professional development training and educational opportunities that assist Hamline University staff members in

- developing knowledge, awareness and skills for strengthening their work in and with our diverse community of learners and workers;
- supporting student learning, acclimation and success in the university community;

- achieving their individual professional and personal diversity goals as outlined in their annual performance reviews; and
- assisting Hamline University to achieve our diversity goals and aspiration in their respective roles, responsibilities, and units.[48]

Apart from this, faculty members have support for teaching diversity in the form of pedagogical support, curriculum development, and assessment resources. The Race, Gender and Beyond Faculty Development Program "offers a range of activities from individual consultations, to drop-in reading groups, to workshops, on-going reading groups as well as summer institutes."[49]

Hamline University reinforces its experience and knowledge about institutional value of "diversity" among academic community from external organizations:

Since May 1999, Hamline University has been sending a team of staff, students, faculty and administrators to the National Conference on Race and Ethnicity (NCORE) in American Education.[50]

NCORE's purpose is to support the development of Hamline-based diversity leadership and Hamline's teams, in turn, provide on-campus programs tailored to the particular learning needs of our university community.[51]

Having analyzed the spectrum of activities undertaken at the Hamline University for institutionalization of the "diversity" value, there emerges an impression that the school is replete with diversity. In effect, this university has created a specific culture of diversity. Immersion in an organization that actively fosters such diversity is the best way for this value to become embedded within students. Hamline University constantly offers activities in the form of diversity workshops, programs, and training opportunities that are aimed at helping students prepare to live, serve, and succeed in a diverse university and in the world. The Hedgeman Center for Student Diversity Initiatives and Programs or the Safe Zone Network are two prime examples of this fine attention to diversity.

Authorities at Hamline University also remember that the substantial element of core values maintaining is motivating and rewarding for behavior compliant with them. The choice of awards and distinctions is very impressive in this field. They include awards and distinctions such as Wesley Award for students, staff, and faculty, Diversity Research Award, or the Honorary Degrees.

> The Hamline Diversity Research Award is given annually to an undergraduate who demonstrates excellent facility with scholarly research materials to produce a project on a diversity topic.[52]

> On the other hand

> Honorary degrees are awarded to outstanding high-achieving individuals who have made contributions in their respective fields, and who live lives that demonstrate the highest ethical integrity and commitment to the greater good. (…)While not all recipients have close Hamline connections, all such individuals exemplify Hamline's core mission, vision, and values.[53]

When describing management by values of academic ethos in the Hamline University, we cannot forget that it is the first and the oldest university in the state of Minnesota. Its identity derived from its nearly 200-year-old traditions. This immersion in tradition is visible at every step in the Hamline University, starting from the Hamline Seal that includes three values: religion, learning, and freedom,[54] through architecture symbols such as The Bishop Statue, Bridgman Memorial Court, and Hamline United Methodist Church, ending up with stories like these:

> This quote from John Wesley is the cornerstone of what Hamline is all about it. It's recited by the President at the Matriculation ceremony and at Commencement—and a few times in between.

> Do all the good you can, by all the means you can, in all the ways you can, in all the places you can, at all the times you can, to all the people you can, as long as ever you can.[55]

and The Piper:

In the 1920s, Hamline athletics were quite successful. As interest in the teams grew, the St. Paul Pioneer Press-Dispatch writers felt that a new team name was needed to replace the traditional name, "Red and Gray." Suggestions came in, among them "Red Sox," "Red Legs," and "Cardinals." But the suggestion that caught on was "Pipers," taken from Robert Browning's poem "The Pied Piper of Hamelin." Throughout the years, students have shown their school spirit by bringing the Piper to life.[56]

Not all traditions hearken back to older times. In 2005, Hamline's president Linda N. Hanson decided to "light up Hewitt Avenue" for the Christmas holidays by gathering the community around the Bishop statue and flipping the switch for the many lights adorning the festive tree. Now, holiday celebrations include cocoa, candy canes, and camaraderie during the Annual Tree Lighting Ceremony at the school.

This example not only clearly shows that Hamline University cultivates its identity and its core values through stories from the past but also participates in the process of continually developing those traditions. Authorities not only talk but also listen to what the academic community members are talking about, what jokes and stories they are saying. The University's leaders choose those that reflect university's core values.

Through the evidence above, Hamline University clearly shows itself to be a model for managing core values that constitute cultural identity of the university. This identity is a set of core values (its central characteristics) that can distinguish a higher school, not only grounding it in the ideals of *university* that have come down through the ages but also remaining on the tip of twenty-first century advancements and concerns. Core value management is an important catalyst for the continued success of a higher school. Hamline University has proved that for the past 200 years, it has been excellent in this process.

CHAPTER 9

Recommendations from Cases

Toward the Concept of Academic Integrity Development by Academic Ethos Management

The conclusions and recommendations from qualitative research conducted in this field provide vital rationales when formulating the concept of academic integrity through management of the core values of academic ethos. Key research has been conducted in six deliberately chosen higher schools located in different countries: the United States, Argentina, Iceland, and Poland. The criterion of choice was the age of the school, its ownership form, and phase of development.

Case studies of DePaul University, Hamline University, Wright University, IAE Business School, Jagiellonian University, and Reykjavik University after the process of its merger provide rich empirical material. Synthesis and reference to the theoretical proposals furthers the existing state of knowledge about the methods of academic integrity creation and of academic ethos management, as well as offers guidelines to better understanding the concept of academic integrity development through managing the core values of academic ethos.

The assumptions of this concept are included in the following statements.

1. The source for the persistence and development of contemporary universities is finding the golden mean (the balance) between the stability of core values of academic ethos (cultural identity) and the

constantly changing mechanisms of their enactment and maintenance in order to make them compliant with internal and external
requirements.

2. Universities throughout the world, regardless of their age, size, or
ideology, have managed and still are managing the academic ethos.
However, they do this in a more or less aware, institutionalized way
following developed sets of deliberate actions.

3. Managing of academic ethos values is the process of managing a
university's cultural identity and transferring the university's core
values from one management generation to another by taking over
responsibilities resulting from core values and their protection for
the benefit of the organization and its members through their institutionalization in a morally positive manner.

4. The level of academic integrity in a substantial way depends on the
extent of managing the core values of academic ethos.

5. The process of managing core values of academic ethos is of a cyclic
character and consists of the following phases: discovering and developing, enacting, and maintaining the core values of academic ethos.

6. Academic integrity is the result of a compound process of coordinated actions in the following areas: leaders' integrity, integrity of a
higher school as an organization, integrity of members of academic
community, and integrity of environment of a higher school.

7. The key differentiation among higher schools lies not in the general
core values statement (many universities have very similar or nearly
identical core values) but in the effectiveness of transmitting the
chosen academic ethos to the academic community and transferring
academic ethos core values (cultural identity) into university behavior.

8. Core values of academic ethos emanate from various sources. Most
often they are academic tradition, ideology, the institutional history
with ideology, and the leader's personality.

9. Representatives of all the groups constituting the academic community should be involved in the process of discovering and redefining
core values of academic ethos.

10. Higher schools with a high level of awareness of academic ethos core
values place a special emphasis on enacting these values by supporting

them in the university's goals, objectives, and measures, formulating university's policies, procedures, and codes as well as maintaining them by recruitment, actions taken in order to explain core values, training on core values for members of academic community and the way of awarding and promotion system and control the behavior compliance of academic community members with the behaviors ascribed to core values of academic ethos.

11. The persistence of core values of academic ethos in the process of a university's development has its source in the clear definition and continuous updating of definitions in the context of desirable and unacceptable behaviors.

12. Each participant of the academic community should sign an academic pledge and be trained on core values of academic ethos, behaviors and policies, procedures and codes created on this basis. Training should be supplemented with the appropriate materials in paper and electronic form.

13. A university should call into being the unit responsible for the control of policies, procedures, and compliance with core values of academic ethos.

14. A university should create a formal system for communicating core values of academic ethos. One of its objectives should be to inform the members of academic community about the achievements and activities undertaken for academic ethos enactment.

15. A motivation system should regard the compliance of actions of a university employee with the values of academic ethos.

16. The key elements to the success of universities' merger are the organizational cultures analysis of the combined organizations and recognition and respect for their traditions and values of academic ethos of those organizations.

17. Core values of the higher school created as a result of a merger should be the effect of consensus regarding traditions of both the universities.

This set of statements is not a closed list of suggestions. The practice of managing the higher schools, as well as the importance and present-day interest of this topic in the scientific discourse, will probably result in the identification of particular conditions and deviations from the statements.

However, the assumptions of this concept are compliant with the main development trajectory within this research area in management sciences, and the importance of this topic provokes further cognitive efforts to be taken in this field.

CHAPTER 10

Positive Academic Ethos

The Frame for Integrity in Managerial Education

The Process of Academic Ethos Management

A university does not simply exist; rather, it happens, becomes, and transforms. For a contemporary company, it is the consciousness and stability of its academic ethos core values that conditions the way it evolves. Empirical studies[1] have found that organizations that have survived for a long period of time and outperformed their competitors have a homogeneous and intense identity, which at the same time is complex and abstract enough to survive over time. By discovering and defining academic ethos core values, management makes general statements about the central characteristics (core values) of the university, which in the existing conditions are commonly shared and preferred, shaped by the entrepreneurial attitudes and behaviors of people at the university. They therefore create foundations for the development of social ties among academic community members and build the relationship of loyalty, trust, and cooperation—the necessary conditions for the development of a learning company.[2]

The key differentiation among higher schools lies not in the general core values statement (many universities have very similar or nearly identical core values) but in the effectiveness of transmitting the chosen academic ethos to the academic community and transferring academic ethos core values (cultural identity) into university behavior.

A particular logic of transferring academic ethos values into an organization's developmental behavior is the university's individual paradigm, typical for a given higher school—its cultural identity. The instrumentarium of the cultural identity management of a university is what we call Academic Ethos Management (AEM). Entrepreneurs, founders, and other business leaders used to manage and do manage, consciously (and unconsciously), in an operationalized way, more or less institutionalized, in the form of specific methods (special and intentional sets of managerial actions), the university's cultural identity to ensure its efficient and effective process of development. In a contemporary university, cultural identity management takes place in a conscious and organized way through AEM,[3] so the instrumentarium of academic ethos core values management and its transmission to the members of academic community and other stakeholders is a process of academic ethos management.

On the basis of our previous study,[4] we may conclude that academic ethos management is a process of managing university culture identity and transferring the university's core values from one management generation to another by taking over responsibilities resulting from core values and their protection for the benefit of the organization and its members through their institutionalization (enacting and maintaining) in a morally positive manner. The development of particular phases (stages) of AEM is presented in Table 10.1.

The objective of AEM is to establish a university culture of integrity by acquiring a favorable image of university and consequently a positive identity of the university among employees so that, in the long run, this can result in the acquisition of a favorable reputation of the university; this, in turn, leads to members of the academic community displaying positive behavior toward the university.[5]

Mark Twain once said, "It is curious that physical courage should be so common in the world and moral courage so rare."[6] The development of a university's cultural identity as well as its effective AEM does not guarantee a higher school to be free from corruption and unethical behavior. Numerous cases of vulgarization of this process are known from managerial practice. Undoubtedly, core values may be cultivated in a morally negative, neutral, as well as positive way.[7]

Table 10.1. *Characteristics of Academic Ethos Management Phases*

Academic Ethos Management Phase	Phase Component	Characteristics

Discovering and developing core values of academic ethos	Discover core values of academic ethos	Values should be discovered by representatives of all groups that constitute an academic community (president, deans, heads of departments, faculty staff, administration staff, students)
		
		Values should be identified on:
		  – Individual level
		  – University level
		The discovered values should be: authentic, shared, constant, few, guaranteeing the flourishing of individuals and a university

	Description (definition) of core values	– The university level – The university's unit level – The individual level
	Definition of desired behaviors	The definition of academic core values, desirable behaviors should concern the whole academic as well as its particular groups like: students, academic teachers, scientists, administration staff, and even for students' parents or guardians.
	Definition of unacceptable behaviors	The definition of unacceptable behaviors should concern the whole academic as well as its particular groups like: students, academic teachers, scientists, administration staff, and even for students' parents or guardians.

(Continued)

Table 10.1. (*Continued*)

Academic Ethos Management Phase	Phase Component	Characteristics
Enacting the core values of academic ethos	Supporting core values of academic ethos in university's goals, objectives, and measures	University leaders should communicate to academic community what will be done for core values implementation (goals), how it will be done (objectives), and how the effect of core values implementation will be measured Each core value should be expressed by a university through particular objectives, tasks for its realization, and measures enabling to assess the effectiveness of its activity.
	Formalization university's policies, procedures, and codes	Involves: – Developing policy statement or goal statement – Developing core values statement – Defining communal responsibilities and rights – Defining academic pledge (general pledge, student pledge, faculty members pledge, and parent pledge) – Description of definitions and consequences of prohibited behaviors – Descriptions of tips to prevent academic misconduct – Description of reporting and adjudication process – Developing procedures of whistleblowers protection – Developing procedures for sanctions and appeals
	Communicating core values of academic ethos	The spectrum of communication tools includes: involvement of top management (values modeling), cultural models, declarations of core values language, university traditions reflected in myths, story tales, legends, academic rituals and ceremonies, songs or architecture symbols (monuments, logos), physical symbols (gowns, rings, mascots), or symbols of prestige (presidential costume, chain, mace) University should also use modern technology (social media: Facebook, LinkedIn, Second Life, etc.) and chatterbots for communicating core values of academic ethos.

Maintaining core values of academic ethos	Protecting core values	Comprises:

		– Recruitment (cultural adequacy of prospective employees)
		– Core values explaining with the use, for example, new student conferences, first meeting of every course, new faculty orientation, graduate teaching assistant training, faculty/staff job application materials, handbooks, catalogue, admission application materials, student rules and handbooks, course syllabus, university's www site, special publications for students act
		– Cyclic training for both current and new employees equipping with the capabilities to act in compliance with a particular value of academic ethos
		– Training for students on values of academic ethos:
		1. in the classroom by
		   • positive classroom climate,
		   • exemplar pattern of academic teacher's behavior during classes,
		   • specifying desirable as well as reprehensible behaviors in syllabus,
		   • discussions with students,
		2. out of the classroom by:
		   • creating on university's website a FAQ section concerning values of academic ethos issues,
		   • organizing contests for slogan, poster, T-shirt, or a comic that shows positive behaviors compliant with core values,
		   • organizing movie festivals, symposium, seminars, lectures of scientific personages or discussion panels for students, faculty members, focused on core values of academic ethos.

(Continued)

Table 10.1. (*Continued*)

Academic Ethos Management Phase	Phase Component	Characteristics

	Controlling and redefining core values of academic ethos	– Motivating and awarding:
		    Formal and informal rewarding (diplomas, praise, awards),
		    Formal punishments and reporting about reprehensible behaviors.
		Regular monitoring of core values implementation level through checking compliance between academic community members' behaviors and the behavioral patterns assigned to core values of academic ethos.
		Supplementing core value sets or changing their definitions that result from, for example, a merger, changes in the university's environment, development, the atmosphere of distrust and hostility, cynicism and pessimism inside the university.

Source: Author's own study.

Positive Organizational Scholarship—the Treatment for Misbehavior and Dishonesty in Academic Context

Taking efforts to redefine and reconstruct academic ethos and to create the fundamentals for academic integrity, we should adopt a different perspective to observe and study this process than the one that has caused the crisis (erosion) of academic ethos. It seems that we have wasted too much energy and time for elaborating policies and codes aimed at spying on and punishing those members of academic community who have behaved in an unethical way. We also have spent too much time on creating the tools for preventing unethical behavior inside the higher school that were focused on reducing opportunities for such actions. However, the academic life is very creative, and unethical behavior such as corruption may be compared with a pandemic, a virus that incessantly mutates, changes, creates new strains, and forms immunities to existing medicines such as policies and codes of ethics. At the same time, as noted by Dr. Charles Wankel and I,[8] reaction to highly publicized corporate scandals and instances of management misconduct that have eroded public faith (such as Enron, WorldCom, Tyco, Adelphia, and Arthur Andersen) have even suggested that current managerial theories actually contribute to unethical practices.[9]

This is not to say that the approach to creating academic integrity, based on policies, procedures, and codes focused on preventing from dishonest, unethical behaviors of academic community members, is wrong or inappropriate. These actions should be supported by programs such as the Positive Organizational Scholarship, which promotes academic integrity and human values and virtues. The "old" institutional theory focused on the value-based aspects of leading and organizing;[10] in the selfsame manner, Positive Organizational Scholarship returns to basics on topics such as:

1. collective concern about "flourishing," or succeeding;
2. development of strengths and talents;
3. the dynamics of organization (individual as part of a dynamic, organic group).[11]

Many intellectual disciplines serve as models, including appreciative inquiry,[12] community psychology,[13] and humanistic psychology.[14]

The greatest influence stems from positive psychology, the organizational dynamics allowing individuals, groups, and entire organizations to strive for excellence and flourish. Such flourishing on an organizational level may be manifested in creativity, innovation, growth, resilience, kindness, or other markers revealing that a group is healthy and is performing "above normal."[15]

In my study on positive organizational identity, "Virtuousness can be understood as internationalization of moral rules that produces social harmony[16] and can be examined as a study of capacity, attributes, and reserve in organizations that facilitate the expressions of positive deviance among organization members."[17] Virtuous organizations "move individuals toward better citizenship, responsibility, nurturance, altruism, civility, moderation, tolerance, and work ethic."[18] Many researchers have reported[19] that virtuous organization leads to the development of human strength and healing and cultivates extraordinary individual and organizational performance; this, in turn, leads to flourishing outcomes and the best of the human condition and fosters virtuous behaviors and emotions such as compassion, forgiveness, dignity, respectful encounters, optimism, and integrity, as well as faith, courage, justice, and wisdom."[20]

Through a virtues approach to creating academic integrity, schools of higher education strive to develop a specific culture of integrity, promoting an environment in which members behave in responsible, honest, right ways, not because they are afraid of sanctions or because they treat work as their duty but because their "internal self" determines the right way to behave, the only way that can flourish. As noted in my previous works, the formal, ethical infrastructure as well as its external mechanisms cannot guarantee the integrity within academia.[21] Every regulation and formal system, even knowledge itself, has limitations. Ethical and moral decisions are made by human beings who have their individual life experience, character, and system of values. Therefore, one can presume that the positive identity of an organization can be managed by developing the company's morality (by way of developing the moral competences of the staff and implementing the Academic Ethos Management process) and placing more emphasis on abiding and respecting the law and external regulations. It has to be stated, however, that this will not be achieved by implementing institutional reforms or internal systems.

Sooner or later, even a well-functioning system or institution can be perverted by the wrong culture or wrong customs. The problem is that, as far as it is easy to improve the infrastructural dimension of an organization, it is much more difficult to reduce the human-related risk because it became established in the culture. It needs to be emphasized that, although a company's culture is usually resistant to change, one should make efforts to do so because, unlike Bakan[22] who stated in his diagnosis of a contemporary corporation, good people are able to change bad enterprises—they only need to be people with strong moral character and integrity.

The Quest for Integrity in Management Education

It is not necessarily true to state that it is generally known that integrity is essential, "is at heart of what effective business and education is about," or is a basic characteristic of a leader. The legendary former CEO of General Electric, however, has been known to say that he never held a management meeting where integrity was not mentioned. Great leaders of the past, Weinberger (2010) notes,[23] would more likely be cited for courage, wisdom, and integrity.[24] Covey and Kouzes and Posner[25] put integrity on the top of the list of essential characteristics for effective leadership.[26] Organizational leaders are responsible for creating a caring atmosphere within their organizations and for creating norms of integrity and justice in the larger competitive and societal context.[27]

However, relatively little is known about how management education can prepare managers and professionals to cope effectively with challenges of leading with integrity in multicultural environments.[28] Developing future business leaders with capabilities of leading is a challenging but an important task for management educators,[29] especially when, as observed by Sandra Waddock, "Trust is central to the effective functioning of all markets. Trust is destroyed, however, when individuals and institutions act without integrity."[30]

The quest for integrity in business and education is only partly a reaction to highly publicized corporate scandals and instances of management misconduct that have eroded public faith (such as Enron, WorldCom, Tyco, Adelphia, and Arthur Andersen). As Wankel and I have noted,[31]

"The quest for integrity is also a result of changes and new demands in the global business environment[32] as well as the latest economic crisis.[33] Among the sources of these new demands are the expectations of stakeholders that corporations and their leaders will take more active roles as citizens within society and in the fight against some of the most pressing problems in the world, such as poverty, environmental degradation, defending human rights, corruption, and pandemic diseases."[34] In truth, "The collapse of giants like Enron and Arthur Andersen signaled a major turning point in the conversation about corporate ethics and integrity."[35]

Business schools can teach the techniques, skills, and tools of, for example, marketing, finance, and operations, but they have lost their ability to install a sense of integrity or moral responsibility in students.[36] As Palmer claims,[37] education should focus on the "who am I," rather than solely on the "what" and "how." Integrity is therefore the use of that wisdom that resides within ourselves.[38] But what constitutes the integrity of an individual? Is it possible to teach it, or can the higher schools only encourage ethical behavior through the educational process? And what constitutes the integrity of the whole organizations such as higher schools?

Individual Integrity and the Integrity of a Higher School

The origin of the word "integrity" is grounded in the Latin root *integer*, which refers to a whole number, suggesting the idea of wholeness. The broadest meaning given to the term *integrity* in the Oxford English Dictionary[39] presents two definitions of integrity: the physical and the moral. Integrity applies to the physical state of undivided wholeness, whether of a united land or unbroken body. Alternately, integrity connotes an unimpaired moral state, characterized by innocence, uprightness, honesty, sincerity, and being without sin.[40]

According to Kaiser and Hogan,[41] the concept of integrity includes two components: honesty and consistency. *Honesty* is defined as the way in which a person acts within shared ethical standards to meet the expectations of society; *consistency* is the connection between words and deeds, by behaving in a logical, orderly manner over a period of time and in a variety of contexts.[42]

Baltimore sees integrity as "the state or quality of being complete, undivided, [and] unbroken."[43] According to Sawyer, Johnson, and Holub, integrity refers to "a consistency across time, consistency across individuals, and consistency across decisions."[44] With regard to the individual, integrity means the successful unity of intellectual, physical, emotional, and spiritual levels.[45] Individuals with integrity tell the truth, are trustworthy, hold high moral standards for themselves, and, quite simply, do what they say they are going to do.[46]

Ayn Rand and Leonard Peikoff define integrity as "loyalty in action to a morally justifiable code of principles and values that promotes the long-term survival and well-being of individuals as rational beings."[47] Carson states that integrity is "an unwavering commitment to acting for the benefit of others, standing up for those who are under attack, loyalty to people to whom we have committed ourselves, acting honorably, and so on."[48] In Solomon's view, integrity is a balance between institutional loyalty and moral autonomy and is associated with moral humility.[49] While principles and policies are important, integrity "involves a pervasive sense of social context and a sense of moral courage that means standing up for others as well as oneself."[50]

When we are speaking about leadership, a leader of integrity is aware of his values and acts in a way that keeps those values and their actions aligned.[51] According to Peter Drucker, integrity is the "congruence between deeds and words, between behaviour and professed beliefs and values."[52] Only under such conditions will a manager be able to develop the positive university identity and cultivate under core values in a morally positive way as well as effectively manage the organization with the aid of Academic Ethos Management process.[53]

However, the integrity of a university's leaders is not enough to build the integrity of the school as a whole. The integrity of a higher school also depends on integrity and moral characteristics of the other participants of academic community, both students and employees. Taking employees into consideration, a higher school may create appropriate recruitment systems based on cultural adequacy of an applicant as well as on his/her level of moral intelligence. But what about students? Is it possible to teach them integrity?

Research indicates that moral development begins at a young age,[54] and some state that, rather than teach ethical behavior, universities can only encourage it.[55] However, pedagogical support can be developed through carefully designed training of individual awareness for realizing and maintaining integrity. The first quality of integrity is exhibiting strong moral principles regarding what is acceptable and what is not. Students, in effect, must examine what they stand for. The person with integrity knows his or her moral principles and strives to live by them. Such a person is prepared to peacefully defend values and beliefs. Integrity is therefore forged in the activities of day-to-day experience.[56]

However, the best way to develop the moral character of students and to encourage them to behave with integrity is through example, in one of the best "laboratories" on earth: the university itself.[57] Immersing students in a university with integrity helps them to gain insight how to create and perpetuate a culture of integrity.[58]

- Helps students to develop and enhance their innate capacity to act with integrity in the unexpected and new situations.
- Helps students to become better aware of their values.[59]
- Helps students to discover their core values as they learn to know themselves holistically.[60]
- Influences development of students new professional identities.[61]
- Helps student to experience the benefit of culture of integrity.

But there is still a question: What exactly characterizes the integrity of a higher school? While discussion of the topic naturally begins with human beings, it can also refer to educational systems and business paradigms. For example, LeClair, Ferrell, and Fraedrich defined the notion of integrity management as "uncompromising implementation of legal and ethical principles" that are themselves embodied in the strategic planning process of the firm.[62] Paine sees organizational integrity in a broad sense as "honesty, self-governance, fair dealing, responsibility, moral soundness, adherence to principle, and consistency of purpose."[63]

We can assume that, according to Paine, organizational integrity is a result of consequent managing by values of a particular organization. This author has also emphasized that it is impossible to create organization's integrity without the integrity of its participant, and vice versa—the integrity of participants is not enough to construct the integrity of a whole organization. The ethical infrastructure is necessary here. But how does it function in the educational process? Terms such as academic integrity and educational integrity appear frequently in the literature of ethos; the terms, however are a many-headed beast, a mythological, multiheaded Hydra of sorts,[64] twisting in many directions with a multiplicity of meanings (with abstract ideas such as "policy" and "right"). In general, the terms have to do with the difference between honest and dishonest practices in educational settings—sometimes blatantly obvious, sometimes subtle, and hidden in nuances and shadows of gray. A generally accepted definition of academic integrity is "honesty in all manners relating to endeavors of the academic environment,"[65] but the term also comes to light through behavior such as honesty, trust, fairness, respect, and responsibility.[66] Hall and Kuh suggest that one can better understand academic integrity and related behavior by gazing at them through a "cultural lens," which adjusts to particular foci.[67]

However, we cannot and should not limit the definition of a university's integrity solely to academic honesty—the integrity of a higher school transcends honesty. It is a specific organizational culture that is supported with values such as wisdom, courage, humanity, justice, respect, responsibility, fairness, and compassion. It inspires virtuousness of individuals and organizations, and in turn helps an academic community truly flourish. That is why the term of "integrity of higher schools" is a consequence of awareness, a deliberate and consequent managing of values of academic ethos in an ethical way. Constructing academic integrity starts at the top. Academic leaders must exhibit a high level of moral intelligence, wisdom and knowledge, courage, humanity, justice, temperance, and transcendence.[68] They must discover and define university ethos and thus make key statements about the central characteristics (core values) of a university. These characteristics form the set of meaning that leaders want an academic community to follow.

Leaders are responsible for transferring a university's core values from one management generation to another by taking over responsibilities resulting from academic ethos core values and their protection in the name of and for the benefit of a university and academic community through this institutionalization (enacting and maintaining academic ethos core values) in a morally positive manner. Academic leaders model through their day-to-day interactions with the members of academic community and other stakeholders. Moreover, leaders make necessary efforts to maintain core values of academic ethos by appropriate recruitment process, explaining core values, training, rewarding, motivating, and providing mechanisms to control the compliance of academic community members' activity with the values of a university as well as by action taken to redefine those values. These are the only conditions that will enable a manager to develop the positive academic ethos and cultivate core values in a morally positive way. Positive corporate identity is vital; it must be communicated to all employees and stakeholders through Academic Ethos Management. The critical point for the future behavior of the company's employees and the organization itself is the way in which employees interpret the organization's actions. It is never easy to make sense of an organization's goals, achievements, and position.

Every organization is a complex structure that has its own history, traditions, and set of activities enabling members to understand the organization's activities, goals, and values. Each member analyzes the organization's actions in order to better understand them. The member infers what an organization stands for and interprets organizational actions in response to specific events.[69]

Interpretation of an organization's actions influences the way in which members perceive the organization. A member's interpretations relates to some degree to the kind and degree of virtuousness of actions. "Virtuous organizational action" is the perceived exercise of collective behavior that indicates that the organization follows core values leading improvement on both moral and ethical levels.[70] The financial performance of an organization is directly proportional to the degree of virtuousness of their actions.

This is evidence that positive organizational identity and members' identification with and attachment to their organization results, to some extent, from the perceived virtuousness of organization's actions. Therefore, if an organization acts in accordance with its core values (walking the talk), and its behaviors are perceived as humane, just, and courageous, it has a positive influence on organizational identity (meaning that members recognize their collectives).[71] This, in turn, contributes to positive behavior toward the organization's positive word-of-mouth recommendations, encourages employees to act ethically and legally, strengthens positive emotions of an organization's members, and reflects in the virtuous self-constructs of members.[72]

A typical organization's actions can be described as "walking the talk," while the positive corporate identity (core values) requires implementing the Academic Ethos Management process in a morally positive way. Organizational action can be described as humane when it involves actions such as helping and taking care of organizational members or a larger society, through which they feel appreciated and are treated with dignity and respect. Moreover, courageous organizational action is undertaken by the organization in a spontaneous way in order to pursue "what is right," irrespective of the risks it may bring, and which aims at securing social well-being and moral improvement.[73] Only such an organization, which meets all the aforementioned attributes, can be perceived as one that is able to build a prosperous academic community, distinguished by its integrity in teaching, learning, conducting research, and providing services.

However, we need to remember that a college or university does not act in a vacuum but in a specific environment, the micro and macro one. The external environment of a higher school has an impact on the integrity of a higher school. The general environment (sociocultural, political, or economic, for example) has an indirect impact on a university; the external-task environment (like government regulation, funding for scientific work, job opportunities for trainees and researchers, journal policies and practices, and the policies and practices of scientific societies)[74] has a direct impact on the integrity of a higher school. When they are implemented, government regulations concerning scientific research conduct, reporting study results, reviewing scientific works, protection of authorship rights or reporting unethical behaviors in a scientific environment regulate academic work and have a profound impact on the members of an academic community. A similar situation may be observed in policies and practices implemented by scientific journals, stating that their editors must be vigorous in their dissection of work, particularly "in such areas as authorship practices, disclosure of conflicts of interest, duplicate publication, and reporting of research methodologies, the scientific community receives an important message about the role of integrity in research."[75]

We should not forget about the current labor market that becomes more and more competitive for scientists and for academic teachers. It causes a specific pressure on people of science to strive more and perform better in the short term. It may result in unethical behavior such as taking shortcuts, for example, through disseminating sensational research results that are not honest or by gaining funds for scientific research through unethical practices and agreements with external organizations.

The practice provides us with numerous examples of such unethical conduct. Well-known Dutch psychologist Diederick Stapel admitted that,

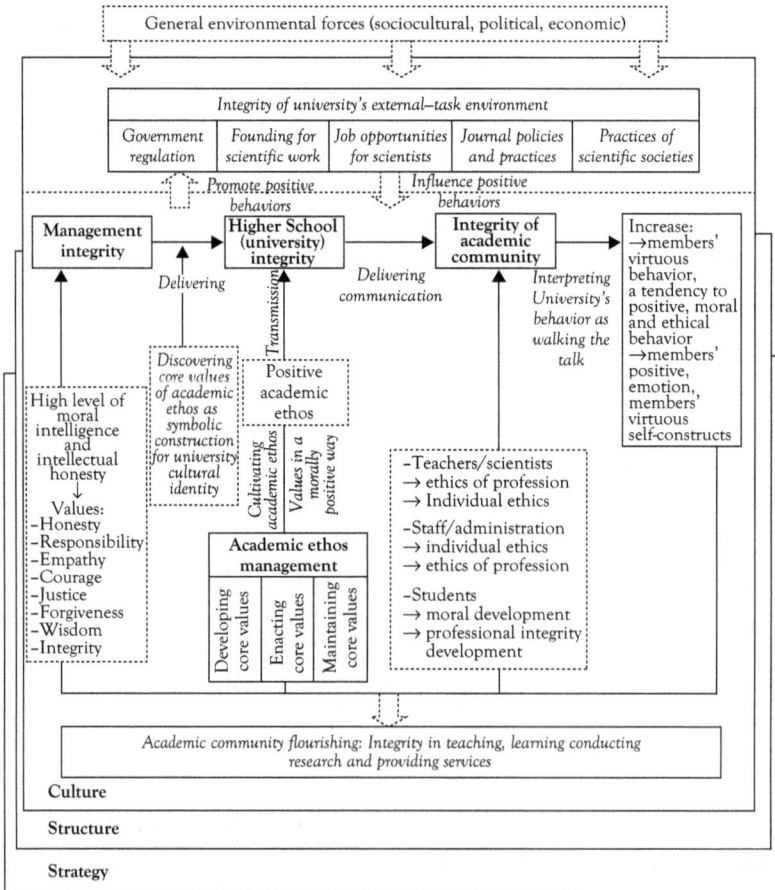

Figure 10.1. Conceptual framework of academic integrity based on Positive Academic Ethos.
Source: Author's own study.

for many years, he has been falsifying research results that were published in renowned journals such as *Science*.[76] Wicher from the University of Amsterdam confirmed that Stapel was not an exception, as in psychology the results usually are not commented by others. Jonathan Schooler, a psychologist from the University of California in Santa Barbara, affirmed that some scientists embellish their research results to be more interesting for their publication. That is why the challenge for a higher school is to create an organizational culture supported by appropriate ethical infrastructure that will maintain a high level of integrity within the academic community.

In conclusion, academic integrity is the effect of a compound process of coordinated actions in the following areas:

- leaders' integrity;
- integrity of a higher school as an organization;
- integrity of members of academic community;
- integrity of environment of a higher school.

Figure 10.1 illustrates a conceptual framework of academic integrity based on positive academic ethos.

I have a deep conviction and belief that a combination of a positive academic ethos and the integrity of academic community with positive meaning that academic communities impute to their collectives (as a result of implementing university actions as virus) with positive leadership and integrity of academic environment can install values, meaning, and purpose in university's life and results in academic flourishing demonstrated by integrity in teaching, learning, conducting research, and providing services.

The road to academic integrity is a very difficult and long process, but it is the only possibility for a university to fulfill its mission of discovering the truth, developing knowledge, playing a leading role in the development of democratic principles and free thinking, and educating citizens who will make this world a better place.

Conclusion

Integrity in the business world and in the realm of higher education is a topic that seizes the minds and imaginations of many of today's top thinkers. We stand at crossroads, looking back at the sources of a university's greatness in the past and looking ahead at the features that will characterize outstanding educational institutions in the years to come.

The proofs for the increasing importance of these research areas for the management of contemporary universities were addressed during the Third Global Forum for Responsible Management Education in Rio de Janeiro in 2012, as well as during the United Nations Conference on Sustainable Development (Rio +20). The topic of integrity in the scientific and business worlds, the responsibility of the academic environment for educating ethical leaders who will be the active, responsible citizens in multicultural world was the theme of debates conducted within both global scientific events. Moreover, the participants at the conferences elaborated a declaration called "The Future We Want: A Road Map for Management Education to 2020," which is cited below:

> "We, the representatives and stakeholders of the world's management and business schools and Higher Education Institutions (HEIs) assembled at the Third Global Forum for Responsible Management Education, 14–15 June 2012, the official platform for management-related HEIs at the 2012 United Nations Conference on Sustainable Development (Rio+20), reaffirm our commitment to the role that management and leadership education will play in society according to sustainable development—meeting the needs of the present without compromising the ability of future generations to meet their own needs."

The activity of the scientific world in the development of particular guidelines and methods for shaping academic integrity go beyond joint declarations. The meaningful contribution to the development of this research area of the process for shaping the academic integrity includes, for example, the publication by Mary C. Gentile entitled "Giving Voice to Values" or numerous books by Dr. Charles Wankel, such as "Managing Education for Global Sustainability."

This topical and much-needed book constitutes an important part of the debate on the integrity in an academic context as a sine qua non for responsible management education and responsibility of the business world. Such discussion in management education occurred partly in reaction to highly publicized corporate scandals and instances of management misconduct that have eroded public faith.

During the past decade, the educational system in general and business education in particular were immersed in a wave of criticism as being responsible for moral ignorance of the business world and for the failure to inculcate in students the standards of good conduct.[1] Current thought even suggests that the educational systems have actually weakened the moral character of students. Critics of today's educational system (and business education particularly) more frequently regard not only the system of higher education but also the university as an institution. With alarming frequency, episodes of unethical conduct come from behind university walls, such as cases of plagiarism, master theses written on request, or the unreliability of conducted research, cheating, and academic dishonesty (such as fabricating or falsifying a bibliography).

Questions also arise as to whether the academic environment truly shapes the moral attitudes of young people and creates the appropriate exemplars for them. Does the academic ethos and core values that constitute it (that are included in some declarative documents, such as mission statements, codes of ethics, and core values statements) really shape the behavior of the academic community (students, staff members, and university officials)?

Next, there emerges a clear necessity for the indication of the way to redefine academic ethos to create the fundamentals for reconstruction and development of academic integrity. The first step toward redefinition of academic ethos is to become aware of the causes of the current state. Those causes may be defined (in the easiest and most logical way) as a consequence and continuum of pathological phenomena and behaviors happening outside the university, such as the global problem of corruption or the moral crisis of business world.

However, adopting this view seems to be insufficient. Causes of the erosion of a university's core values can be found in the "marketization of education," which results in mass and commercialized academic education[2] as well as the transformation of the university from a "temple of wisdom" into a "higher school" or even into a "professional service firm."[3] Schools adopting many rules of organizational culture of a corporate world have made the same mistakes. Those mistakes of managing the university made by authorities of higher schools may be perceived as the next cause of erosion of academic ethos.

There are many more causes for the erosion of values of academic ethos, but the most important is the fact that the current crisis of academic ethos has inspired colleges and universities to be more introspective and to draw lessons from very public mistakes; in this way, they redefine their ethos in order to better educate honest and responsible future leaders in the world. This should enhance the response of the scientific world to the phenomenon of corruption through prevention within its own community. A sine qua non condition for this process is the return of higher schools to their fundamentals—to the core values that consolidate academic ethos and an academic community.

This book is an attempt to answer the question about ways of redefining and reconstructing the core values of academic ethos to create the fundamentals for academic integrity development. The author has adopted a different perspective to study the processes that have caused the crisis (erosion) of academic ethos. This is not to say that the approach to creating academic integrity, based on policies, procedures, and codes focused on preventing from dishonest, unethical behavior of academic community members is wrong or inappropriate. These actions should be supported by virtue ethics and Positive Organizational Scholarship, which promot academic integrity and human values and virtues.

Virtuous organization leads to the development of human strength and healing and cultivates extraordinary individual and organizational performance; this, in turn, leads to flourishing outcomes and the best of the human condition and fosters virtuous behaviors and emotions such as compassion, forgiveness, dignity, respectful encounters, optimism, and integrity, as well as faith, courage, justice, and wisdom.[4]

Through a virtuous approach to creating academic integrity, schools of higher education strive to develop a specific culture of integrity, promoting an environment in which members behave in responsible, honest, right ways, not because they are afraid of sanctions or because they treat work as a duty but because their "internal self" determines the right way to behave, the only way that can flourish.

It is also the best way to shape the integrity among students, future business leaders. The best way to develop the moral character of students and to encourage them to behave with integrity is by giving students the opportunity to work in an organization with integrity: the university itself.[5]

Inspired by the assumption of Positive Organizational Scholarship such as the usage of research results (case studies) in six leading academic entities from different parts of the world, this author has presented the conceptual framework of academic integrity based on positive academic ethos and has offered a new, holistic approach involving developing academic integrity based on human fulfillment and development of man's virtuous nature.

This book also provides the empirically grounded theoretical insight for redefining academic ethos as a result of the last economic crisis, which had its roots in the unethical behavior of contemporary organizations and their leaders.

Through qualitative research in universities such as DePaul University, Wright State University, Reykjavik University, IAE Business School at Austral University, Jagiellonian University, and Hamline University, the phases of the process of academic ethos management were discovered and described as well as an elaboration on the assumptions (guidelines) for the concept of academic integrity development through academic ethos management. The proposed model and recommendations from case studies in the form of concepts for academic integrity development through academic ethos management may be an inspiration and a signpost for future research on integrity development in the organizational world.

This book utilizes stimulating examples of how universities should bring their core values of academic ethos to life. Using case studies and examples from universities throughout the world, this book offers what few other title can: practical advice and guidance, explaining in detail how administrators and educators should discover, articulate, and maintain core values of academic ethos in daily academic activities and create foundations for academic integrity. The universities, administrators, and instructors committed to socially responsible management education will find many valuable tools and pragmatic strategies to effectively spread practice of integrity based on core values of academic ethos across organizational institutions.

This book also provides valuable teaching case studies and should be used by course leaders at undergraduate, Master's, and MBA levels in all business schools. I have a deep conviction that a combination of a positive academic ethos and the integrity of the academic community with positive meaning that academic communities impute to their collectives (as a result of implementing university actions as virus) with positive leadership and integrity of academic environment can install values, meaning, and purpose in university's life and results in academic flourishing demonstrated by integrity in teaching, learning, conducting research, and providing services.

Moreover, I hope that such attitudes toward academic ethos management guarantees that contemporary higher schools experience not only the greatness in these days but also in the future, as the future inevitably brings the meaningful changes in many areas of higher school performance. One cannot help but wonder: What will our population look like? Who and what will the future student be like? What and how will she/he be studying? How many students will take traditional or online forms of studies? All these circumstances undoubtedly will have an impact on organizations such as universities and may cause some crucial changes.[6]

However, the core of a higher school must be stable to survive. It must stand on the rock of reason, on what determines its identity, namely the values of its academic ethos that are reflected in outstanding lecturers, great researchers, and scholarship, outreach to an ever-increasing community and thorough preparation of the student for life.[7] The awareness of what should change in the modern, evolving world of education and what needs to remain unchangeable will be the source of its development and greatness in the future.

I hope that the conceptual framework and empirical findings pre-sented in this book demonstrate how several themes that emerge across the levels of analysis build conceptual and empirical pathways toward a deeper and broader understanding of integrity that enriches both theory and practice.

I would like to close with a quotation that I hope will inspire further research on this fascinating and inspiring topic and that will convince readers to make an effort to implement the process of academic ethos management at their universities. It is truly worthwhile.

"Do not believe in anything simply because you have heard to. Do not believe in anything simply because it is spoken and rumored by many. Do not believe in anything simply because it is found written in your religious books. Do not believe in anything merely on the authority of your teachers and elders. Do not believe in traditions because they have been handed down for many generations. But after observation and analysis, when you find that anything agrees with reason and is conducive to the good and benefit of one and all, then accept it and live up to it."

—Buddha

Notes

Introduction

1. Gregg and Stoner (2008).
2. Purdy and Lawless (2012).
3. Porras and Collins (1997).
4. Posner, Kouzes, and Schmidt (1985); Nohria and Ghoshal (1994); Bowen, Ledford, and Nathan (1991).

Chapter 1

1. Sztompka (2002), pp. 202–203.
2. Stachowicz-Stanusch (2009), p. 11.
3. I am fully aware that there are different types of institutions of higher education: "two-year junior colleges, community colleges, privately endowed colleges and universities, state colleges and universities, military academies, seminaries for religious studies, professional schools (law, medicine, nursing, etc.), and postdoctoral institutes for advanced study." (Source: Robinson and Moulton (2005)). However, following this book, there are used notions such as "higher school" and "university" as they honor the traditional name of those entities.
4. Nęcka (2003).
5. Stachowicz-Stanusch (2010), p. 44.
6. Lennick and Kiel (2006), p. 11.
7. Cragg (2000).
8. Hawawini (2005); Ivory et al. (2006a, 2006b); Lorange (2005); Mintzberg (2004); Mintzberg and Gosling (2002); Pfeffer and Fong (2004); Starkey, Hatchuel, and Tempest (2004).
9. Swanson (2004).
10. Schmidt et al. (2009).
11. Ghoshal (2005).
12. Neubaum et al. (2009); Wankel, Stachowicz-Stanusch, and Tamtana (2011).
13. Delgado-Márquez et al. (2011).
14. Interview with PhD Marek Wroński by Wysocki T. (2009).
15. About 20% of Polish academic students admitted that they would buy a master thesis. Survey by Gazeta Wyborcza; Pacewicz and Pezda (2009), p. 1.

16. The classic example of scientific unreliability or even of academic pathology is a case of polywater—the hypothetic polymerized form of water that had been considered within numerous scientific concepts until its existence was definitely excluded. Source: National Academy of Sciences, National Academy of Engineering, Institute of Medicine (1995), p. 7.

17. Between 60% and 80% of faculty members report having been faced with instances of academic dishonesty. Furthermore, between 3% and 21% of faculty members report having ignored at least one reasonably clear instance of cheating. Cited after: Whitley and Keith-Spiegel (2002), pp. 7–8.

18. http://news.bbc.co.uk/2/hi/6729537.stm

19. Kloc and Chmielewska (2004), pp. 100–105.

20. Kloc and Chmielewska (2004), pp. 15–17.

21. Kloc and Chmielewska (2004), pp. 95–99.

22. Ramaley (n.d.), p. 3.

23. Fragureiro (2011).

24. Lebow (1997), p. 111.

25. Stachowicz-Stanusch (2004), p. 119.

26. Kloc and Chmielewska (2004), p. 10.

27. Harland and Pickening (2011), pp. 27–28.

28. Carnegie Foundation for the Advancement of Teaching (1990).

29. European University Association (2003) *Forward from Berlin: The role of universities*. Available [at] http://www.eua.be/eua/jsp/en/upload/GrazDecENG .1066743764824.pdf

30. Lickona, Schaps, and Lewis (1995).

31. Berkowitz and Bier (2006).

32. The Center for Academic Integrity (1999).

33. The Center for Academic Integrity (1999), p. 4.

34. http://www.ethicsed.org

35. Turknett and Turknett (2002).

36. Paine (1997), p. vii.

37. Delors (1998), p. 85.

38. Delors (1998), p. 95.

39. Stachowicz-Stanusch (2004), p. 35.

40. Peters and Waterman (1982); Collins and Porras (1997); Geus (2002); Jacobs and MacFarlane (1990); Kotter and Heskelt (1992).

41. Anderson (1997); Blanchard and O'Connor (1997); Stachowicz-Stanusch (2007); Nohria and Ghoshal (1994).

42. Kristof (1996); Posner, Kouzes, and Schmidt (1985); Turnipseed (1996).

43. Stachowicz-Stanusch (2004), p. 38. Posner, B., Kouzes, J., & Schmidt, W. (1985).

44. Porras and Collins (2003), p. 89.

45. Senge (2003), pp. 219, 224.

46. www.distlearn.com/Vision00.PDF

47. http://www.louisville.edu/org/sun/research/project.html

48. http://www.nps.gov/training/uc/whcv.htm; cf.: HeathField, S.: *Build a Value-Based Organization*, http://humanresources.about.com/library/weekly/aa0912 00a.htm?once=true&; HeathField S.: *How to Make Values Live in Your Organization*, http://humanresources.about.com/library/weekly/aa101500a.htm

49. Stachowicz-Stanusch (2007).

50. Stachowicz-Stanusch (2004), p. 38.

51. http://www.tamu.edu/about/coreValues.html

52. http://president.msu.edu/statements/core-values/

53. http://www.ucop.edu/ucophome/coordrev/policy/Stmt_Stds_Ethics.pdf

54. http://uca.edu/mission/

55. http://www.washington.edu/discover/visionvalues

56. http://www.stjohns.edu/about/general/core

57. http://www.cauc.ca/about/vision

58. http://www.ncu.edu.jm/discover/core-values.aspx

59. http://www.eafit.edu.co/english/about-eafit/Paginas/english-version-mis sion-vission-institutional-values.aspx

60. http://www.zamorano.edu/english/explore-zamorano/about-us/our-mission/

61. http://www.pucp.edu.pe/EN/content/pagina15.php?pID=916&pIDSeccio nWeb=6&pIDReferencial=

62. http://english.pku.edu.cn

63. http://www.effatuniversity.edu.sa/index.php?option=com_content&task=vi ew&id=482&Itemid=550

64. http://www.ntpu.edu.tw/english/?page_id=40

65. http://www.sim.edu.sg/discover-sim/pages/whoweare.aspx

66. http://www.cityu.edu.hk/provost/strategic_plan/core_values.htm

67. http://www.manipal.edu/AboutUs/Pages/Mission,VisionValues.aspx

68. http://www.utm.my/about/vision-mission/

69. http://www.lums.edu.pk/page.php?xyz=%7C%40~ROU1UQW1jR2xrUF RFPQ%3E%3E

70. http://www.uonbi.ac.ke/node/11

71. http://www.covenantuniversity.edu.ng/About-Us/Our-Core-Values

72. http://www.mogadishuuniversity.com/english/index.php?page=Core-Values

73. http://www.cut.ac.za/web/mission

74. http://www.knust.edu.gh/pages/sections.php?mid=14&sid=94&id=81

75. http://www.nileu.edu.eg/Docs/Nile%20University%20Profile%20-%20 2011.pdf

76. http://www.admin.cam.ac.uk/univ/mission.html

77. http://www.maastrichtuniversity.nl/web/Faculties/SBE/Theme/AboutThe School/CoreValues1.htm

78. http://www.tut.fi/en/about-us/tuts-strategy/index.htm

79. http://www.fu-berlin.de/en/universitaet/leitbegriffe/veritas-lustitia-libertas/index.html
80. http://www.uaic.ro/uaic/bin/view/University/Prezentare
81. http://english.us.edu.pl/one-sentence
82. http://mq.edu.au/about/profile/values.html
83. http://www.otago.ac.nz/about/otago000764.pdf
84. Stachowicz-Stanusch (2009), p. 138.
85. Stachowicz-Stanusch et al. (2009), pp. 132–133.
86. Stachowicz-Stanusch (2004), p. 8.

Chapter 2

1. Collins (2000).
2. Collins and Porras (1997), p. 222.
3. Collins and Porras (1997), p. 222.
4. Stachowicz-Stanusch (2004), p. 118.
5. Stachowicz-Stanusch (2004), p. 116.
6. Kloc and Chmielecka (2004), p. 10.
7. Malphurs (1997), p. 60.
8. Collins (2000).
9. Collins (2000).
10. Hultman and Gellerman (2002).
11. Stachowicz-Stanusch (2004), pp. 130–131.
12. Lebow and Simon (1997), pp. 115–125.
13. Stachowicz-Stanusch (2004), pp. 133–136.
14. Dearlove (2002), p. 21.
15. Stachowicz-Stanusch (2004), pp. 120–122.
16. http://www.utech.edu.jm/about/overview/core_values.html
17. http://update.sxu.edu/Administrative/Mission/core_values.asp
18. http://www.ammanu.edu.jo/en/AAU/AAUHistory.aspx?p=2
19. http://www.hau.ac.kr/english/introduce/initiative1.htm
20. http://www.ferris.edu/htmls/ferrisfaq/mission.htm
21. http://www.llu.edu/central/values.page
22. http://update.sxu.edu/Administrative/Mission/core_values.asp
23. http://www.webster.edu/strategicplan/core_values.shtml
24. http://update.sxu.edu/Administrative/Mission/core_values.asp
25. http://www.ferris.edu/htmls/ferrisfaq/mission.htm
26. http://www.llu.edu/central/values.page
27. http://www.uwp.edu/departments/community.partnerships/home/mission.cfm
28. http://www.education.auburn.edu/aboutus/corevalues.html

29. http://www.humboldt.edu/president/VisionMissionCoreValues.html
30. http://www.ysu.edu/strategicplan/spc_core_values.shtml
31. http://www.mseuf.edu.ph/index.php?option=com_content&view=article &id=124&Itemid=296
32. http://www.stjohns.edu/about/general/core
33. http://www.fu-berlin.de/en/universitaet/leitbegriffe/veritas-lustitia-libertas /index.html
34. http://www.lipscomb.edu/www/Mission-Values-Vision
35. http://www.bethel.edu/about/values
36. http://www.uob.ac.tz/Mission
37. http://uca.edu/mission/
38. http://www.ucop.edu/ucophome/coordrev/policy/Stmt_Stds_Ethics.pdf
39. http://www.uic.edu/home/wowaward.shtml#core
40. http://www.hau.ac.kr/english/introduce/initiative1.htm
41. Graham et al. (1994); Roig (1994).
42. McLeod (1992), p. 12.
43. Stachowicz-Stanusch (2004), pp. 123–124.

Chapter 3

1. Stachowicz-Stanusch (2004), p. 146.
2. Whitley and Keith-Spiegel (2002), p. 150.
3. Anderson et al. (1995); Deming (1986); Freuberg (1986); Hackman and Wageman (1995).
4. Davis and Welton (1991).
5. Hammer and Organ (1978).
6. http://www.ethicsed.org/programs/integrity-works/index.htm
7. http://www.sehs.org/academic-honor-code-policy
8. http://www.saintleo.edu/Campus-Life/Code-of-Conduct
9. http://www.hillsdale.edu/academics/registrar/academic_honor.asp
10. For example, Bok (1995); Greenberg (1990).
11. Examples taken from:
    Jordan High School Academic Honor Policy,
    University of Connecticut Code of Conduct,
    Handbook of University Policies & Procedures, The University of Queensland, Australia,
    Code of Ethics of Academic Staff, The University of Waikato, New Zealand,
    Aggie Honor System Office. Rules and Procedures, Texas A&M University, United States.
12. Examples taken from:

http://www.hillsdale.edu/academics/registrar/academic_honor.asp
http://aggiehonor.tamu.edu/RulesAndProcedures/HonorSystemRules.aspx
Example of Honor Policy. The School For Ethical Education—Integrity
Works! www.ethicsed.org, p. 4.

13. Code of Ethics of Academic Staff. Available at: http://www.waikato.ac.nz/hrm
    /internal/policy/codethic1.html

14. Code of Ethics of Academic Staff. Available at: http://www.waikato.ac.nz/hrm
    /internal/policy/codethic1.html

15. *Honor System Rules.* Texas A&M University. Available at: http://www.aggie
    honor.tamu.edu/RulesAndProcedures/HonorSystemRules.aspx

16. *Code of Ethics of Academic Staff.* Available at: http://www.waikato.ac.nz/hrm
    /internal/policy/codethic1.html

17. Whitley and Keith-Spiegel (2002), p. 131.

18. www.ethicsed.org p. 4–5

19. *Example of an Honor Policy.* The School For Ethical Education—Integrity
    Works! www.ethicsed.org, p. 4–5.

20. Mainland Regional High School, Linwood, NJ—Public.
    Available   at: http://www.mainlandregional.net/school%20information
    /honor%20code.html

21. *Example of an Honor Policy.* The School For Ethical Education—Integrity
    Works! www.ethicsed.org, p. 4–5.

22. *Academic Honor Code Policy. St. Elizabeth High School.* Available at: http://
    www.sehs.org/academic-honor-code-policy

23. Ibidem.

24. http://nfaetyka.wordpress.com/2011/12/29/problemy-jakie-napotykaja
    -whistleblowerzy/

25. *The disciplinary process.* Boston College. Carroll School of Management.

26. *Reporting and Adjudication.* Texas A&M University.
    Available at: http://aggiehonor.tamu.edu/RulesAndProcedures/Reporting
    AndAdjudication.aspx

27. *Academic Honor Policy.* Florida State University, p. 4.

28. *Reporting and Adjudication.* Texas A&M University.
    Available at: http://aggiehonor.tamu.edu/RulesAndProcedures/ReportingAnd
    Adjudication.aspx

29. *Academic Honor Policy.* Florida State University, p. 5.

30. *Reporting and Adjudication.* Texas A&M University.
    Available at: http://aggiehonor.tamu.edu/RulesAndProcedures/Reporting
    AndAdjudication.aspx

31. Ibidem.

32. Stachowicz-Stanusch (2004), pp. 58–59.

33. Examples taken from:

Academic Honor Policy. Florida State University, p. 3,
Whitley and Keith-Spiegel (2002).

34. *Academic Honor Policy*. Florida State University, p. 3.
35. I Suspect a Student Cheated… Now What Do I Do? Texas A&M University. Available at: http://aggiehonor.tamu.edu/Faculty/WhatToDo.aspx
36. Examples taken from:
    Academic Honor Policy. Florida State University, p. 5,
    Whitley and Keith-Spiegel (2002). *Example of an Honor Policy*. The School For Ethi*cal Education—Integrity* Works! www.ethicsed.org, p. 9.

Chapter 4

1. Stachowicz-Stanusch (2004), p. 143.
2. Gardner (1965).
3. Millet (1978); Baldridge et al. (1977).
4. Stachowicz-Stanusch (2004), p. 144.
5. Wilcox and Libbs (1993).
6. Harvey and Lucia (1995).
7. Harvey and Lucia (1995).
8. Krueger (2000).
9. Drucker (1973); Keller (1983); Hartley (2002).
10. Morphew (2006).
11. Harvey and Lucia (1995).
12. Blanchard and O'Connor (1998).
13. Brilman (2002).
14. http://www.au.af.mil/au/awc/awcgate/ndu/strat-ldr-dm/pt4ch16.html
15. Brilman (2002).
16. http://www.corpus.cam.ac.uk/undergraduates/information-for-freshers/traditions
17. http://www.corpus.cam.ac.uk/undergraduates/information-for-freshers/traditions
18. http://www.universityaffairs.ca/tradition.aspx
19. http://ptoniana.ealumni.com/tradition.asp
20. Zbiegień-Maciąg (1999), p. 50.
21. http://www.ocm.auburn.edu/welcome/traditions.html
22. http://ptoniana.ealumni.com/tradition.asp
23. http://ptoniana.ealumni.com/clapper.asp
24. Stachowicz-Stanusch (2004).
25. http://www.lunduniversity.lu.se/o.o.i.s/24815
26. http://www.ocm.auburn.edu/welcome/traditions.html
27. http://www.agh.edu.pl/en/university/about-us/history-and-traditions.html

28. http://www.universityaffairs.ca/tradition.aspx

29. Brilman (2002).

30. http://ptoniana.ealumni.com/fredfox.asp

31. http://tulane.edu/about/traditions.cfm

32. http://www.clemson.edu/about/traditions.html

33. http://www.ttu.edu/traditions/blarney.php

34. http://tulane.edu/about/traditions.cfm

35. http://www.bucknell.edu/x499.xml

36. http://www.nyu.edu/faculty/governance-policies-and-procedures/faculty
-handbook/the-university/history-and-traditions-of-new-york-university
/university-traditions.html

37. http://www.ttu.edu/traditions/seal.php

38. http://www.ou.edu/discover/discover_home/traditions.html

39. http://www.corpus.cam.ac.uk/undergraduates/information-for-freshers/tra
ditions

40. http://www.universityaffairs.ca/tradition.aspx

41. http://www.bucknell.edu/x495.xml

42. http://www.clemson.edu/about/traditions.html

43. http://tulane.edu/about/traditions.cfm

44. http://www.bucknell.edu/x496.xml

45. http://www.gwu.edu/explore/aboutgw/traditions/sealmacecoatofarms

46. Wankel (2010).

47. http://enterprisefeatures.com/2011/05/real-world-artificial-intelligence
-has-arrived-a-chatbot-can-automate-your-customer-service-support-and
-interactions/

48. Based on data from http://chatbots.org

49. http://www.uca.edu.ar/uca/index.php/ingreso/index/es/universidad/ingre
santes/ingreso-buenos-aires/

50. http://www.sarrera.ehu.es/p259-content/es/contenidos/informacion/asistente
_virtual/es_inf/unai_v1.html

51. http://www.tueris.ugr.es:9090/elvira/

52. Stachowicz-Stanusch (2004), p. 146.

Chapter 5

1. Robbins (2004).

2. Stachowicz-Stanusch (2004), p. 149.

3. http://vision2020.tamu.edu/

4. http://nku.edu/about/plan.php

5. Robbins (2004).

6. Whitley and Keith-Spiegel (2002).

7. Sztompka (2002), p. 232.

8. Stachowicz-Stanusch (2004).

9. Robbins (2004).

10. http://dms.tamu.edu/diversityedu/dti.htm

11. Kibler (1994).

12. Keith-Spiegel and Gray-Shellberg (1997).

13. http://www.cmu.edu/academic-integrity/preventing/students.html

14. http://www.cmu.edu/academic-integrity/preventing/instructors.html

15. For example, Rosenfeld (1983).

16. Examples taken from Whitley and Keith-Spiegel (2002).

17. Rodabaugh (1996).

18. http://atmentors.tamu.edu/

19. Stephens and Wangaard (2008).

20. Harland and Pickering (2011).

21. http://www.academicintegrity.org/educational_resources/educational_mate rials/sylbs_ucfl a.php

22. http://www.academicintegrity.org/educational_resources/educational_mate rials/sylbs_gtwnu.php

23. Whitley and Keith-Spiegel (2002).

24. For example, Greenberg (1990).

25. Aiken (1991).

26. http://www.academicintegrity.org/educational_resources/educational_mate rials/sample_posters/index.php

27. Missouri State University. Academic Integrity Days 2011.

28. Donnelly (1999).

29. Academic Integrity: A Panel Discussion to Advance Strategies to Resist Cheating in High Schools. Character Education Partnership's 15th Annual forum. October 17, 2008, Washington DC. Available at: http://www.ethicsed .org/programs/integrity-works/resources.htm

30. http://www.bucknell.edu/x44217.xml

31. Schein (1985).

32. Stansbury and Barry (2007), pp. 254–258.

33. Harmon and Jacobs (n.d.), p. 130.

34. Stachowicz-Stanusch (2004), p. 122.

35. Hultman and Gellerman (2002), p. 104.

36. Malphurs (1997), pp. 83–84.

37. Donnelly (1999).

38. Sztompka (2002), p. 404.

39. Stachowicz-Stanusch (2004).

Chapter 6

1. Each case study is based on interviews with university's employees, internal documentation analysis as well as information available on the University's websites.
2. http://www.president.depaul.edu/Vision2012/Vision2012.html
3. http://www.depaul.edu/about/Pages/history-and-mission.aspx
4. Murphy (1991).
5. http://www.mission.depaul.edu/AboutUs/Documents/Final_Report.pdf
6. http:// www.diversity.depaul.edu/About/index.html
7. http://www.depaul.edu/about/Pages/history-and-mission.aspx
8. http://www.president.depaul.edu/Vision2012/Vision2012.html
9. http://www.president.depaul.edu/Downloads/VISIONtwenty12Brochure.pdf
10. It also refers to the other values of DePaul University.
11. http://www.mission.depaul.edu/AboutUs/Documents/0809ExecutiveSummary.pdf
12. http://www.mission.depaul.edu/Pages/default.aspx
13. http://www.sr.depaul.edu/catalog/catalogfiles/Current/undergraduate%20Student%20Handbook/pg53.html
14. http://www.sr.depaul.edu/catalog/catalogfiles/Current/undergraduate%20Student%20Handbook/pg18.html
15. http://www.sr.depaul.edu/catalog/catalogfiles/Current/undergraduate%20Student%20Handbook/pg106.html
16. http:// www.sr.depaul.edu/catalog/catalogfiles/Current/undergraduate%20Student%20Handbook/pg106.html
17. http://www.sr.depaul.edu/catalog/catalogfiles/Current/undergraduate%20Student%20Handbook/pg106.html
18. http://www.depaul.edu/admission-and-aid/financial-aid/for-parents/Pages/default.aspx
19. http://www.mission.depaul.edu/Ombudsperson/Pages/default.aspx
20. http://www.mission.depaul.edu/AboutUs/Documents/0809ExecutiveSummary.pdf
21. http:// www.mission.depaul.edu/AboutUs/Pages/Survey.aspx
22. http://www.mission.depaul.edu/Programs/Orientation/Pages/default.aspx
23. http://www.mission.depaul.edu/Programs/Orientation/Pages/NewEmployeeOrientation.aspx
24. http://www.mission.depaul.edu/Programs/Orientation/Pages/NewStudentOrientation.aspx
25. http://www.mission.depaul.edu/Programs/Orientation/Pages/MissionforFirstYears.aspx
26. http://www.mission.depaul.edu/Programs/awards/spiritaward/Pages/default.aspx
27. http://www.mission.depaul.edu/Programs/awards/mchugh/Pages/default.aspx

28. http://www.mission.depaul.edu/Programs/Co-SponsoredEvents/Pages/Tag Days.aspx

29. http://www.mission.depaul.edu/Programs/heritagedays/Pages/default.aspx

30. http://www.mission.depaul.edu/Programs/Tours/Pages/default.aspx

31. http://www.mission.depaul.edu/Programs/Tours/Pages/FacultyandStaff.aspx

32. http://www.mission.depaul.edu/Programs/Pages/DePaulReadsTogether.aspx

33. http://www.leadership.depaul.edu/secure/downloads/2006-2007_Annual _Report.pdf

34. http://www.mission.depaul.edu/AboutUs/Documents/Executive%20Sum mary%20-%20DMVSurvey%202003-2006.pdf

35. Each case study is based on interviews with university's employees, internal doc-umentation analysis as well as information available on University's websites.

36. https://www.wright.edu/nca/pdfs/nca_vol1.pdf

37. http://www.wright.edu/administration/vision/index.html

38. https://www.wright.edu/nca/pdfs/nca_vol1.pdf

39. http://www.wright.edu/administration/vision/student.html

40. http://www.wright.edu/administration/vision/exsum.html

41. http://www.wright.edu/administration/vision/fac.html

42. http://www.wright.edu/administration/vision/facility.html

43. http://www.wright.edu/administration/vision/fund.html

44. https://www.wright.edu/nca/pdfs/nca_vol1.pdf

45. http://www.wright.edu/foundational-principles/vision-statement

46. https://www.wright.edu/nca/pdfs/nca_vol1.pdf

47. http://www.wright.edu/foundational-principles/guiding-principles

48. http://www.wright.edu/foundational-principles/guiding-principles

49. http://www.wright.edu/foundational-principles/guiding-principles

50. http://www.wright.edu/foundational-principles/guiding-principles

51. http://www.wright.edu/foundational-principles/guiding-principles

52. https://www.wright.edu/nca/pdfs/nca_vol1.pdf

53. http://www.wright.edu/business/about/mission.html

54. http://www.wright.edu/business/about/mission.html

55. http://www.wright.edu/business/about/mission.html

56. https://www.wright.edu/nca/pdfs/nca_vol1.pdf

57. https://www.wright.edu/nca/pdfs/nca_vol1.pdf

58. https://www.wright.edu/nca/pdfs/nca_vol1.pdf

59. https://www.wright.edu/nca/pdfs/nca_vol1.pdf

60. https://www.wright.edu/nca/pdfs/nca_vol1.pdf

61. http://www.wright.edu/news_events/cultureresources.htm/

62. https://www.wright.edu/nca/pdfs/nca_vol1.pdf

63. https://www.wright.edu/nca/pdfs/nca_vol1.pdf

64. http://www.med.wright.edu/web

65. https://www.wright.edu/nca/pdfs/nca_vol1.pdf

66. http://www.wright.edu/sustainability/
67. http://www.wright.edu/sustainability/transportation.html
68. http://www.wright.edu/administration/physicalplant/recycling/
69. http://www.wright.edu/sustainability/news/
70. http://www.wright.edu/sustainability/news/
71. http://www.wright.edu/sustainability/news/

Chapter 7

1. This case is based on the materials from the year 2007 up to 2009 and takes into account the events and progress at that time. Each case study is based on interviews with University's employees, internal documentation analysis as well as information available on University's websites.
2. The origins of Reykjavík University lie in Computer School of the Commercial College of Iceland (Tölvuskóli Verzlunarskóla Íslands), founded in January 1998. On the establishment of the Reykjavík School of Business (Viðskiptaháskólinn í Reykjavík) in Autumn 1998, the Commercial College of Iceland Computer School became one of two Schools of the new institution. In January 2000 the name was changed to Reykjavík University (Háskólinn í Reykjavík).
3. http://www.menntamalaraduneyti.is/media/MRN-pdf/Sjalfsmatsskyrsla-lagadeild-HR-2010-ENSKA-AGUST-2010.pdf
4. Bjarnadóttir (2005).
5. Deliotte/Braxton M&A Survey.
6. http://www.menntamalaraduneyti.is/media/MRN-pdf/Sjalfsmatsskyrsla-lagadeild-HR-2010-ENSKA-AGUST-2010.pdf
7. http://www.menntamalaraduneyti.is/media/MRN-pdf/Sjalfsmatsskyrsla-lagadeild-HR-2010-ENSKA-AGUST-2010.pdf
8. Strategy of RU (íslenska). Following workshops with staff in the spring of 2007.
9. 2008 workshops handout.
10. http://www.menntamalaraduneyti.is/media/MRN-pdf/Sjalfsmatsskyrsla-lagadeild-HR-2010-ENSKA-AGUST-2010.pdf
11. http://www.menntamalaraduneyti.is/media/MRN-pdf/Sjalfsmatsskyrsla-lagadeild-HR-2010-ENSKA-AGUST-2010.pdf
12. http://www.en.ru.is/media/hr/skjol/Gaedahandbok_EN_Web.pdf
13. http://www.en.ru.is/media/hr/skjol/Gaedahandbok_EN_Web.pdf
14. http://www.en.ru.is/media/hr/skjol/Gaedahandbok_EN_Web.pdf
15. http://www.en.ru.is/media/hr/skjol/Gaedahandbok_EN_Web.pdf
16. http://www.en.ru.is/media/hr/skjol/Gaedahandbok_EN_Web.pdf
17. http://www.en.ru.is/media/hr/skjol/Gaedahandbok_EN_Web.pdf
18. http://www.en.ru.is/media/hr/skjol/Gaedahandbok_EN_Web.pdf
19. http://www.en.ru.is/media/hr/skjol/Gaedahandbok_EN_Web.pdf

20. http://www.menntamalaraduneyti.is/media/MRN-pdf/Sjalfsmatsskyrsla
    -lagadeild-HR-2010-ENSKA-AGUST-2010.pdf
21. To Do Top 10 List. Reykjavik University.
22. http://www.menntamalaraduneyti.is/media/MRN-pdf/Sjalfsmatsskyrsla
    -lagadeild-HR-2010-ENSKA-AGUST-2010.pdf
23. http://www.menntamalaraduneyti.is/media/MRN-pdf/Sjalfsmatsskyrsla
    -lagadeild-HR-2010-ENSKA-AGUST-2010.pdf
24. Strategy of RU (íslenska). Following workshops with staff in the spring of 2007.
25. http://www.en.ru.is/media/hr/skjol/RU_Internal_analysis.pdf
26. http://www.en.ru.is/the-university/hr-strategy-in-research/
27. http://www.en.ru.is/media/hr/skjol/RU_Internal_analysis.pdf.
28. Each case study is based on interviews with University's employees, internal
    documentation analysis as well as information available on University's websites.
29. http://www.iae.edu.ar/SiteCollectionDocuments/20090114_Folleto_insti
    tucional.pdf
30. IAE Business School PRME Report 2012.
31. http://www.iae.edu.ar/SiteCollectionDocuments/AnnualReportResumen.pdf
32. http://www.english.iae.edu.ar/IAEhoy/Escuela/Pages/mision.aspx
33. For complete listing of publications, http://www.english.iae.edu.ar/PI
    /Areas/Pages/ESE.aspx
34. IAE Business School PRME Report 2012.
35. IAE Business School PRME Report 2012.
36. IAE Business School PRME Report 2012 (Introduction from Marcelo
    Paladino, Dean, IAE Business School).
37. http://www.english.iae.edu.ar/IAEhoy/Internacional/Pages/PRME.aspx
38. IAE Business School PRME Report 2012.
39. IAE Business School PRME Report 2012.
40. IAE Business School PRME Report 2012.
41. IAE Business School PRME Report 2012.
42. This goal was achieved and results even overrated expectations as the depart-
    ment managed to build 38 clubs, organized 23 meetings outside Buenos
    Aires in other Argentine Provinces and 33 meetings abroad.
43. IAE Business School PRME Report 2012.
44. http://www.english.iae.edu.ar/PI/centros/Pages/Home.aspx
45. http://www.english.iae.edu.ar/PI/centros/Governance/Pages/Mision.aspx

Chapter 8

1. Each case study is based on interviews with University's employees, internal
   documentation analysis as well as information available on University's websites.
2. http://www.uj.edu.pl/c/document_library/get_file?uuid=bbad4dcc-fac0-46
   59-9aab-4e7ed057f314&groupId=10172

3. http://www.uj.edu.pl/c/document_library/get_file?uuid=bbad4dcc-fac0-46
59-9aab-4e7ed057f314&groupId=10172
4. http://www.uj.edu.pl/uniwersytet/wartosci-akademickie
5. http://www.uj.edu.pl/c/document_library/get_file?uuid=d63b4be0-5eee
-4d94-bd32-3b1ccef396f6&groupId=10172
6. http://www.uj.edu.pl/uniwersytet/wartosci-akademickie
7. http://www.uj.edu.pl/c/document_library/get_file?uuid=d63b4be0-5eee
-4d94-bd32-3b1ccef396f6&groupId=10172
8. http://www.uj.edu.pl/uniwersytet/wartosci-akademickie
9. http://www.krasp.org.pl/pl/kdp/kodeks_dobre_praktyki
10. http://www.uj.edu.pl/c/document_library/get_file?uuid=bbad4dcc-fac0-46
59-9aab-4e7ed057f314&groupId=10172
11. http://www.uj.edu.pl/c/document_library/get_file?uuid=bbad4dcc-fac0-46
59-9aab-4e7ed057f314&groupId=10172
12. Prokop (2007), pp. 20–22.
13. http://www.uj.edu.pl/documents/10172/1315002/Newsletter42.pdf
14. http://www.maius.uj.edu.pl/history.en.html
15. http://www.uj.edu.pl/uniwersytet/muzea/
16. http://www.uj.edu.pl/c/document_library/get_file?uuid=bbad4dcc-fac0-46
59-9aab-4e7ed057f314&groupId=10172
17. http://www.uj.edu.pl/uniwersytet/nagrody-i-wyroznienia/doktorzy-hc
18. http://www.uj.edu.pl/uniwersytet/nagrody-i-wyroznienia/doktorzy-hc
19. http://www.uj.edu.pl/uniwersytet/nagrody-i-wyroznienia/pro-arte-docendi
20. http://www.uj.edu.pl/uniwersytet/nagrody-i-wyroznienia/merentibus
21. http://www.uj.edu.pl/uniwersytet/aktualnosci/video-foto/-/journal_content
/56_INSTANCE_7Cwe/10172/6019177
22. Each case study is based on interviews with University's employees, internal documentation analysis as well as information available on University's websites.
23. http://www.hamline.edu/about/history.html
24. Creating Pathways to distinction. Hamline University Strategic Plan 2011. Update.
25. Creating Pathways to distinction. Hamline University Strategic Plan 2011. Update.
26. http://www.hamline.edu/about/mission.html
27. http://www.hamline.edu/about/mission.html
28. Hamline's Strategic Plan. Pathways 20 2013–2017
29. http://www.hamline.edu/Policy.aspx?id=2147490770
30. http://www.hamline.edu/Policy.aspx?id=2147488077
31. http://www.hamline.edu/Policy.aspx?id=2147488077
32. http://www.hamline.edu/policies/

33. http://www.hamline.edu/students/first-year/piper-preview.html
34. http://www.hamline.edu/students/first-year/piper-passages.html
35. http://www.hamline.edu/parents/
36. http://www.hamline.edu/students/veterans/
37. http://www.hamline.edu/students/veterans/history.html
38. http://sites.hamline.edu/150/4alumni_legacy/4alumni_legacy.html
39. http://www.hamline.edu/offices/ombudsman/
40. http://www.hamline.edu/offices/ombudsman/standards-of-practice.html
41. http://www.hamline.edu/offices/diversity/director.html
42. http://www.hamline.edu/offices/diversity/definition.html
43. http://www.hamline.edu/offices/diversity/
44. http://www.hamline.edu/offices/diversity/
45. http://www.hamline.edu/offices/diversity/
46. http://www.hamline.edu/offices/diversity/director.html
47. http://www.hamline.edu/offices/diversity/director.html
48. http://www.hamline.edu/offices/diversity/staff/
49. http://www.hamline.edu/offices/diversity/rgb.html
50. http://www.hamline.edu/offices/misa/ncore.html
51. http://www.hamline.edu/offices/misa/ncore.html
52. http://www.hamline.edu/offices/diversity/student-awards.html
53. http://www.hamline.edu/Content.aspx?id=4294969060
54. http://sites.hamline.edu/150/6historical_hamline/chist_seal.html
55. http://www.hamline.edu/offices/brand-experience/traditions.html
56. http://www.hamline.edu/offices/brand-experience/traditions.html

Chapter 10

1. Stachowicz-Stanusch (2004).
2. Stachowicz-Stanusch (2008).
3. Stachowicz-Stanusch (2008).
4. Stachowicz-Stanusch (2007, 2010).
5. Vella and Melewar (2008).
6. Lennick and Kiel (2005), p. 214.
7. Stachowicz-Stanusch (2010).
8. Wankel and Stachowicz-Stanusch (2011).
9. Ghoshal (2005).
10. Selznick (1957).
11. Dutton and Glynn (2008).
12. Cooperrider and Srivastva (1987).
13. Jahoda (1958).
14. Maslow (1968).

15. Stachowicz-Stanusch (2010).
16. Baumeister and Exline (1999).
17. Cameron (2003).
18. Seligman and Csikszentmihalyi (2000), p. 5.
19. Cameron, Dutton and Quinn (2003); Manz et al. (2001, 2003, 2004, 2006).
20. Stachowicz-Stanusch (2010).
21. Stachowicz-Stanusch (2004, 2010).
22. Bakan (2004).
23. Weinberger (2010).
24. Audebrand and Burton (2011).
25. Covey (1991); Kouzes and Posner (2007).
26. Heaton, Travis, and Subramaniam (2011).
27. Delios (2010); Purdy and Lawless (2012).
28. Stachowicz-Stanusch and Wankel (2011).
29. Purdy and Lawless (2012).
30. Waddock (2005), p. 147.
31. Wankel and Stachowicz-Stanusch (2011).
32. Wankel and Malleck (2011).
33. For example, Berger et al. (2007); Maak and Pless (2006); Rodriguez et al. (2006).
34. Pless, Maak, and Stahl (2010).
35. Waddock (2005), p. 145.
36. Audebrand and Burton (2012).
37. Palmer (1998).
38. Pavlowich (2012).
39. Oxford English Dictionary (1989).
40. Stachowicz-Stanusch and Wankel (2011).
41. Kaiser and Hogan (2010).
42. Purdy and Lawless (2012).
43. Baltimore (1999), p. 260.
44. Sawyer, Johnson, and Holub (2009); Stachowicz-Stanusch and Wankel (2011).
45. Audenbrand and Burton (2012).
46. Purdy and Lawless (2012).
47. Rand (1964); Peikoff (1991).
48. Carson (1995), p. 6.
49. Solomon (1992).
50. Solomon (1992), p. 174.
51. Audebrand and Burton (2012).
52. Drucker (1992), p. 115; Heaton, Travis, and Submaniam (2011).
53. Stachowicz-Stanusch (2010), p. 44.
54. Kohlberg (1969).

55. Davis and Welton (1991). cf. Purdy and Lawless (2012).

56. Pavlovich (2011).

57. Purdy and Lawless (2012).

58. Purdy and Lawless (2011).

59. Audebrand and Burton (2012).

60. Influence cognitive, emotional, and behavioral development, thereby increasing the likelihood of future integrity on the part of students. Source: Purdy and Lawless (2012).

61. Purdy and Lawless (2011).

62. LeClair, Ferrell, and Fraedrich (1998); Stachowicz-Stanusch and Wankel (2011).

63. Paine (1997), p. vii.

64. Steer and Gentle (2007).

65. Turner and Beemsterboer (2003), p. 1122.

66. Center for Academic Integrity (1999); cf. Randall, Bender, and Montgomery (2007).

67. Hall and Kuh (1998), p. 3; Stachowicz-Stanusch and Wankel (2011).

68. Sauser and Sims (2011).

69. Rhee, Dutton, and Bagozzi (2006), p. 3.

70. Rhee, Dutton, and Bagozzi (2006), p. 3.

71. Cropanzano et al. (2001); Worline, Wrzesniewski, and Rafaeli (2002).

72. Rhee et al. (2006); Houghton, Gabel, and Williams (2008).

73. Rhee et al. (2006).

74. Committee on Assessing Integrity in Research Environments, National Research Council, Institute of Medicine (2002). Integrity in Scientific Research: Creating an Environment that Promotes Responsible Conduct. Available at: http://www.nap.edu/catalog.php?record_id=10430

75. Committee on Assessing Integrity in Research Environments, National Research Council, Institute of Medicine (2002). Integrity in Scientific Research: Creating an Environment that Promotes Responsible Conduct. Available at: http://www.nap.edu/catalog.php?record_id=10430

76. On-line source.

References

Aiken, I. R. (1991). Detecting, understanding, and controlling for cheating on tests. *Research in Higher Education 32*, 725–736.

Anderson, C. (1997). Values-based management. *Academy of Management Executive 9*(4), 25–46.

Anderson, J., Rungtusanatham, M., Schroeder, R., & Devaraj, S. (1995). A path analytic model of a theory of quality management underlying the Deming management method: Preliminary empirical findings. *Decision Sciences 26*, 637–658.

Audebrand, L. K., & Burton, J. W. (2011). Chapter 21: Nurturing integrity in management education with the development of an alternative web of metaphors. In: Ch. Wankel, & A. Stachowicz-Stanusch (Eds.), *Handbook of research on teaching ethics in business and management education* (pp. 359–373). US: IGI Global.

Bakan, J. (2004). *The corporation: The pathological pursuit of profit and power.* New York, NY: Free Press.

Baldridge, J. V., Curtis, D. V., Ecker, G. P., & Riley, G. L. (1977). Alternative models of governance in higher education. In G. L. Riley, & J. V. Baldridge (Eds.), *Governing academic organizations* (pp. 2–25). Berkeley, CA: McCutchan.

Baltimore, J.P.D. (1999). *Public integrity.* London: John Hopkins University Press.

Barnard, C. (1958). *The functions of the executive.* Cambridge, MA: Harvard University Press.

Berger, L. E., Cunningham, P. H., & Drumwright, M. E. (2007). Mainstreaming corporate social responsibility. *California Management Review 49*, 132–157.

Berkowitz, M., & Bier, M. (2006). *What works in character education.* Washington, DC: Character Education Partnership. Available at: www.characterandcitizenship.org

Blanchard, K., & O'Connor, M. (1997). *Managing by values.* San Francisco, CA: Berret-Koehler.

Blanchard, K., & O'Connor, M. (1998). *Zarządzanie Poprzez Wartości.* Warszawa: Studio Emka.

Bok S. (1995). *Common values.* Columbia, SC: University of Missouri Press.

Bowen D.E., Ledford G.E., Nathan B.R. (1991). Hiring for the organization not for the job. *Academy of Management Executive 5*, 35–51.

Brilman, J. (2002). *Nowoczesne koncepcje i metody zarządzania.* Warszawa: PWE.

Cameron, K., Dutton, J., & Quinn, R. E. (2003). *Positive organizational scholarship: Foundations of a new discipline*. San Francisco, CA: Berret-Koehler.

Carson, A. S. (1995). The nature of a moral business person. *Review of Business 17*(2), 16–22.

Center for Academic Integrity (1999). *The fundamental values of academic integrity: Honesty, trust, respect, fairness, responsibility*. Durham, NC: Duke University.

Collins, J. (2000). *Aligning action and values. The forum*.

Available at: http://www.jimcollins.com/article_topics/articles/aligning-action.html

Collins, J., & Porras, J. (1997). *Built to last. Successful habits of visionary companies*. New York, NY: Harper-Collins Publishers.

Collins, J., & Porras, J. (2003). *Wizjonerskie organizacje. Praktyki zarządzania najlepszych firm*. Warszawa: Jacek Santorski—Wydawnictwa Biznesowe.

Cooperrider, D. L., & Srivastva, S. (1987). Appreciative inquiry in organizational Life. *Research in Organizational Change and Development 1*, 128–169.

Covey, S. (1991). *Principle-centered leadership*. New York, NY: Simon & Schuster.

Cropanzano, R., Byrne, Z. S., Bobocel, D. R., & Rupp, D. E. (2001). Moral virtues, fairness heuristics, social entities, and other denizens of organizational justice. *Journal of Vocational Behavior 58*, 164–209.

Davis, J. R., & Welton, R. E. (1991). Professional ethics: Business students' perceptions. *Journal of Business Ethics 10*(6), 451–463.

Davis, J. R., & Welton, R. E. (1995). Professional ethics: Business students' perceptions. *Journal of Business Ethics 10*(6), 451–463. Cited after: Purdy J. M., & Lawless J. (2011). Chapter 25: Building a culture of integrity. In: Ch. Wankel, & A. Stachowicz-Stanusch (Eds.), *Handbook of research on teaching ethics in business and management education*. US: IGI Global.

Dearlove, D., & Coomber, S. (2002). *Corporate values*. Louisville, KY: BrownHerron Publishing.

Delgado-Márquez, B. L., Aragón-Correa, J. A., & Hurtado-Torres, N. E. (2011). Fostering integrity in business education: An analysis of academic administrators' perceptions at Spanish business schools. In Ch. Wankel, & A. Stachowicz-Stanusch (Eds.), *Management education for integrity: Ethically educating tomorrow's business leaders* (pp. 89–104). US: Emerald Group Publishing Limited.

Delios, A. (2010). How can organizations be competitive but dare to care? *Academy of Management Perspectives 24*(3), 25–36.

Delors J. (Ed.) (1998). *Edukacja—jest w niej ukryty skarb*. Warszawa: UNESCO.

Deming W. E. (1986). *Out of crisis*. Cambridge, MA: Center for Advanced Engineering Study, Massachusetts Institute of Technology.

Donnelly, C. (1999). Differences in schools: A question of ethos? Paper presented at the British Educational Research Association Annual Conference.

University of Sussex in Brighton, September 2–5 1999. Available at: http:// www.leeds.ac.uk/educol/documents/00001274.htm

Drucker, P. (1973). *Management: Tasks, responsibilities, practices*. New York, NY: Harper & Row.

Drucker, P. (1992). *Managing for the future*. New York, NY: Penguin Group.

Dutton, J. E., & Glynn, M. A. (2008). Positive organizational scholarship. In J. Barling, & C. L. Cooper (Eds.), *Handbook of organizational behavior*, vol. 1 (pp. 693–712).

European University Association (2003) *Forward from Berlin: The role of universities.*

Available [at] http://www.eua.be/eua/jsp/en/upload/GrazDecENG.1066743764824. pdf

Feuberg D. (1986). *The corporate conscience: money, power, and responsible business*. New York, NY: American Management Association.

Fragueiro, F., & Thomas, H. (2011). *Strategic leadership in the business school: Keeping one step ahead*. UK: Cambridge University Press.

Gardner, J. W. (1965). The Antileadership Vaccine. Annual report. New York, NY: Carnegie Corp. Cited after: Wilcox, J. R., & Libbs, S. (1993). Ethical leadership. Successfully communicating institutional values. *NACUBO Business Officer*, pp. 36–41.

Geus, A. (2002). *The living company. Habits for survival in a turbulent business environment*. Boston, MA: Harvard Business School Press.

Ghoshal, S. (2005). Bad management theories are destroying good management practices. *Academy of Management Learning & Education 4*(1), 75–91.

Graham, M. A., Monday, J., O'Brien, K., & Steffen, S. (1994). Cheating at small colleges: An examination of student and faculty attitudes and behaviors. *Journal of College Student Development 35*, 255–260.

Greenberg, J. (1990). Employee theft as a reaction to underpayment inequity: The hidden costs of pay cuts. *Journal of Applied Psychology 75*, 561–568.

Gregg, S., & Stoner, J. R. Jr. (Eds.) (2008). *Rethinking business management: Examining the foundations of business education* Princeton, NJ: Witherspoon Institute.

Hackman J. R., & Wageman R. (1995). Total quality management: Empirical, conceptual, and practical issues. *Administrative Science Quarterly 40*, 309–342.

Hall, T. L., & Kuh, G. D. (1998) Honor among students: Academic integrity and honor codes at state-assisted universities. *National Association of Student Personnel Administrators Journal 36*(1), 2–18.

Hammer W. C., & Organ D. W. (1978). *Organizational behavior: An applied psychological approach*. Dallas, TX: Business Publications.

Harland, T., & Pickering, N. (2011). *Values in higher education teaching*. London, New York, NY: Routledge Taylor & Francis Group.

Harmon, F. G., & Jacobs, G. (n.d.). *The vital difference. Unleashing the powers of sustained corporate success.* Available at: http://mirainternational.com/books/difference/CHAP12.htm

Hartley, M. (2002). *A call to purpose: Mission-centered change at three liberal arts colleges.* New York, NY: RoutledgeFalmer.

Harvey, E., & Lucia A. (1995). *Walk the talk. And get the results you want.* Dallas, TX: Performance Publishing.

Hawawini, G. (2005). The future of business schools. *Journal of Management Development 24*(1), 770–783.

Heaton, D. P., Travis, F., & Subramaniam, R. (2011). Chapter 4: A consciousness-based approach to management education for integrity. In Ch. Wankel, & A. Stachowicz-Stanusch (Eds.), *Handbook of research on teaching ethics in business and management education* (pp. 68–82). US: IGI Global.

Houghton, S. M., Gabel, J. T., & Williams, D. W. (2008). Connecting the two faces of CSR: Does employee volunteerism improve compliance? *Journal of Business Ethics 87*, 71–89.

Hultman, K., & Gellerman, B. (2002). *Balancing individual and organizational values. Walking the tightrope to success.* San Francisco, CA: Jossey-Bass/Pfeiffer.

Ivory, C., Miskell, P., Shipton, H., White, A., Moeslein, K., & Neely, A. (2006a). *UK business schools: Historical contexts and future scenarios.* London: Advanced Institute of Management.

Ivory, C., Miskell, P., Shipton, H., White, A., Moeslein, K., & Neely, A. (2006b). *UK business schools: Historical contexts and future scenarios.* London: Advanced Institute of Management.

Jacobs, G., & MacFarlane, R. (1990). *The Vital Corporation. How American businesses large and small double profits in two years or less.* Englewood Cliffs, NJ: Prentice-Hall.

Jahoda, M. (1958). *Current concepts of positive mental health.* New York, NY: Basic Books.

Kaiser, R. B., & Hogan, R. (2010). How to (and how not to) assess the integrity of managers. *Consulting Psychology 62*(4), 216–234.

Keith-Spiegel, P., & Gray-Shellberg, L. (1997). 1997–1998 honor roll for character-building colleges. Radnor, PA: Author. Cited after: Whitley B. E., Jr., & Keith-Spiegel P. (2002). *Academic dishonesty. An educator's guide.* Mahwah, NJ: Lawrence Erlbaum Associates.

Keller, G. (1983). *Academic strategy: The management revolution in American higher education.* Baltimore, MD: Johns Hopkins University Press.

Kibler, W. L. (1994). Addressing academic dishonesty: What are institutions of higher education doing and not doing? *NASPA Journal 30*, 8–18.

Kloc, K. & Chmielewska, E. (Eds.) (2004). Dobre obyczaje w kształceniu akademickim. *Conference Proceedings.* 20-21.05.2004 Krakow. Warszawa.

Kohlberg, L. (1969). Stage and sequence: The cognitive-developmental approach to socialization. In D. A. Goslin (Ed.) *Handbook of socialization theory and research* (pp. 347–480). Chicago, IL: Rand McNally.

Kotter, J. P., & Heskelt, J. (1992). *Corporate culture and performance.* New York, NY: The Free Press.

Kouzes, J. M., & Posner, B. Z. (2007). *The leadership challenge* (4th ed.). San Francisco, CA: Jossey-Bass.

Kristof, A. (1996). Person—organization fit: An integrative review of its conceptualizations, measurement and implications. *Personnel Psychology 49,* 1–49.

Krueger Ch. (2000). Elements of High Performing People Process Type Cultures. Available at: http://www.ppc.uwstout.edu/high_performing.html

Lebow, R., & Simon, W. (1997). *Lasting change. The shared values process that makes companies great.* New York, NY: John Wiley & Sons.

LeClair, D. C., Ferrell, O. C., & Fraedrich, J. P. (1998). *Integrity management: A guide to managing legal and ethical issues in the workplace.* Tampa, FL: University of Tampa Press.

Lennick, D., & Kiel, F. (2005). *Moral intelligence: Enhancing business performance & leadership success.* Upper Saddle River, NJ: Wharton School Publishing. Cited after: Stachowicz-Stanusch, A. (Ed.) (2010). *Corruption immunity based on positive organizational scholarship towards theoretical framework.* In A. Stachowicz-Stanusch (Ed.), Organizational Immunity to Corruption. Building Theoretical and Research Foundations (pp. 35–51).

Lennick, D., & Kiel, F. (2006). In the balance capitalism and ethics. Available at: http://www.moralcompass.com/MNCPA_Feature_April_06.pdf.

Lickona, T., Schaps, E., & Lewis, C. (1995). *Eleven principles of effective character education.* Washington, DC: Character Education Partnership. Available at: www.character.org

Lorange, P. (2005). Strategy means choice: Also for today's business school. *Journal of Management Development 24*(9), 783–791.

Maak, T., & Pless, N. M. (2006). Responsible leadership in a stakeholder society. A relational perspective. *Journal of Business Ethics 66,* 99–115.

Malphurs A. (1997). *Values-driven leadership. Discovering and developing your core values for ministry.* Grand Rapids, MI: BakerBooks. Cited after: Stachowicz-Stanusch A. (2004). *Zarządzanie Poprzez Wartości. Perspektywa rozwoju współczesnego przedsiębiorstwa.* Gliwice: Wydawnictwo Politechniki Śląskiej.

Manz, C. C., Manz, K. P., & Marx, R. D. (2003). *The search for wisdom at work.* Leadmotiv, Stockholm: Stockholm School of Economics, 2, pp. 42–53.

Manz, C., Manz, K., Marx, R., & Neck, C. (2001). *The wisdom of Solomon at work: Ancient virtues for living and leading today.* San Francisco, CA: Berret-Koehler.

Manz, C.C., Manz, K.P., Marx, R.D., & Neck, C.P. (2004). Spiritual beliefs and scholarship: A journey with the wisdom of Solomon. *Management Communication Quarterly 17*, 611–620.

Manz, K. P., Marx, R. D., Neal, J., & Manz, C. C. (2006). The language of virtues: Toward an inclusive approach for integrating spirituality in management education. *Journal of Management Spirituality and Religion 3*, 104–122.

Maslow, A. (1968). *Towards a psychology of being* (2nd edition) New York, NY: Van Nostrand.

McLeod, S. H. (1992). Responding to plagiarism: The role of the WPA. *WPA: Writing Program Administration 15*(3), 7–16.

Meyer, J. W., & Rowan, B. R. (1977). Institutionalized organizations: Formal structure as myth and ceremony. *American Journal of Sociology 83*(2), 340–363.

Millet, J. D. (1978). *New structures of campus power: Success and failures of emerging forms of institutional governance.* San Francisco, CA: Jossey-Bass.

Mintzberg, H. (2004). Managers not MBAs: *A hard look at the soft practice of managing and management development.* London: Pearson Education.

Mintzberg, H., Gosling, J. (2002). Educating managers beyond borders. *Academy of Management Learning and Education 1*(1), 64–76.

Morphew, C. C. (2006). Mission statements: A thematic analysis of rhetoric across institutional type. *The Journal of Higher Education 77*(3), 456–471.

Murphy, J. P. (1991). *Visions and values in Catholic higher education.* Kansas City, MO: Sheed & Ward, p. 148.

N/A (1990). *Campus life—In search of community.* Princeton, NJ: Carnegie Foundation for the Advancement of Teaching.

National Academy of Sciences, National Academy of Engineering, Institute of Medicine (1995): On Being a Scientist: Responsible Conduct in Research, Second Edition. US.

Nęcka, E. (2003). *Inteligencja. Geneza, Struktura. Funkcje.* Gdańsk: Gdańskie Wydawnictwo Psychologiczne.

Neubaum, D. O., Pagell, M., Drexler, J. A. Jr, McKee-Ryan, F. M. & Larson, E. (2009). Business education and its relationship to student personal moral philosophies and attitudes toward profits: An empirical response to critics. *Academy of Management Learning and Education 8*(1), 9–24.

Nohria N., & Ghoshal S. (1994). Differentiated fit and shared values: Alternatives for managing headquarters-subsidiary relations. *Strategic Management Journal 15*(6), 491–502.

Pacewicz P., & Pezda A. (2009). Wyższa szkoła zachwytu, *Gazeta Wyborcza*, October 19, 2009.

Paine, L. S. (1997). Cases in leadership, ethics and organizational integrity. A strategic perspective. Chicago, IL: Irwin. Cited after: Rendtorff, J. D.

(2011). Business ethics, strategy and organizational integrity: The importance of integrity as a basic principle of business ethics that contributes to better economic performance. In: Ch. Wankel, A. & Stachowicz-Stanusch (Eds.), *Handbook of research on teaching ethics in business and management education* (pp. 276–290). US: IGI-Global.

Palmer, P. (1998). *The courage to teach.* San Francisco, CA: Jossey-Bass.

Pavlovich, K. (2011). Chapter 6: Management education for developing spiritual integrity. In Ch. Wankel, & A. Stachowicz-Stanusch (Eds.), *Handbook of research on teaching ethics in business and management education* (pp. 103–116). US: IGI-Global.

Peikoff, L. (1991). *Objectivism: The philosophy of Ayn Rand.* New York, NY: Meridian.

Peters, T. J., & Waterman, R. H. Jr. (1982). *In search of excellence: Lessons from America's best-run companies.* New York, NY: Harper and Row.

Pfeffer, J., & Fong, C.T. (2004). The business school business: Some lessons from the US experience. *Journal of Management Studies 41*(8), 1501–1520.

Pless, N., Maak, T, & Stahl, G. (2010). Developing Responsible Global Leader Through Integrated Service Learning–Program Ulysses at PWC. Paper presented on Academy of Management, Montreal 2010.

Posner, B., Kouzes, J., & Schmidt, W. (1985). Shared values make a difference: An empirical test of corporate culture. *Resource Management 24*(3), 293–309.

Purdy, J. M., & Lawless, J. (2011). Chapter 25: Building a Culture of Integrity. In: Ch. Wankel, & A. Stachowicz-Stanusch (Eds.), *Handbook of research on teaching ethics in business and management education* (pp. 429–442). US: IGI Global.

Purdy, J. M., & Lawless, J. (2012). Learning about governance through nonprofit board service. *Journal of Management Education 36*(1), 33–65.

Ramaley J. A. (n.d.). From 'My work' to 'Our Work': Realigning Faculty Work with College and University Purposes. Paper presented at Third AAHE Conference on Faculty Roles and Resources.

Rand, A. (1964). *The virtue of selfishness: A new concept of egoism.* New York, NY: Signet.

Randall, K., Bender, D. G., & Montgomery, D. M. (2007). Determining the opinions of health sciences students and faculty regarding academic integrity. *International Journal for Educational Integrity 3*(2), 27–40.

Rhee, S. Y., Dutton, J. E., & Bagozzi, R. P. (2006). Making sense of organizational actions in response to tragedy: Virtue frames, organizational identification and organizational attachment. *Journal of Management, Spirituality and Religion 3*, 34–59.

Robbins, S. P. (2004). *Zachowania w organizacji.* Warszawa: PWE.

Robinson G. M., & Moulton J. (2005). *Ethical problems in higher education.* US: iUniverse, Inc.

Rodabaugh, R. C. (1996). Institutional commitment to fairness in college teaching. In L. Fisch (Ed.), *Ethical dimensions of college and university teaching* (pp. 37–45). San Francisco, CA: Jossey-Bass. Cited after: Whitley B. E., Jr., and Keith-Spiegel P. (2002). *Academic dishonesty. An educator's guide.* Mahwah, NJ: Lawrence Erlbaum Associates.

Rodriguez, P., Siegel, D. S., Hillman, A., & Eden, L. (2006). Three lenses on the multinational enterprise: Politics, corruption, and corporate social responsibility. *Journal of International Business Studies 37*, 733–746.

Roig, M., and Ballew, C. (1994). Attitudes toward cheating of self and others by college students and professors. *Psychological Record 44*, 3–12.

Rosefeld, L. B. (1983). Communication climate and coping mechanisms in the college classroom. *Communication Education 32*, 167–174. Cited after: Whitley B. E., Jr., and Keith-Spiegel P. (2002). *Academic dishonesty. An educator's guide.* Mahwah, NJ: Lawrence Erlbaum Associates.

Sauser, W. I., Jr., and Sims, R. R. (2011). Showing business students how to contribute to organizational cultures grounded in moral character. In Ch. Wankel, and A. Stachowicz-Stanusch (Eds.), *Handbook of research on teaching ethics in business and management education* (pp. 235–255). US: IGI-Global.

Sawyer, K. R., Johnson, J., and Holub, M. (2009). Decline in academe. *International Journal for Educational Integrity 5*(2), 10–28.

Schein, E. H. (1985). *Organizational culture and leadership.* San Francisco: Jossey-Bass. Cited after: Whitley B. E., Jr., and Keith-Spiegel P. (2002). *Academic dishonesty. An educator's guide.* Mahwah, NJ: Lawrence Erlbaum Associates.

Schmidt, C. D., McAdams C. R., & Foster V. (2009). Promoting the moral reasoning of undergraduate business students through a deliberate psychological education-based classroom intervention. *Journal of Moral Education 38*(3), 315–334.

Seligman, M., and Csikszentmihalyi, M. (2000). Positive psychology: An Introduction. *American Psychologist 55*, 5–14.

Selznick, P. (1957). *Leadership in administration.* New York, NY: Harper and Row.

Senge, P. M. (2003). *Piąta dyscyplina. Teoria i praktyka organizacji uczących się.* Kraków: Oficyna Ekonomiczna.

Sims, R. L. (1995). The severity of academic dishonesty: A comparison of faculty and student views. *Psychology in the Schools 32*, 233–238.

Solomon, R. C. (1992). Corporate roles, personal virtues: An Aristotelean approach to business ethics. *Business Ethics Quarterly 2*, 317–339.

Stachowicz-Stanusch, A. (2004). *Zarządzanie Poprzez Wartości. Perspektywa rozwoju współczesnego przedsiębiorstwa.* Gliwice: Wydawnictwo Politechniki Śląskiej.

Stachowicz-Stanusch, A. (2007). *Potęga wartości: Jak zbudować nieśmiertelną firmę.* Gliwice: Helion.

Stachowicz-Stanusch, A. (2008). The role of management by values in the process of company development based on HP case study. In J. Sepp (Ed.), *The economics of education and innovation for sustainability and growth*. Wilkes: Congress of Political Economists (COPE), Wilkes University.

Stachowicz-Stanusch, A. (Ed.) (2009). *Główne wartości uczelni wyższych w kontekście różnych kultur narodowych. Koncepcja badań i wyniki badań sondażowych*. Gliwice: Wydawnictwo Politechniki Śląskiej.

Stachowicz-Stanusch, A. (Ed.) (2010). Corruption immunity based on positive organizational scholarship towards theoretical framework. In A. Stachowicz-Stanusch (Ed.), *Organizational immunity to corruption. Building theoretical and research foundations* (pp. 35–51).

Stachowicz-Stanusch, A., Grzanka, I., Mendel, I., Krannich, M., Aleksander, A., & Sworowska, A. (2009). 9. Główne wartości uczelni wyższych—wyniki badań. In A. Stachowicz-Stanusch (Ed.), *Główne wartości uczelni wyższych w kontekście różnych kultur narodowych. Koncepcja badań i wyniki badań sondażowych* (pp. 125–143). Gliwice: Wydawnictwo Politechniki Śląskiej.

Stachowicz-Stanusch, A., and Mendel, I. (2009). 1. Główne wartości uczelni wyższych jako podstawa etosu akademickiego. In A. Stachowicz-Stanusch (Ed.), *Główne wartości uczelni wyższych w kontekście różnych kultur narodowych. Koncepcja badań i wyniki badań sondażowych* (pp. 9–26). Gliwice: Wydawnictwo Politechniki Śląskiej.

Stachowicz-Stanusch, A., and Wankel, Ch. (2011). The principle for responsible management education—a pathway to management education for integrity. *Organizacja i Kierowanie 5*(147).

Stansbury, J., and Barry, B. (2007). Ethics Programs and the Paradox of Control. *Business Ethics Quarterly 17*(2), 239–261.

Starkey, K., Hatchuel, A., & Tempest, S. (2004). Rethinking the business school. *Journal of Management Studies 41*(8), 1521–1530.

Steer, M., and Gentle, F. (2007). Ensuring integrity in educational assessment. *International Journal for Educational Integrity 3*(1), 26–34.

Stephens, J. M., and Wangaard, D. B. (2008). *Teaching for Integrity: Steps to Prevent Cheating in Your Classroom*. http://www/ethicsed.org/programs/integrity-works/index.htm

Swanson, D. L. (2004). The buck stops here: Why universities must reclaim business ethics education. *Journal of Academic Ethics 2*(1), 43–61.

Sztompka, P. (2002). *Socjologia. Analiza społeczeństwa*. Krakow: Wydawnictwo Znak.

Taylor, B. (n.d.). Academic Integrity: A Letter to My Students. A letter based upon ideas contained in the first draft of "The Fundamental Values of Academic Integrity."

Available from the Center for Academic Integrity, http://www.acaemicintegrity.org/. Text in constant development.

The Center for Academic Integrity (1999). The Fundamental Values of Academic Integrity.

Turknett, R., & Turknett, L. (2002). Three essentials for rebuilding trust: Code, character and conversation. GoodBusiness. Vol. 1(2), pages unnumbered. Cited after: Sauser W. I. Jr., & Sims R. R. (2011). Chapter 14: Showing business students how to contribute to organizational cultures grounded in moral character. In Ch. Wankel, and A. Stachowicz-Stanusch (Eds.), *Handbook of research on teaching ethics in business and management education* (p. 238) US: IGI Global.

Turner, S.P. Beemsterboer, P.L. (2003). Enhancing academic integrity: Formulating effective honor codes. *Journal of Dental Education 67*(10), 1122–1129.

Turnipseed, D. (1996). Organization citizenship behavior: An examination of the influence of the workplace. *Leadership and Organization Development Journal 17*(2), 42–47.

Vella, K. J., & Melewar T. C. 2008. Explicating the relationship between identity and culture: A multi-perspective conceptual model. In: T. C. Melewar (Ed.), Facets of corporate identity, communication and reputation, Routledge. Cited after: Stachowicz-Stanusch, A. (Ed.) (2010). Corruption Immunity Based on Positive Organizational Scholarship Towards Theoretical Framework. In A. Stachowicz-Stanusch (Ed.), *Organizational immunity to corruption*. Building theoretical and research foundations (pp. 35–51).

Waddock, S. (2005). Hollow men and women at the helm ... Hollow accounting ethics? *Issues in Accounting Education, 20*(2), 145–150.

Wankel, Ch. (Ed.) (2010). *Cutting-edge social media approaches to business Eeducation: Teaching with LinkedIn, Facebook, Twitter, Second Life, and Blogs.* Charlotte, NC: Information Age Publishing.

Wankel, Ch, and Malleck, S. (Eds.) (2011). *Globalization: Ethical Models and Applications.* Hershey, PA: IGI-Global.

Wankel, Ch., Stachowicz-Stanusch, A., & Tamtana, J. S. (2011). The impact of the national culture dimension and corruption on students' moral competencies-Research results. *Journal of Intercultural Management, 3*(2), 19–45.

Weinberger, D. (2010). The American leader's love affair with integrity (Conversations Blog). Retrieved from Harvard Business Review. Available at: http://blogs.hbr.org/cs/2010/10/the_american_leaders_love_affa.html

Whitley, B.E., and Keith-Spiegel, P. (2002). *Academic dishonesty. An educator's guide.* Mahwah, NJ: Lawrence Erlbaum Associates.

Wilcox, J. R., and Libbs, S. (1993). Ethical leadership. Successfully communicating institutional values. *NACUBO Business Officer*, pp. 36–41.

Worline, M. C., Wrzesniewski, A., & Rafaeli A. (2002). Courage and work: Breaking routines to improve performance (pp. 295-330). In: R. Lord,

R. Klimoski, & R. Kanfer (Eds.), *Emotions in the workplace: Understanding the structure and role of emotions in organizational behavior* (pp. 295–330). San Francisco, CA: Jossey-Bass.

Zbiegień-Maciąg, L. (1999). Kultura w organizacji. Identyfikacja kultury znanych firm. Warszawa: PWN.

http://aggiehonor.tamu.edu/Faculty/WhatToDo.aspx

http://aggiehonor.tamu.edu/RulesAndProcedures/HonorSystemRules.aspx

http://aggiehonor.tamu.edu/RulesAndProcedures/HonorSystemRules.aspx

http://aggiehonor.tamu.edu/RulesAndProcedures/ReportingAndAdjudication.aspx

http://atmentors.tamu.edu/

http://blogs.hbr.org/cs/2010/10/the_american_leaders_love_affa.html

http://chatbots.org

http://diversity.depaul.edu/About/index.html

http://dms.tamu.edu/diversityedu/dti.htm

http://en.ru.is/media/hr/skjol/Gaedahandbok_EN_Web.pdf

http://en.ru.is/media/hr/skjol/RU_Internal_analysis.pdf

http://en.ru.is/the-university/hr-strategy-in-research/

http://english.iae.edu.ar/IAEhoy/Escuela/Pages/mision.aspx

http://english.iae.edu.ar/IAEhoy/Internacional/Pages/PRME.aspx

http://english.iae.edu.ar/PI/Areas/Pages/ESE.aspx

http://english.iae.edu.ar/PI/centros/Governance/Pages/Mision.aspx

http://english.iae.edu.ar/PI/centros/Pages/Home.aspx

http://english.pku.edu.cn

http://english.us.edu.pl/one-sentence

http://enterprisefeatures.com/2011/05/real-world-artificial-intelligence-has-arrived
    -a-chatbot-can-automate-your-customer-rvice-support-and-interactions/

http://humanresources.about.com/library/weekly/aa091200a.htm?once=true&

http://humanresources.about.com/library/weekly/aa101500a.htm

http://leadership.depaul.edu/secure/downloads/2006-2007_Annual_Report.pdf

http://mission.depaul.edu/AboutUs/Documents/0809ExecutiveSummary.pdf

http://mission.depaul.edu/AboutUs/Documents/Executive%20Summary%20
    -%20DMVSurvey%202003-2006.pdf

http://mission.depaul.edu/AboutUs/Documents/Final_Report.pdf

http://mission.depaul.edu/AboutUs/Pages/Survey.aspx

http://mission.depaul.edu/Ombudsperson/Pages/default.aspx

http://mission.depaul.edu/Pages/default.aspx

http://mission.depaul.edu/Programs/awards/mchugh/Pages/default.aspx

http://mission.depaul.edu/Programs/awards/spiritaward/Pages/default.aspx

http://mission.depaul.edu/Programs/Co-SponsoredEvents/Pages/TagDays.aspx

http://mission.depaul.edu/Programs/heritagedays/Pages/default.aspx

http://mission.depaul.edu/Programs/Orientation/Pages/default.aspx

http://mission.depaul.edu/Programs/Orientation/Pages/MissionforFirstYears.aspx

http://mission.depaul.edu/Programs/Orientation/Pages/NewEmployeeOrient
ation.aspx

http://mission.depaul.edu/Programs/Orientation/Pages/NewStudentOrien
tation.aspx

http://mission.depaul.edu/Programs/Pages/DePaulReadsTogether.aspx

http://mission.depaul.edu/Programs/Tours/Pages/default.aspx

http://mission.depaul.edu/Programs/Tours/Pages/FacultyandStaff.aspx

http://mq.edu.au/about/profile/values.html

http://news.bbc.co.uk/2/hi/6729537.stm

http://nfaetyka.wordpress.com/2011/12/29/problemy-jakie-napotykaja-whistle
blowerzy/

http://nku.edu/about/plan.php

http://president.depaul.edu/Downloads/VISIONtwenty12Brochure.pdf

http://president.depaul.edu/Vision2012/Vision2012.html

http://president.msu.edu/statements/core-values/

http://ptoniana.ealumni.com/clapper.asp

http://www.ptoniana.ealumni.com/fredfox.asp

http://www.ptoniana.ealumni.com/tradition.asp

http://www.sites.hamline.edu/150/4alumni_legacy/4alumni_legacy.html

http://www.sites.hamline.edu/150/6historical_hamline/chist_seal.html

http://www.sr.depaul.edu/catalog/catalogfiles/Current/undergraduate%20
Student%20Handbook/pg53.html

http://www.tulane.edu/about/traditions.cfm

http://www.uca.edu/mission/

http://www.update.sxu.edu/Administrative/Mission/core_values.asp

http:www.//vision2020.tamu.edu/

http://www.academicintegrity.org/educational_resources/educational_materials
/sylbs_ucfla.php

http://www.academicintegrity.org/educational_resources/educational_materials
/sylbs_gtwnu.php

http://www.academicintegrity.org/educational_resources/educational_materials
/sample_posters/index.php

http://www.admin.cam.ac.uk/univ/mission.html

http://www.agh.edu.pl/en/university/about-us/history-and-traditions.html

http://www.ammanu.edu.jo/en/AAU/AAUHistory.aspx?p=2

http://www.au.af.mil/au/awc/awcgate/ndu/strat-ldr-dm/pt4ch16.html

http://www.bethel.edu/about/values

http://www.bucknell.edu/x44217.xml

http://www.bucknell.edu/x495.xml

http://www.bucknell.edu/x496.xml

http://www.bucknell.edu/x499.xml

http://www.cauc.ca/about/vision

http://www.characterandcitizenship.org

http://www.cityu.edu.hk/provost/strategic_plan/core_values.htm

http://www.clemson.edu/about/traditions.html

http://www.cmu.edu/academic-integrity/preventing/instructors.html

http://www.cmu.edu/academic-integrity/preventing/students.html

http://www.corpus.cam.ac.uk/undergraduates/information-for-freshers
    /traditions

http://www.covenantuniversity.edu.ng/About-Us/Our-Core-Values

http://www.cut.ac.za/web/mission

http://www.depaul.edu/about/Pages/history-and-mission.aspx

http://www.depaul.edu/admission-and-aid/financial-aid/for-parents/Pages
    /default.aspx

http://www.distlearn.com/Vision00.PDF

http://www.eafit.edu.co/english/about-eafit/Paginas/english-version-mission
    -vission-institutional-values.aspx

http://www.education.auburn.edu/aboutus/corevalues.html

http://www.effatuniversity.edu.sa/index.php?option=com_content&task=view
    &id=482&Itemid=550

http://www.ethicsed.org

http://www.ethicsed.org/programs/integrity-works/index.htm

http://www.eua.be/eua/jsp/en/upload/GrazDecENG.1066743764824.pdf

http://www.ferris.edu/htmls/ferrisfaq/mission.htm

http://www.fu-berlin.de/en/universitaet/leitbegriffe/veritas-lustitia-libertas
    /index.html

http://www.gwu.edu/explore/aboutgw/traditions/sealmacecoatofarms

http://www.hamline.edu/about/history.html

http://www.hamline.edu/about/mission.html

http://www.hamline.edu/Content.aspx?id=4294969060

http://www.hamline.edu/offices/brand-experience/traditions.html

http://www.hamline.edu/offices/diversity/

http://www.hamline.edu/offices/diversity/definition.html

http://www.hamline.edu/offices/diversity/director.html

http://www.hamline.edu/offices/diversity/rgb.html

http://www.hamline.edu/offices/diversity/staff/

http://www.hamline.edu/offices/diversity/student-awards.html

http://www.hamline.edu/offices/misa/ncore.html

http://www.hamline.edu/offices/ombudsman/

http://www.hamline.edu/offices/ombudsman/standards-of-practice.html

http://www.hamline.edu/parents/

http://www.hamline.edu/policies/
http://www.hamline.edu/Policy.aspx?id=2147488077
http://www.hamline.edu/Policy.aspx?id=2147490770
http://www.hamline.edu/students/first-year/piper-passages.html
http://www.hamline.edu/students/first-year/piper-preview.html
http://www.hamline.edu/students/veterans/
http://www.hamline.edu/students/veterans/history.html
http://www.hau.ac.kr/english/introduce/initiative1.htm
http://www.hillsdale.edu/academics/registrar/academic_honor.asp
http://www.humboldt.edu/president/VisionMissionCoreValues.html
http://www.iae.edu.ar/SiteCollectionDocuments/20090114_Folleto_institu
    cional.pdf
http://www.iae.edu.ar/SiteCollectionDocuments/AnnualReportResumen.pdf
http://www.jimcollins.com/article_topics/articles/aligning-action.html
http://www.knust.edu.gh/pages/sections.php?mid=14&sid=94&id=81
http://www.krasp.org.pl/pl/kdp/kodeks_dobre_praktyki
http://www.lipscomb.edu/www/Mission-Values-Vision
http://www.llu.edu/central/values.page
http://www.louisville.edu/org/sun/research/project.html
http://www.lums.edu.pk/page.php?xyz=%7C%40~ROU1UQW1jR2xrUFRFP
    Q%3E%3E
http://www.lunduniversity.lu.se/o.o.i.s/24815
http://www.maastrichtuniversity.nl/web/Faculties/SBE/Theme/AboutTheSchool
    /CoreValues1.htm
http://www.maius.uj.edu.pl/history.en.html
http://www.manipal.edu/AboutUs/Pages/Mission,VisionValues.aspx
http://www.med.wright.edu/web
http://www.menntamalaraduneyti.is/media/MRN-pdf/Sjalfsmatsskyrsla
    -lagadeild-HR-2010-ENSKA-AGUST-2010.pdf.
http://www.mogadishuuniversity.com/english/index.php?page=Core-Values
http://www.moralcompass.com/MNCPA_Feature_April_06.pdf
http://www.mseuf.edu.ph/index.php?option=com_content&view=article&id=1
    24&Itemid=296
http://www.nap.edu/catalog.php?record_id=10430
http://www.ncu.edu.jm/discover/core-values.aspx
http://www.nileu.edu.eg/Docs/Nile%20University%20Profile%20-%202011.pdf
http://www.nps.gov/training/uc/whcv.htm
http://www.ntpu.edu.tw/english/?page_id=40
http://www.nyu.edu/faculty/governance-policies-and-procedures/faculty
    -handbook/the-university/history-and-traditions-of-new-york-university
    /university-traditions.html

http://www.ocm.auburn.edu/welcome/traditions.html

http://www.otago.ac.nz/about/otago000764.pdf

http://www.ou.edu/discover/discover_home/traditions.html

http://www.pucp.edu.pe/EN/content/pagina15.php?pID=916&pIDSeccionWe
    b=6&pIDReferencial=

http://www.saintleo.edu/Campus-Life/Code-of-Conduct

http://www.sehs.org/academic-honor-code-policy

http://www.sim.edu.sg/discover-sim/pages/whoweare.aspx

http://www.stjohns.edu/about/general/core

http://www.tamu.edu/about/coreValues.html

http://www.ttu.edu/traditions/blarney.php

http://www.ttu.edu/traditions/seal.php

http://www.tut.fi/en/about-us/tuts-strategy/index.htm

http://www.uaic.ro/uaic/bin/view/University/Prezentare

http://www.ucop.edu/ucophome/coordrev/policy/Stmt_Stds_Ethics.pdf

http://www.uic.edu/home/wowaward.shtml#core

http://www.uj.edu.pl/c/document_library/get_file?uuid=d63b4be0-5eee-4d94
    -bd32-3b1ccef396f6&groupId=10172

http://www.uj.edu.pl/documents/10172/1315002/Newsletter42.pdf

http://www.uj.edu.pl/uniwersytet/aktualnosci/video-foto/-/journal_content/56
    _INSTANCE_7Cwe/10172/6019177

http://www.uj.edu.pl/uniwersytet/muzea/

http://www.uj.edu.pl/uniwersytet/nagrody-i-wyroznienia/doktorzy-hc

http://www.uj.edu.pl/uniwersytet/nagrody-i-wyroznienia/merentibus

http://www.uj.edu.pl/uniwersytet/nagrody-i-wyroznienia/pro-arte-docendi

http://www.uj.edu.pl/uniwersytet/wartosci-akademickie

http://www.universityaffairs.ca/tradition.aspx

http://www.uob.ac.tz/Mission

http://www.uonbi.ac.ke/node/11

http://www.utech.edu.jm/about/overview/core_values.html

http://www.utm.my/about/vision-mission/

http://www.uwp.edu/departments/community.partnerships/home/mission.cfm

http://www.vision/ministries.org/resources/developing_core_values.pdf

http://www.waikato.ac.nz/hrm/internal/policy/codethic1.html

http://www.washington.edu/discover/visionvalues

http://www.webster.edu/strategicplan/core_values.shtml

http://www.wright.edu/administration/physicalplant/recycling/

http://www.wright.edu/administration/vision/exsum.html

http://www.wright.edu/administration/vision/fac.html

http://www.wright.edu/administration/vision/facility.html

http://www.wright.edu/administration/vision/fund.html

http://www.wright.edu/administration/vision/index.html
http://www.wright.edu/administration/vision/student.html
http://www.wright.edu/business/about/mission.html
http://www.wright.edu/foundational-principles/guiding-principles
http://www.wright.edu/foundational-principles/vision-statement
http://www.wright.edu/news_events/cultureresources.htm/
http://www.wright.edu/sustainability/
http://www.wright.edu/sustainability/news/
http://www.wright.edu/sustainability/transportation.html
http://www.ysu.edu/strategicplan/spc_core_values.shtml
http://www.zamorano.edu/english/explore-zamorano/about-us/our-mission/
https://www.wright.edu/nca/pdfs/nca_vol1.pdf

Index

A
Academic administrators
    responsibility, 49–50
Academic community
    fundamental values, 9
    hearing process principles and
        employees' and students'
        rights, 56–57
    IAE Business School, 162–163
    pledge
        faculty member, 51
        parent, 51
        student, 50–51
    reporting and adjudication,
        51–54
    responsibility
        academic administrators, 49–50
        academic staff, 49
        student, 47–48
        teacher, 48
    sanctions and appeals, 57–59
    whistleblowers' protection,
        54–56
Academic ethos management (AEM)
    characteristics, 207–210
    crisis of, 1–5
    definition, 9, 206
    erosion, 5–10
    objective, 206
Academic honesty, 45
Academic integrity. *See also* Integrity
    assumptions, 201–204
    compound process, 221
    conceptual framework, 220–221
    definition, 8–9
Academic pledge
    faculty member, 51
    parent, 51
    student, 50–51
Academic publicity, 64
Academic staff responsibility, 49
Administrative Hearing, 109

AEM. *See* Academic ethos
        management
Anonymous reporting, 53
Architectural symbols, 71–72

B
Behavioral core values
    desirable behaviors, 24, 31
    higher school, 25–28
    particular, 29–30, 32
    threatening, 34–36
    unacceptable behavior, 31, 33, 37
Business practice, ethical lapses, 4

C
CAI. *See* Center for Academic
        Integrity
*Campus Life—In Search of
        Community,* 7–8
Center for Academic Integrity (CAI),
        8–9
Chatterbots, 77–78
Code of Ethics for Academic Staff, 49
Code of Student Responsibility, 108
Communicating core values
    academic publicity, 64
    declarations, 63
    higher learning, 61–62
    language as tool, 63–64
    new technology
        aim/goal, 74
        benefits, 76–77
        chatterbots, 77–78
    university's traditions
        architectural symbols, 71–72
        cultural models, 69–70
        myths and folk tales, 65–67
        physical symbols, 72–73
        rituals and ceremonies, 67–69
        symbols of prestige, 73
Confidential reporting, 53
Consistency, 214

Cooper and Cartwright model,
140–141
Core values
academic ethos
higher schools, 13
universities, 15–18
websites, 13–14
behavioral terms
desirable behaviors, 24, 31
higher school, 25–28
particular, 29–30, 32
threatening, 34–36
unacceptable behavior, 31, 33, 37
case study-DePaul University
brief history, 95–97
examples of achievements, 106
institutionalization, 99–102,
105, 107–115
mission, 97–98
particular goals and objectives,
103–104
vision, 97, 99
case study-Hamline University
brief history, 181–184
institutionalization, 185–186,
191–199
mission, 185
strategic directions and
initiatives, 187–190
vision, 185
case study-IAE Business School
academic community, 162–163
brief history, 153–154
institutionalization, 156–163
mission statement, 155–156
Vision 2015, 155
case study-Jagiellonian University
brief history, 165–170
core values, 172–174
institutionalization, 174–181
mission statement, 170–171
case study-Reykjavik University
brief history, 137–138
institutionalization, 143–153
mission, 141
strategy for, 142
vs. Technical University of
Iceland, 140–141
vision of, 141–142

case study-Wright State University
brief history, 115–116
goals, objectives and
implementation results,
126–127
institutionalization, 125,
128–135
mission statement, 121
Vision 2020, 117–121
communicating
academic publicity, 64
declarations, 63
higher learning, 61–62
language as tool, 63–64
new technology, 74–78
university's traditions, 65–73
definition, 12
discovery of, 19–23
maintaining
control issues, 92
explaining protection issues,
81–82
motivating and awarding,
90–91
recruitment, 80–81
redefining, 92–94
training levels, 82–90
scientific research results, 10–13
Webster definition, 11
Culture Due Diligence, 140–141
Culture of integrity, 8

D
The DePaul Leadership Project,
113–114
DePaul University
brief history, 95–97
core values, 98–99
examples of achievements, 106
institutionalization, 99–102, 105,
107–115
mission, 97–98
particular goals and objectives,
103–104
vision, 97, 99
Desirable behavior, 24, 31
Diversity Training Institute
(DTI), 83
DTI. See Diversity Training Institute

E
ELIZA chatterbots, 75
Enacting academic ethos
   academic community
      hearing process principles and
         employees' and students'
         rights, 56–57
      pledges, 50–51
      reporting and adjudication, 51–54
      responsibilities, 47–50
      sanctions and appeals, 57–59
      whistleblowers' protection,
         54–56
   communicating core values, 44
   formalizing a university's policies,
      procedures, and codes, 41, 44
   policy statements, 45
   reflecting and supporting core
      values in university's goals,
      objectives, and measures,
      40–43
European University Association, 8

F
Financial Times, 154

G
General reporting, 53
Georgetown University websites,
   87–88
Government Program for Local
   Community Leadership
   Development, 160

H
Hamline University
   brief history, 181–184
   core values, 185
   institutionalization, 185–186,
      191–199
   mission, 185
   strategic directions and initiatives,
      187–190
   vision, 185
Higher school core values, 25–28
Honesty, 214
Honor code violations reporting, 53
Honor System, 88
Human interaction, 10

I
IAE Business School
   academic community, 162–163
   brief history, 153–154
   core values, 156
   institutionalization, 156–163
   mission statement, 155–156
   Vision 2015, 155
Integrity. *See also* Academic integrity
   components, 214
   culture of, 216
   of higher schools, 217
   moral, 214
   organizational, 216–217
   physical, 214
   quest for, 214–215
   views of, 215

J
Jagiellonian University
   brief history, 165–170
   core values, 172–174
   institutionalization, 174–181
   mission statement, 170–171
Judicial Board Hearing, 109
Judicial hearings, 109

L
Language
   definition, 63
   tool for core value articulation,
      63–64

M
Maintaining core values
   control issues, 92
   protection
      explaining core values, 81–82
      motivating and awarding, 90–91
      recruitment, 80–81
      training on core values, 82–90
   redefining, 92–94
Moral integrity, 214

N
National Conference on Race and
   Ethnicity (NCORE), 197
NCORE. *See* National Conference on
   Race and Ethnicity

O
Office of Diversity Integration, 196
Office of Institutional Diversity
   core values, 99
   mission, 98
   vision, 99
Ombudspersons, 55
Organizational culture, 18
Organizational integrity, 216
   definition, 9
   Wright State University, 131
Organizational psychology, 23

P
Parent E-Newsletter, 193
Parent Network, 193
Particular core values, 29–30, 32
Physical integrity, 214
Physical symbols, 72–73
Piper Preview, 192–193
Positive organizational scholarship,
   211–213
Principles for Responsible
   Management Education
   (PRME), 162
PRME. See Principles for Responsible
   Management Education

Q
Quest for integrity, 214–215

R
Regional Leadership Training, 159
Reykjavik University (RU)
   brief history, 137–138
   institutionalization, 143–153
   mission of, 141
   strategy for, 142
   vs. Technical University of Iceland,
      140–141
   vision of, 141–142

S
S.A.I.L. See Student Academic
   Integrity and Leadership

Staff Diversity Development
   Initiative, 196–197
Student Academic Integrity and
   Leadership (S.A.I.L.), 90
Student's responsibility of academic
   community, 47–48
Symbols
   architectural, 71–72
   physical, 72–73
   of prestige, 73

T
Teacher's responsibility of academic
   community, 48
Technical University of Iceland,
   140–141
Threatening core values, 34–36

U
UCF. See University of Central
   Florida
Unacceptable behavior, 31, 33, 37
University of Central Florida
   (UCF), 87
University traditions, core values
   architectural symbols, 71–72
   cultural models, 69–70
   myths and folk tales, 65–67
   physical symbols, 72–73
   rituals and ceremonies, 67–69
symbols of prestige, 73

W
Wright State University
   brief history, 115–116
   core values, 122–124
   goals, objectives and
      implementation results,
      126–127
   institutionalization, 125,
      128–135
   mission statement, 121
   Vision 2020, 117–121
Writing across the Curriculum
   (WAC) Program, 132

Endorsements

Among salient strengths of the book is its development of a conceptual framework of academic integrity founded on a positive academic ethos; a holistic approach; an empirical grounding with theoretical implications for developing an academic ethos that will stem inclinations towards unethical behavior in the future; an integration of qualitative research from North America, South America, and Europe; a discerning overview of the process of academic ethos management; and notably an overview of the spectrum of methods and tools for managing the core values of an academic ethos aimed at the fostering of academic and career integrity.

—Professor Charles Wankel,
St. John's University, New York

[In this book] Agata Stachowicz-Stanusch places academic institutions squarely in the same arena and on the same foundation as the many companies and other institutions where their graduates will build careers. She asks the same questions of higher education that have been asked of society's other core institutions with regard to ethics and fundamental values. This volume will be an invaluable resource for educational leaders and administrators and faculty who want to ensure that their institutions reflect the same values they espouse.

—Mary C. Gentile, PhD,
Babson College

Dr. Stachowicz-Stanusch's new book arrives at just the right time with just the right focus and content. [This] book shows how universities and their business schools can discover their core values, make them real on a day to day basis, and truly walk the talk of ethical commitment and leadership. Rich in examples from around the world, [it] provides a valuable, scientific roadmap that can be followed and adjusted for individual situations and opportunities by educational leaders committed to setting the kind of ethical leadership example we all need from our universities and their business schools.

—Professor James A.F. Stoner, Fordham University,
New York

OTHER TITLES IN OUR PRINCIPLES OF RESPONSIBLE MANAGEMENT EDUCATION COLLECTION

Oliver Laasch, Monterrey Institute of Technology, Collection Editor

- *Managing Corporate Responsibility in Emerging Markets: Issues, Cases, and Solutions* by Jenik Radon
- *Business Integrity in Practiced: Insights from International Case Studies* by Agata Stachowicz-Stanusch
- *Responsible Management: Understanding Human Nature, Ethics, and Sustainability* by Kemi Ogunyemi
- *Marketing to the Low-Income Consumer* by Paulo Cesar Motta
- *Educating for Values-Driven Leadership: Giving Voice to Values* by Mary Gentile

---

Announcing the Business Expert Press Digital Library

Concise E-books Business Students Need for Classroom and Research

This book can also be purchased in an e-book collection by your library as
- a one-time purchase,
- that is owned forever,
- allows for simultaneous readers,
- has no restrictions on printing, and
- can be downloaded as PDFs from within the library community.

Our digital library collections are a great solution to beat the rising cost of textbooks. e-books can be loaded into their course management systems or onto student's e-book readers.

The **Business Expert Press** digital libraries are very affordable, with no obligation to buy in future years. For more information, please visit **www.businessexpertpress.com/librarians**. To set up a trial in the United States, please contact **Adam Chesler** at *adam.chesler@businessexpertpress .com* for all other regions, contact **Nicole Lee** at *nicole.lee@igroupnet.com*.

www.ingramcontent.com/pod-product-compliance
Lightning Source LLC
Chambersburg PA
CBHW060332200326
41519CB00011BA/1911